Baseball and the Mythic Moment

ALSO BY JAMES D. HARDY, JR.
AND FROM McFARLAND

*The New York Giants Base Ball Club: The Growth of
a Team and a Sport, 1870 to 1900* (1996; paperback 2006)

Baseball and the Mythic Moment

How We Remember the National Game

JAMES D. HARDY, JR.

McFarland & Company, Inc., Publishers
Jefferson, North Carolina, and London

All photographs used by permission of the National Baseball Hall of Fame Library, Cooperstown, New York.

LIBRARY OF CONGRESS CATALOGUING-IN-PUBLICATION DATA

Hardy, James D. (James Daniel), 1934–
    Baseball and the mythic moment : how we remember the national game / James D. Hardy, Jr.
        p.   cm.
    Includes bibliographical references and index.

    ISBN-13: 978-0-7864-2650-8 (softcover : 50# alkaline paper)

    1. Baseball — Anthropological aspects— United States.
    2. Baseball — United States— History.   I. Title.
    GV867.54.H37   2007
    796.357 — dc22   2006036341

British Library cataloguing data are available

Cover art: "Poor Vic(S)tory," Opie Otterstad, acrylic on canvas 58" × 46", 2000 (www.opieart.com)

Manufactured in the United States of America

McFarland & Company, Inc., Publishers
    Box 611, Jefferson, North Carolina 28640
        www.mcfarlandpub.com

To the memory of
my mother and my Uncle George,
who introduced me to
baseball.

And to my
wife, Claudia, who has come to
accept this peculiar affection
in her husband.

Contents

Preface

In *The Leopard*, Giuseppe di Lampedusa remarked that a noble family lived on its memories. So does a culture, and baseball is part of the general American cultural memory. The resonance of baseball appears in something so basic as the language itself, with three-strike laws in penal legislation, and extends to the huge and growing number of books on baseball which raise the game beyond the ephemera of the summer sports pages. But only fragments of baseball story and anecdote have entered the national memory as myth, propelled into familiarity by cultural preference and popular mood. Collective memory in baseball preserves from the whole history of the game a few moments of high excitement, unexpected success, hideous failure, sudden reversals of fortune, all described by Aristotle in the *Poetics* (ix.ii;1452a) as "incidents that cause fear and pity, and this happens most of all when the incidents are unexpected, yet one is a consequence of the other."

Memorable moments that stick in the popular imagination vary from a single pitch, through a play, to an inning, a critical game, a World Series, or even an entire season. They find their way into the statistical record of the game, and into books that celebrate the event. Joe DiMaggio's fifty-six-game hitting streak, or Cal Ripken surpassing Lou Gehrig's record for playing in consecutive games become moments of general recall and public reference. Moments of exceptional drama, such as Babe Ruth's "called" home run in the 1932 World Series, rise above the rest of the game, or rather the rest of the games, teams, seasons, or decades, and become part of the tapestry of American lore. Described by Stephen Jay Gould as adamantine in memory, they stitch individual and communal memory together into what Americans recognize as the national pastime.

Baseball has been part of the American memory for more than a century, and that tenacity indicates that baseball is an enduring American metaphor for life. It is not alone, of course. The wilderness experience, therapy, the attentions of the police, and the rituals and retributions of the law also suggest themselves as metaphors for life, but baseball is incomparably the most beautiful and the most joyful. Baseball describes the nature of heroism, illustrates the virtues of perseverance, shows that character is of greater utility and value than indulgence, and, in a hundred box scores daily, illuminates the tragic view of life through defeat and disappointment accepted and borne. Baseball has endured from the Gilded Age through war, depression, prosperity, scandal, excess, and the therapeutic society to this day, and likely beyond.

In a society generally, though not invariably, addicted to the newest fad of the moment, baseball has still descended from generation unto generation. Popular trends and fads, as with songs and costume, come and (mercifully) go so rapidly that one can hardly keep up. The hula hoop came and went and came again and went again, in the usual way, while Barbie dolls came and stayed and multiplied and metastasized. Social persistence is not a quality to be despised, and it is reasonable to assume a culturally qualitative difference between things that appear only to disappear and things that remain. That difference can be found in the areas of memory and myth.

Economics, the most respected of the current social disciplines, has an alternate description of the differences between things that leave and things that last. Economists emphasize the difference in kind between consumables, such as bread, beer, fashion in dress or music, which are used up and then replaced, and consumer durables, such as furniture, china, houses, or even automobiles, which are retained for years or decades and can increase in value over time. Baseball is one of the cultural consumer durables of current American interest and national memory, like the old West and the Civil War.

Memory that is ubiquitous and dramatic can be transformed by general approval into myth. Myth is a vehicle for existential truth and responds to the whole culture, to values and attitudes both current and remembered, and to the need that all experience to bring meaning, order, and importance, either real or symbolic and especially symbolic, to the vagaries of life. Because myth describes essential truth, the story itself may be fantastic, involving gods, heroes, and suspension of natural law. Some respond to myth by suspending disbelief in deference to truth; others react skeptically in recognition that the mythic tale is often false in fact. In either case, the myth retains its charm, in part, certainly, because it functions in the most logical manner imaginable, moving from the known, though often misunderstood, to illuminate the unknown. Myth commonly uses the narrative of the hero journey as a matrix into which variant versions of detail and elaboration may be poured, and this is the standard mode for baseball mythology as well as it was for the Greeks. The mythic moments become the cultural property of all, whether we saw Babe Ruth hit his home run, or heard it, or read about it, or heard of it, or came across it as merely a reference. In every case, mythic meaning enhances the value of current attitude and of personal memory, and moment has become symbol as well as having been fact, or perhaps fact. In baseball, as much as any area of modern American life, this is ongoing cultural reality.

This book is an extended comment on the content and variety of myth and memory in baseball, about what is lost as much as about what abides. Things teeter on the brink of being forgotten and ignored, as was Gothic architecture, style, and iconography during the Renaissance. This book deals with events and anecdotes that fit both categories. There are chapters on the New York Yankees and Chicago Cubs, still with us, and on the Brooklyn Dodgers, sadly not. A chapter describes play-offs remembered only by historians, and another examines Babe Ruth, remembered by all. Since baseball centers memory more on individuals than teams, there are chapters dealing with hitting, pitching, and the process whereby a player becomes a hero or a bum. There are major moments of great drama forgotten, and insignificant incidents remembered. Finally, there are chapters on baseball as a general source of myth and as a measurement of time and memory.

This book had its origins in the ordinary world of conversation over the lunch table. Remembrance rambled through the artifacts of time and the quality of living, from military service to sports, history, religion, politics, and persons, all mingled with professional observations and gossip, along with horror stories about the latest enormous stupidity proposed or practiced by our university administrators. Over the years certain tales were constantly retold; others, once heard, then vanished into silence. Myth has humble as well as heroic origins, and the everyday lunch conversations over a couple of decades brought myth and memory from the realm of study to that of experience. Most authors thank those who read and commented on a book, but here I express my debt to those who inspired it. My appreciation goes to professors James Geer, Nathan Gottfried, Perry Prestholdt, Bill Seay, and Bill Waters, all in psychology; to Chris and Bainard Cowan and to Karen Powell, from English; to Leonard Hochberg, in geopolitics; to Leonard Stanton, who teaches Russian; and to my longtime coauthor in matters of Renaissance English religion and literature, the late Gale H. Carrithers, Jr. I came to the lunch bunch well after the group had formed, but they accepted me anyway. And now, by way of thanks, they are blamed for a book.

Finally, there is always the vexing matter of errors. One hopes there will be no errors, but in a fallen world there always are. Though I would much prefer to blame others for the errors, the responsibility, alas, is entirely my own. I will try to do better, but writing is like baseball. "Wait 'till next year," as the Brooklyn Dodgers fans used to say. The perfect season or the perfect book is easily imagined but always lies just beyond reach.

1

Myth and Memory

In the fall of 1932 America was in the midst of a presidential election. The race had more of desperation than excitement about it. The Democratic candidate, Franklin Delano Roosevelt, was clearly ahead by early October, not so much for what he promised to do about the Depression but because incumbent Republican Herbert Hoover had already done too little. Moreover, Roosevelt exuded a jaunty and infectious optimism, giving the impression that whatever he might do, he would certainly do something and that something would work. President Hoover had become identified with the unfortunate notion that "prosperity was just around the corner." Alas, for Hoover, this was not true, and, more to the point, almost no one thought it would be true anytime soon. If this were not bad enough, Hoover also supported Prohibition. The "great social and economic experiment, noble in motive and far-reaching in purpose," as Hoover had described Prohibition, had become an ignoble failure to increasing numbers of Americans.[1] Roosevelt was for repeal; he had said so in his acceptance speech in Chicago in July 1932.

Roosevelt's promise to repeal Prohibition addressed an issue that four years earlier had symbolized the cultural differences between an older, more rural, and more Protestant America and the great cities that industry and immigration had built in the generation since 1880. Although Prohibition had once been a main plank of the women's movement, it had recently become identified with Protestant churches, which stuck with it, while the women's movement, searching for new wrongs to be righted, supported Roosevelt. Now, in 1932, the economic, social, and employment crisis had grown so great that Prohibition was a peripheral issue to all but the dry zealots, and Roosevelt could safely pronounce his position on it. Repeal was about his only specific pledge. On other matters, he confined himself to generalizations and platitudes. He campaigned by displaying what Supreme Court Justice Oliver Wendell Holmes, Jr. called "a first-class temperament," along with what Holmes also called "a second-class intellect."[2] For the rest, Roosevelt's actual program was mainly a mystery, certainly to the press and perhaps to himself. The only firm clue came in his acceptance speech in Chicago. There he had said: "I pledge you, I pledge myself, to a new deal for the American people."[3] In the ordeal of the Great Depression, that was enough.[4]

Campaigning for public office means more than position papers that few read and speeches that few believe. The candidate must also make public appearances, and Franklin D. Roosevelt made one in a securely Democratic venue, the city of Chicago. He came to the third game of the 1932 World Series. Smiling and waving, at which Roosevelt excelled, the candidate gave every appearance of taking time off from the race to see a ball game, be with friends, and enjoy himself. He threw out the first pitch of the game to the cheers of the crowd. No one did this sort of ceremonial occasion better.

Great enthusiasm for Roosevelt in Chicago was only to be expected, but the citizens of the Second City had also greeted the New York Yankees with a good-natured mob in and around the La Salle Street Station. The Yanks had won the first two games of the Series in New York, but the fans at the station, apparently glad to see the World Series come to town, overlooked those inconvenient losses. So great was the crush of fans that only

> with the help of a special detail of police the Yankees managed to extricate themselves from the station and made their way to a row of waiting cabs. Then followed a triumphal procession that also had difficulty in getting under way, for outside the station thousands milled in the streets.[5]

The good humor of the crowd at La Salle Street Station did not carry over to the Chicago sports writers, who fanned discontent between the two teams. Joe McCarthy managed the Yankees, and he had been the Chicago manager when they won the pennant in 1929. But the Cubs had lost the Series that year, as they usually do, and the Chicago owner, Phil Wrigley, fired McCarthy toward the end of the 1930 season on the grounds that he was coming in second and would never win a Series. McCarthy wanted to win this Series very badly. So did Phil Wrigley.

By the time the Yankee caravan reached the Edgewater Beach Hotel the mood of the crowd had become decidedly testy. According to Babe Ruth,

> the Chicago fans were in a lather. Especially the lady fans. The Cubs had gone in very strongly for ladies' days that season, and had made a lot of fanatics out of the otherwise orderly housewives of Chicago. I've seen some nutty fans in my life, but never any quite like those gals....
> Most of their wrath was directed against me, and during that rough trip to the front door I heard some words even I had never heard before.[6]

The Chicago players had not enjoyed being trounced in New York, nor were they pleased to read and hear that the Yanks were going to win the next two in Chicago, particularly since these predictions seemed likely to be right. These dire forecasts began to come true in the first inning of the third game. With two men on and no one out, the Cubs' pitcher, Charlie Root, made a pitch to the Babe a little too fat, and Ruth hit a three-run homer. But the

Cubs fought back, and at the end of four innings the game was tied at four runs each. In the top of the fifth the Yankees broke the game open. With one out, the Babe came to bat. "Ruth had a spirited debate with the Cub substitutes on the bench while Root was serving three balls and two strikes, then swung at the sixth pitch and hit a tremendous drive which sailed over the bleachers' screen and came down at the base of the flag pole beside the score board in deepest centre for his second homer of the game."[7] The *New York Times* said nothing about Babe Ruth pointing his bat to the bleachers and calling the home run. The home movie taken of that Ruthian at bat shows the slanging match between the Babe and the Cubs bench, with Ruth pointing his bat at the dugout. But these facts, observed and reported, like all facts remain subject to revision, interpretation, wishful thinking, reconsideration, adjustment, improvement, and correction. Fortunately, there are plenty of facts to reconsider, since testimony survives from both of the participants in this mythic drama. Much of the detail described by Charlie Root coincides with the story told by the Bambino. But not all. Root recalled: "Players on both sides were razzing one another and Ruth, in particular, was singled out for a lot of ribbing. The first pitch was a called strike and Ruth raised one finger, signifying that was only the first strike. Then he took a second strike, raised two fingers. The next pitch landed in the center field stands."[8] The Babe remembered all this, and something more.

> While he [Root] was making up his mind to pitch to me I stepped back again and pointed my finger at those bleachers, which only caused the mob to howl that much more at me. Root threw me a fast ball....
>
> I swung from the ground with everything I had and as I hit the ball every muscle in my system, every sense that I had, told me I would never hit a better one, that as long as I lived nothing would feel as good as this. I didn't have to look but I did. That ball just went on and on and hit far up in the center-field bleachers in exactly the spot I had pointed to. To me, it was the funniest, proudest moment I had ever had in baseball.[9]

Root remembered less illustrative detail. He merely said in reply to the question of whether Babe Ruth had called his shot: "No. You might consider me an authority on this subject since I was pitching for Chicago when Ruth hit that famous home run."[10]

The mythic dimension of that home run overtook the facts pretty quickly, and became fact itself, not describing what actually happened but what should happen when a hero takes the stage. Popular American culture has remembered and enshrined William Bendix, a determined look on his unglamorous mug, pointing his bat directly and unambiguously at the center-field bleachers. The myth become movie is now the central cultural fact of the called home run.

What matters is not the hit but the hero. No one but the mighty Babe *could* have called a home run. Other sluggers, from teammate Lou Gehrig, who followed Ruth's homer with one of his own knocking Root out of the game, to the current champ, Henry Aaron, or Willie Mays, Jimmie Foxx, or Barry Bonds, all have lacked the Ruthian mythic dimension. In hard fact, they may have called as many homers as Ruth, or even more, but the Babe stands alone. Someone may, and probably will, hit 1,000 major league homers, and hit 100 in a single season, but that will not eclipse the mighty Babe. Ruth created the modern power game, and his winning good nature and essential insouciance has had a permanent cultural resonance. The Babe never forgot, and the nation believed that the Babe never forgot, that baseball is a game. Americans loved the Babe then and they still do, making the called home run a tribute to that affection as well as to Babe Ruth's bat.

I

Once upon a time, off-season discussion of baseball was called the Hot Stove League, a name that dated from the nineteenth century when America thought of itself as a people of small towns. In the winter — and Major League Baseball was then confined to areas where there *was* a winter — men (women had too much work to do) gathered at the general store/post office, sat around an iron pot-bellied stove, and discussed the passing parade. Baseball, along with weather, politics, the police blotter and the churches, belonged in that company. The always absorbing pastime of talking baseball could also be found in saloons, but the hot and fetid breath of the Anti-Saloon League burned too fiercely to permit sportswriters to allude to such booze-assisted sociability. The pastoral ideal was much preferred to grubby urban reality, and the cracker barrel (source of philosophy) always trumped the whiskey barrel (source of social irresponsibility). Baseball was firmly situated in the America of Robert Frost, of stone walls and fallen leaves, cold morning air raising steam from the cattle, and waves of warmth from the stove that sustained soul as well as body. It evoked an America of horse and railroad, of the intimacy of family and the nearness to Nature, and the Hot Stove League tied the game to what was thought good in America, a social attitude that was kindly meant and kindly remembered for three generations.[11]

The Hot Stove League remained an emblem for newspaper accounts of talking baseball until the Second World War. After Hiroshima, the technologically obsolete gradually changed from approved memory into social embarrassment. The local, the rural and the regional sank steadily as national emblems, in spite of the best efforts of Andy Griffith, Aunt Bea and Mayberry, to be replaced by the urban, the innovative, and the new and improved. Eventually, the Hot Stove League was heard from no longer, along with the venerable newspaper phrase that the pitcher was "knocked out of the box," dating to the time before 1893 when pitchers worked within a box rather than from the rubber. Both fell into the obsolescence of the quaint, appropriate for use by garrulous old fogies. Time had first preserved and later abandoned these images along with the evocation of things past that accompanied them. In modern America, life has come to imitate popular art.

Baseball today is discussed electronically on radio and television, usually by "experts" who formerly played the game or by sports writers turned into media stars. Actual fans occasionally add comments by calling in, but these are usually uninformative, combative and mercifully brief. Then the experts blather on, alternating punditry with bellow, indignation with raucous laughter, and often advancing positions even more extreme than those of the fans. As always, the emphasis is on the latest doings and sayings of sporting celebrities, for electronic communication creates celebrities the way drums create noise. The whole system functions as an opportunity to sell something, and the media maintain fan interest by exposure rather than discussion.[12] Electronically talking baseball has, in its need for commercial survival, all the attributes of the modern, impersonal, and up-to-date, but stories told over the hot stove did not differ much from those seen and heard electronically, though they were inevitably more local and subdued. In the end, however, stove and tube function alike as media of communication, and the medium is not always the entire message.

II

Within the tales told about baseball, advocacy and imagination always replaces accuracy, regardless of stove or tube. What actually happened usually functions as a starting point, or at least it can. But the story outweighs the event, if for no other reason than the story is endless and variable, fitting many speakers and circumstances, while the event remains fixed in fact and forever the same. Gradually and appropriately, the story assumes the nature of the fabulous, existing in the lively realm of sociability where all grows and changes; the event, however, can be nothing but itself.

Baseball stories, if they are well told and worth repeating, enter the realm of oral culture. They become twice-told tales, appropriate for conviviality, bringing the listener into the life and memory of the storyteller and connecting both to a game that is national in scope. Passed on to children, baseball tales connect generations as they do friends. As living anecdotes, baseball stories are not only fun but also make an intellectual point about the nature of life, love, and the world, connecting those who speak and those who hear into a social and historical community of shared values, attitudes, and memories.

In modern America, of course, the oral anecdote remains formally subordinate to the written record.[13] "You could look it up," wrote Ring Lardner, and he referred to authority of the written word. Baseball record books, and there are many with the number growing, have the official last word as the fount of all fact.[14] But oral tales, whether or not accompanied by a hot stove, exude a charm that the presence of the speaker enhances. My mother loved to tell the tale of opening day at the Polo Grounds in 1946. In the first inning the Giants put the game away as Mel Ott hit his last home run, number 511. Neither Mel nor my mother knew this was his last homer; that detail could only be added later. As for 1946 Giants, that opening day win, putting the Giants in a tie for first place, was the high point of a long season, and my mother suffered with Mel Ott and his team through a terrible year. They came in last, but the excitement of seeing her favorite player hit a homer and her team win never faded from my mother's memory or recitation of the moment. Memory cherished and tales retold shape the meaning of baseball, which, for the fan, consists of the endless tales and moments carrying the game from the field of play into individual lives and the general culture of America.

Baseball stories that fans continue to relate have transcended reality to become myth. We all learned in high school that myth meant stories patently untrue about religions utterly false. Like so much that happens in high school, this definition of myth is itself both utterly false and intensely persistent. The late Meg Greenfield, a Washington journalist of uncommon grace and wit, wrote that regardless of how high we rise in the world, we never get over what happened to us in high school. She meant the anxiety, insecurities and emotional scars inflicted then, but it pertains also to the misinformation so generously ladled out in high school to our fortunately resistant minds. But sometimes something does seep through, and the false definition of myth seems to be one of those things.

Myth is a narrative exposition of truth, in which everything is true but the story itself. And even that could be true, sort of, after a fashion, *un petit peu*. The truth that myth illustrates is existential rather than factual; thus myth illuminates the nature of things rather than describes a specific set of facts. Mythic stories are easy to remember and charming to hear. The more fantastic and outrageous the mythic tale, the better we like them, and the more easily the listener can understand the essential mythic truth behind the varying surface detail. The realistic and recognizable serve both as contrast for the fabulous and as roots in the world that myth would instruct.[15]

As well as being a narrative, myth also relates tales of a certain magnitude, an element of representation that Aristotle found indispensable for tragedy.[16] Magnitude in myth or tragedy depends not on particular details or characters, but rather on enduring questions about the meaning of justice, of the ethical foundations of human society, of the connection to the divine or the nature of humanity. Mythic narration embraces the origins and ends of all things; myth explores gods as well as people, society and history, nature and culture, love and death. These themes deal with the core of human life, and not unexpectedly exhibit a high tolerance for multiple versions of the same story, often with widely differing details, which serve also as reminders of the relative insignificance of a shifting story when compared to basic human truth. For myth, the story itself is illustrative and indicative, and is to be judged by its charm, while magnitude lies in the existential truth that the myth illuminates.

The mode of myth, therefore, resembles that of epic, and, like epic, myth characteristically begins both *in medias res* and *in medias tempora*. "In the beginning" refers only to the myth, though mythic tales may well be sufficiently cosmic to be rooted in time and things unknowable to the teller of the tale.[17] Myth, however, eschews the grandeur of epic, and places existential truth in terms as ordinary, personal, and unforgettable as gossip. Once upon a time, Arachne, a young woman inordinately proud of her skill in weaving, challenged the Olympian goddess Pallas Athena to a weaving contest. Arachne compounded the inordinate pride of *hybris* with incredible folly (*ate*) by weaving as well as Athena, perhaps even better. Driven by surprise, wrath, envy, spite, and humiliation, Athena turned Arachne into a spider.[18] She was transformed into what she had always been, a vessel for a single skill, and her character, once hidden inside, became visible externally, though now at a lower level of the Aristotelian tripartite division of the soul.[19] A quotidian tale of female jealousy and pride, comprehensible to all because experienced by all, became a comment on divine disfavor personalized as malice, with clear implications about the cost of royal disfavor as well. In Athena's all-too-human vice and Arachne's remarkable transformation, the myth combined a universality denoting magnitude with an ordinary specificity that assured resonance and recognition.

Although myth is normatively regarded as an expression of theology, and does often deal with divine intervention, birth, justice and injustice, another appropriate comparison, more secular in nature, is the law. Like myth, the law begins in the middle of time and things, and attempts to bring sense and order to the jumble of ordinary life caught in exceptional circumstances. Even in the dry and technical language of appellate briefs and decisions, legal cases remain short narratives of civil or criminal contretemps and the accompanying individual distress.[20] The law seeks always to uncover the general principles hiding in the singular event, so that human affairs may exhibit a sense of general order beyond the discrete event, and the single case illustrate a general pattern that most can understand. Like myth, the law moves always in the direction of a coherence and consistency that connects the particular to the general, *simul, semper, ubique et ad omnibus*.[21] Myth and law, at their best, seek fundamental truth, not just what has happened in this particular case, but also what it means. Truth, as Greek philosopher Heraclitus observed, remains obscure, because "nature likes to hide."[22] It is the function of myth and law to make the hidden visible, and make a simple narrative illustrate a complicated truth.[23]

A myth that illustrates the characteristics of the genre concerns Semele, daughter of Cadmus, king of Thebes. A beautiful young girl, she attracted the attention of Zeus, king of the gods, who apparently spent a fair proportion of his working hours in pursuit of mortal maidens. As always, Zeus seduced the damsel of his choice, and, as always, word filtered back to his jealous and angry wife, Hera. Deciding to deal with this directly, Hera, disguised as an old crone, went to Thebes, knocked at Semele's door, and asked for water. Semele got the water and Hera, fixing her with a gimlet glance, asked if Zeus loved her. Oh, yes, replied Semele, Zeus loves me more than he loves his wife. If that is so, Hera replied, ask Zeus to show himself to you in his true form, as he does to his wife. Semele remembered this, and the next time Zeus came to visit, she asked him to grant her a wish, without mentioning what it might be. Not paying as much attention to what she said as how she looked, Zeus granted her request. Show yourself to me in your true form, Semele asked. Zeus said he couldn't do that. Semele, dissatisfied, nagged on. Finally, Zeus did as she asked, appeared in his true form, and Semele was utterly consumed.[24] Semele was buried in Thebes under a pile of rocks, which has smoked from that day and to this and will forever.[25]

The story of Semele has everything, from everyday life and its consequentiality to insight into the wholly otherness of the divine. Character is destiny for people, wrote Heraclitus, but intelligence, knowledge and keeping your head in the game also helps a lot.[26] Poor Semele; she was like Rodney McCray, who came up, briefly, with the Mets. Rodney was put in to pinch run at first base, in the bottom of the ninth with one out, the bases loaded, and the Mets down, 5 to 4. McCray was promptly picked off first base. Like Semele, he did not have his head in the game, and, like Semele, one single moment utterly consumed him. He was sent down.

Baseball is as rich in myth and memory as classical Greece and Rome. In baseball one may choose among the endless stories and anecdotes, players and positions, games and teams, statistics and seasons, all constantly expanding to furnish the memory of even the longest life. Being a metaphor for life, baseball lives on memory as much, if not more, than on either the fleeting present or receding future. Time passes and hope may fade, but memory, like the greatness it chronicles, is always ours.

III

In *Remembrance of Things Past*, Marcel Proust uncovered the buried vistas of memory in a single instant. A madeleine cookie dipped in tea recalled a long-forgotten taste that opened extended reminiscence of the French aristocracy during the Belle Epoque before 1914. All memory is connected, expanding in surprising directions, even rising to consciousness. In modern

America, however, a single moment of unexpected recovery is not required. The electronic media function as a continuing "madeleine," endlessly pelting individuals and the general culture with memory real and virtual, some our own, most belonging to others but about to become ours, and all part of the collective cultural memory of post–Thomas Edison America. The relationship of the individual to the past has been reversed since the discreet years before the war that Proust chronicled. Now, instead of recovery, we filter, sifting through an inexhaustible supply of real and ersatz memory pertaining to others far more than ourselves in order to find memory appropriate to our lives. Instead of being recovered, memory in modern America is culturally rejected to make room for new memories; there are "madeleines" to spark recall but none to limit or judge it, and memory is now culturally collective and ubiquitous.

The cultural homogenization of memory can be seen most easily in radio and television, modern equivalents of the church bulletin board, the town crier, and the neighborhood gossip. The electronic media contrive an endless persistence, exemplifying William Faulkner's remark that in the South (and America as a whole) the past is not only not over, it is not even in the past. Everything old is new again in America, as radio and television stations devoted to "golden oldies" continually demonstrate. There are so many "golden oldies" that stations specialize. Some replay televised comedies, such as *I Love Lucy* or *The Andy Griffith Show*, others do game shows, still others concentrate on drama about love and loss, while some specialize in cops and action. The details of syndication are less significant than the genre, which is always growing to encompass new memories and new types of television. Radio has adopted the same programming technique with some stations replaying the noise of the nineties, long enough ago to be both "old" and "golden" and whose listeners, with a span of less than a decade, can relive the alleged music of their lost youth. Other stations concentrate on the eighties, at the edge of young memory, while others play the disco racket popular in the seventies, a full generation ago. Stations also play the music of grandparents, heard first in the fifties and sixties, and recalling the way it was when they and Elvis were young and strong and good.

Though youth is short, it is the interval of life when we acquire a life-long interest in baseball, if we get it at all. The enthusiasms of youth never depart completely; though they may abate under the pressure of everyday life, they remain a reservoir of what once made us happy. Moreover, the good things from our youth will be good for our own kids, so parents and family elders take the kids to ball games. The multi-generational nature of baseball attendance and support participates in the phenomenon of life relived, of lost youth and youth renewed, of nostalgia, the bittersweet memory of what was pure, innocent, and happy. It has been caught by William Shakespeare in sonnet form.

When to the sessions of sweet silent thought
I summon up remembrance of things past,
I sigh the lack of many a thing I sought,
And with old woes new wail my dear Time's waste.[27]

Here is haunting whisper of nostalgia, that always unsatisfied longing drawn
from the Greek words for pain and return. Sweet or not, the pain of return
becomes an exercise in understanding as well as memory, part of the process
in which meaning and beauty are both discovered and defined. We live busily
in time, moving from event to event, encounter to encounter, relentlessly carried forward, while the past steadily grows more beguiling in memory and
affection, and more inviting in revisiting the beauty and hope that has been
lost. The more a moment recedes in time the more layered and subtle understanding becomes. Baseball marks the passing time of life; as the details of
the moment and the game and the season dim, the richer and more mythic
memory becomes. What was once only a game, a diversion of an afternoon
or evening, becomes in continual remembering a moment of great meaning.

IV

American culture has its preferences in nostalgia, as do individuals. In
the decade of the 1990s, when fifty years had passed, World War II became a
matter of intense general interest. Tom Brokaw's book *The Greatest Gener-*
ation was more than a best-seller; it also defined the nation for those who
had fought and worked during those years. The works of Stephen Ambrose
on the war in Europe achieved a similar iconic status, and a D-Day Museum
was successfully established in New Orleans, a town more given to sin then
remembrance.[28] The core of baseball nostalgia has reflected a similar preference for times and events old enough to be distant and recent enough to be
remembered, and begins with the extraordinary season of 1941 (Joe DiMaggio's fifty-six-game hitting streak and Ted Williams' .406 season average) and
extends through the two decades or so after Hiroshima. These years became
the time in baseball that the nation remembered in song ("Talking Baseball"
and "Van Lingle Mungo"), in personal memoir (Billy Crystal, Doris Kearns
Goodwin, George Will) and in building ball parks, such as Camden Yards in
Baltimore, Jacobs Field in Cleveland, and the variously named park in Houston. The era from 1941 to 1965 in baseball has become a symbol of a country
that was more comfortable with itself and more certain of who the good guys
were, and more interested, therefore, in cultivating the memory and the tune
of those times. Those times have become celebrated on an age of national
comfort and prosperity, at least in the pastel tints of memory. America produced cars one could love, such as the Mustang, or the 1955–57 Chevrolets,
the Buicks with portholes and Cadillacs with fins. They could be enjoyed in

a time of expanding opportunity, as the GI Bill and state colleges and universities put higher education within reach of most and professional education within reach of the clever. Looking back, the years from 1945 to 1965 or so seemed to be an age of social virtue and cultural support for approved values. In hard historical fact, this was all unevenly distributed, and many were excluded almost altogether. It was the era of civil rights struggles, and a comfortable age for some was a heroic age for others.

In nostalgia, of course, reality of place, time or event matters less than remembrance. Golden ages are not based on facts but are constructed as myths. Whatever the fifties might have been, they now seem good in memory, and the artifacts which remain are pleasing reminders of a happy time. Nostalgia finds the good, whether it was there or not. But the core of nostalgia is always time itself, filled with incident, personality, folly, and fortune, both good and ill. In the fullness of time, as the bureaucratic ideal goes, chronology imperceptibly gives way to mythic and trans-historical time, where events and heroes acquire meaning beyond the moment and begin to inform the culture. But the base of the process is not the content of the past but rather that it is past, and sufficiently past that we can look at it again with an Augustinian eye.[29]

British writer Philip Gosse has suggested that what grips us relentlessly in nostalgic awareness is the time just beyond our reach. For many American adults, some part of that quarter-century between Joe DiMaggio's streak and the Koufax-Drysdale era fits Gosse's observation. That cannot last. No matter how satisfying the remembrance of and by the Greatest Generation, their time slips by. Already, fans consider Kirk Gibson's home run in the 1988 World Series to be the most dramatic hit ever, ignoring, among others, the Bambino's called shot. But the Babe hit his in 1932, long ago, beyond the reach of memory for anyone younger than eighty-five. In time, Gibson will become a childhood memory barely grasped. The current crop of adults remembers the quarter-century between 1941 and 1966 fondly because they are the right age. Eventually, of course, people will become — indeed, have already become — nostalgic over the unlovely events from the assassination of President Kennedy through Jimmy Carter, the Watergate crisis, hippies, crime, riots, gas lines and inflation that afflicted America through the Iran hostage crisis. The distress of that time will be no bar to fond memory. Time trumps beauty always.

V

In baseball, myth and nostalgia center on particular players more often than on collective personality of teams or the collective impersonality of the clubs. "Sing me a song for a Lad that is gone," runs the Caledonian ballad drawn from Robert Louis Stevenson, and it expresses the sense of inclusion of oneself with the player. Fans have long identified with individual players, and even the most mediocre have had a small cadre who followed their fortunes, rooting that talent would hold back time. Sometimes for a few years, talent did triumph, and youth, both the player's and our own, was magically extended. It is one of the game's greatest gifts.

To move beyond the coterie of childhood friends and current neighbors and acquire a larger following, players established a public persona which intrigued sports writers and fans generally. Some of the players were merely eccentric, though in a charming way. Boots Poffenberger, a right-handed pitcher who had a good year with Detroit in '37 and several chances after that, used to present himself to sports writers as having a "million dollar arm and a ten cent brain." His record, however, indicates that he may have overvalued both.

Poffenberger didn't play long enough or well enough to establish a significant public presence. He was an amusing part of the background. Other players, who were better at the game and also had engaging personalities, stayed around long enough to establish a public role. Floyd Caves "Babe" Herman was one such player. His tour with the Brooklyn Dodgers, though it lasted only half of his thirteen-year career, established a public persona that combined superb talent with a penchant for the off-beat. Babe Herman hit .324 over his career, and in 1930 hit .393. That was pretty good, but not good enough for the National League batting title. Bill Terry hit .401. But no one doubted Babe Herman could hit, and in 1945, after he had been out of the major leagues for seven years, the Dodgers signed him as a pinch hitter. Even at forty-two, Babe Herman was better than many of the wartime players, hitting .265, and driving in nine runs with his nine hits. Part of the reason for signing Babe Herman was publicity and entertainment, and he contributed that as well. On one of his pinch-hits, Babe stumbled over the bag while rounding first. This was not his first contretemps on the base paths. John Lardner wrote: "Floyd Caves Herman never tripled into a triple play, but he once doubled into a double play, which is the next best thing."[30]

Much newspaper comment centered on Herman's adventures afield. Where Joe DiMaggio displayed elegant grace, Babe Herman specialized in awkwardness. He was not a bad outfielder, to be compared with Smead Jolley who set the record for three errors in one play, and went down permanently after 1933, even though he had a .305 lifetime average. Herman merely made each play look harder than it was, establishing a reputation for being a poor fielder. But Babe Herman was good enough, and he usually, somehow, made the play. Sports writers used to write that fly balls hit him in the head, but Babe Herman denied that ever happened, though he did admit that a fly ball once hit him on the shoulder.

The secret of Babe Herman's popularity seems to have been an unselfconscious good humor. He did not try to create an image, he was just himself. He did not object to unflattering newspaper comments about his fielding or base-running. He played ball, hit superbly (no subsequent Brooklyn outfielder, including Dixie Walker, had as high a lifetime average), and fit into the Brooklyn way of seeing the world. Babe Herman might not have been as big a personal success had he played for the humorless Bronx Bombers, though they would have been a better team had they had him. But in Brooklyn he was just what the fans wanted, a cheerful and slightly offbeat player who was really good. After retirement, the fans did not forget him. He used to appear with Red Barber on the Dodgers radio broadcasts now and then. On one occasion Red commented that Babe's son, Robert Herman, was one of the directors of the Metropolitan Opera. Yeah, Herman replied, he certainly was, and then added in a tone of resignation that you can never tell how kids will turn out.

Brooklyn had a mediocre team when Babe Herman played there (1926–1931), and so he never occupied the center ring by playing in a World Series. But he evoked genuine and lasting affection across the Big Bridge, when Brooklyn was still a distinct and provincial entity, not quite the object of vaudeville ridicule that Philadelphia was, but still far from Broadway or Yankee Stadium.

There may be baseball fans who have never heard of Babe Herman, but all Americans, regardless of generation, have heard of Joe DiMaggio. He has been a national figure for sixty-five years as a baseball player, as a husband, as a pitchman on television, ever a constant model of grace, elegance and character, always to be admired. The canonization (and institutionalization, since this is America) of the DiMaggio legend as a permanent part of the American psyche took place in 1941, the last of DiMaggio's six great baseball years. In 1941, Joe DiMaggio hit safely in fifty-six consecutive games.

The hitting streak, from May 15 through July 16, was the longest in Major League history by a factor of 25 percent, and instantly became a celebrated on-going event.[31] Fans followed the streak day by day, and the newspapers followed it as closely as the pennant race, indeed more closely, since the Yanks again ran away from the rest of the American League, clinching the pennant on September 4 and winning by seventeen games. In Boston, Ted Williams, hearing from the scoreboard operators about the streak, used to yell over to center fielder Dom DiMaggio that Joe had gotten his hit. The streak became the centerpiece of the entire season, something wonderful and unique. People would see pennants won and lost, but DiMaggio's hitting streak was once in a lifetime.

In mythic terms, transforming Joe DiMaggio into a permanent national memory, the streak approximated the labors of Hercules, the homecoming of Odysseus, or the flight of Lindbergh. It was the defining heroic moment that combined undeniable fact with dream fulfilled. Stephen Jay Gould expressed this dual reality with his usual felicity.

A man may labor for a professional lifetime, especially in sport or in battle, but posterity needs a single transcendent event to fix him in permanent memory. Every hero must be a Wellington on the right side of his personal Waterloo; generality of excellence is too diffuse. The unambiguous factuality of a single achievement is adamantine. Detractors can argue forever about the general tenor of your life and works, but they can never erase a great event.[32]

The streak was that great event for reasons involving the extended event itself and its cultural context. As Gould and Stanford psychologist Amos Tversky have repeatedly shown, most sports statistics concerning streaks fall within the range of a standard random model, which is simply illustrated by tossing a coin. Heads or tails; over the long haul there will be about the same number of each. Making allowance for skill differential among players, their slumps and streaks still fall into the standard random model. Players hitting around the Mendoza Line (.200) will have more slumps than did Stan Musial, a lifetime .331 hitter, higher than Joe DiMaggio. Even after he went 0 for 4, Ray Oyler, a .175 hitter, was not "due" for a hit, though he may have been ready for a pinch-hitter. And Stan Musial will have more hot spells than Roy Smalley (.227), though in some games Stan the Man would go hitless and now and then Smalley got two or three hits. This also applies to teams. In 1916 the New York Giants won twenty-four games in a row, and finished fourth, seven games behind Brooklyn. In 1988, the Baltimore Orioles lost their first twenty-one games. They didn't win the pennant either. Both streaks and slumps were within the coin toss model. The standard random model always works. Once in a while, and baseball has been played for a great while, heads will come up twenty-six times in a row, and Jim Dyck, who had twenty-six lifetime home runs, will hit two in one game.

The single exception to the iron law of streaks and slumps is Joe DiMaggio's fifty-six-game hitting streak, which is a sufficient number of standard deviations for the normal distribution that it cannot have happened. For fifty-six consecutive games, Joe DiMaggio pitted his skill and will against pitchers, who possess a structural advantage over the hitters. Beyond that, DiMaggio had to face threats of rain shortening the game, bases on balls, errors, great fielding plays, and, most unkind and inevitable of all, bad luck. He did it every day for two months, starting from zero in every game. Three hits yesterday meant nothing; he must get a hit again today. And there was the pressure, as the streak lengthened against all probability and the sports writers made DiMaggio their main object of attention. Day after day, with the graceful reserve that marked his public persona, DiMaggio got another hit, just increasing the pressure within to continue and the determination by the other team to stop him. And, of course, each new hit in yet another game further displeased the Goddess Fortune, against whose capricious inconstancy no one can stand.[33]

The DiMaggio streak has been studied extensively, game by game, by

Michael Seidel in *Streak*, a fine book, making a further recounting, here or elsewhere, of the streak itself a work of supererogation. But DiMaggio's hitting streak in 1941 had a cultural resonance beyond baseball.[34] The most immediate and obvious impact emerged, as is so often the case, with Tin Pan Alley. Popular songs provide instant comment on things of note. Sometimes songwriters worked quickly to catch the moment, and no song caught the spirit of midsummer 1941 in American better than "Joltin' Joe DiMaggio." The basic theme was less how good DiMaggio was than how much the country needed him. The song's refrain was a tiny nugget of perfection: "We want you on our side."

In a baseball context, no one could disparage that simple sentiment. Joe DiMaggio had come to the Yankees in 1936, and the Bronx Bombers, after a three-year hiatus, won the American League pennant and the World Series. They did it again in 1937, 1938 and 1939, four consecutive pennants and Series. That hadn't been done before, and only the Yankees would do it again (1949–1953). After the stumbling in 1940, the Yankees would win the pennant again in 1941, and, of course, they would also win the Series. Five pennants and five Series in six years. The impact Joe DiMaggio had on the Yankees rivaled even that made by Babe Ruth.

DiMaggio's cultural influence rippled beyond the continued Yankee dominance in baseball. Joltin' Joe was simply the most beautiful player in baseball. He radiated a reserved and effortless elegance on and off the field. He lived Hemingway's definition of a gentleman, one who had grace under pressure, and no one in American sport flourished under greater and more constant pressure. He played in New York. He put his streak on the line in every game, his team relied on him every year, and the fans watched and listened and discussed his exploits with rapt admiration. Ty Cobb, a different sort of man altogether, believed that his dead father watched every game, demanding that Ty play hard, and Cobb never let his father down. Joe DiMaggio had a wider, and more vocal, audience, and he never let the fans, the team or the game down. He returned baseballs sent in by small boys to be signed. He bore his cultural responsibilities as a hero with public ease, keeping the strain inside where it belonged. Polite and generous, Joe DiMaggio lived, perhaps not always comfortably, the aristocratic ideal of a gentleman.

DiMaggio was Italian at a time when Italians were held in cultural disapprobation in America. A recent immigrant group, Italians did not seem to fit the English model of social attitudes or religious practices that defined approved norms in America. Italians had worked and prospered through the discrimination, but disapproval had hardly begun to soften in the years before Pearl Harbor. Part of this lack of social respect certainly stemmed from what Americans not Italian in ethnicity regarded as the quintessential Italian contribution to American life, and that was organized crime. By the late thirties, most had forgotten that Prohibition was the joint creation of the women's movement, Puritans, and small-town Protestantism. People saw only boot-leggers, illegal stills and breweries, the St. Valentine's Day Massacre and Al Capone. None of that looked socially useful or virtuous, and Italians got much of the blame, and if one threw in vice and gambling and union corruption, and many did, Italians did not appear to have made a positive contribution to American life.

Into that social milieu came Joe DiMaggio, who personified grace and beauty and the constant drive of perfection. He displayed the artistry of the game; a player must master the fundamentals and make the right play. DiMaggio always did. He carried that beyond the field into life. He was a silent and standing reproach to discrimination against Italians and disapproval of things Italian. His elegant persona, playing excellence, and social approval were so great that he began the cultural shift in how Italians were perceived in America. Like Othello, he has "done the state some service."[35]

The summer of 1941 was a good time for Joe DiMaggio's hitting streak. He provided a bright contrast to the gloom and death of war. All the world but America was already at war, and war could easily be seen approaching across both oceans. Assorted pacifists and America First denounced war and called for remaining neutral "in thought, word, and deed," but passionate longing and pious hope seldom prevail against geopolitical reality. A popular song expressed American concern with the world around them. Unlike "Joltin' Joe DiMaggio," it had not been composed for the immediate occasion, but had been pulled out of a filing cabinet by Irving Berlin and given to Kate Smith. "God Bless America" caught the larger anxieties, just as "Joltin' Joe DiMaggio" expressed the more parochial joy. Perhaps war approached; there still remained one last bit of innocent escape and joy before winter and Pearl Harbor. In the summer and fall of 1941, more and more Americans began to feel the travail ahead. In time of war, the whole nation would need the qualities of character that so distinguished Joe DiMaggio.

The fifty-six-game hitting streak in 1941 increased the standard national attention on baseball. Attention can also move from baseball to the world outside the game, again the result of the fame and approval given to a single player. This occurred in 1949, when a temperature inversion hit Donora, Pennsylvania. Donora was an ugly and impoverished town in the Pennsylvania metallurgical belt, where work was mainly in coal and iron, and where World War II had provided temporary relief from the Depression. The inversion became so serious that Donora literally experienced dusk at noon, and the air grew so acid with particulates and acids that people could not breathe. Smog would get attention when it occurred in Los Angeles and fog was famous in London, but why should anyone notice a bad air day in Donora? Stan Musial came from Donora, and he was generally regarded as the best player in the National League and one of the best liked. He had come up to the Cardinals in 1941, and had shown some promise by hitting .426 in twelve games.

Thereafter, Stan the Man became an iconic figure, less heroic than Joe DiMaggio but sufficiently beloved so that a statue of him was placed in front of Busch Stadium. Donora might be a dismal tank town, but a terrible incident of air pollution from Musial's hometown deserved coverage. Baseball is, after all, the national pastime, and part of the national myth and memory.

VI

Since myth and memory are so closely aligned in personal and cultural function it is hardly surprising that they share the characteristics of circularity. Both myth and memory invite constant reconsideration, as experience deepens understanding and understanding gives meaning to experience in an endless cycle of insight and action. We live forward to new experience but understand backward to new perspective. Augustine explained the nature of distance in the *Confessions*. The mind

> ... looks forward, it considers, it remembers, so that the reality to which it looks forward passes through what it considers into what it remembers. Who then denies that future things are not yet existent? Yet that is already in the mind an expectation of things to come. Who denies that past things no longer exist? Yet there is still in the soul the memory of past things.[36]

From moment to memory to myth is an Augustinian journey of time and perspective from event through ever greater understanding to genuine insight. This Augustinian journey occurs on both the individual level and within the entire culture, thus exhibiting the basic and clarifying difference between memory cherished locally and memory become myth. The process is contiguous with the movement of the culture itself. George Kubler, in *The Shape of Time*, described the movement of artistic style in the river of time in terms of waxing and waning of cultural approval, once operative over centuries, now the work, as all see in popular music, of mere decades. Included in this is myth. The insights on the otherness of the divine remain the same from Semele to Paul Tillich, but the mythic style has given way to the modern penchant for psychological explanation. Albert G. Spalding claimed that the success of baseball lay in its values, which were: "American Courage, Confidence, Combativeness; American Dash, Discipline, Determination; American Energy, Eagerness, Enthusiasm; American Pluck, Persistency, Performance; American Spirit, Sagacity, Success; American View, Vigor, Virility."[37] Today this seems a bit much; most commentators make do with unspoken concepts embodied in the word "hustle." The journey of myth discards as it adds, but myth itself remains constant. "Plus ça change, plus c'est la même chose," the more things change the more they stay the same, runs the French proverb.

Though constant, the change of memory and myth moves always in the same direction, around back to the beginning. The moment itself may be lost, and for all but the most exceptional and dramatic it usually is, but reflection on the memory replaces the moment, and the persistence of reflection leads to mythic meaning, to "A kinde of tune, which all things heare and fear," ending in "something understood."[38] The Hot Stove League, like "American vim, vigor, virility" mark moments and memories that have lost their cultural resonance. The mythic remnant, "something understood," continues, changing with the ephemera of style, continuing as an Augustinian reflection on the meaning the past gives the present, moving from moment about to be forgotten to moment about to be remembered, from Mel Ott's World Series home run in 1933 to Kirk Gibson's in 1988. The cultural cycle of myth-making and the personal process of transforming memory into meaning finds its modern expression with T. S. Eliot:

> We shall not cease from exploration
> And the end of all our exploring
> Will be to arrive at where we started
> And know the place for the first time.[39]

I

Hero Journey

2

The Big Hit

The hardest thing to do in sports is to hit a pitched baseball. This is the dictum of Ted Williams, and popular wisdom and literature gave Ted anterior confirmation of his observation. The most famous hit in the history of the game is not a hit. It is a strikeout, the most celebrated whiff of all. The victim of this far from uncommon disaster was Mighty Casey of the Mudville Nine, documented for all to see in Ernest Thayer's "Casey at Bat."[1] This lyric of baseball, first recited by DeWolfe Hopper, in 1888, and repeated by him thousands of times subsequently, transcends the personal, though that is the usual subject of lyric. It approaches epic, embracing the entirety of baseball as a game and as a metaphor for life.

Mighty Casey was not the only player to strike out in a crucial situation when the fans expected better.[2] Even the best hitter fails more than 60 percent of the time, and the fans always expect better. Baseball is organized to favor the defense, but the mythology cherished by fans usually concerns offense. Hope and reality collide, but hope that leads to myth matters more. The facts show a winning hit in almost every game, and the winning single in the fifth inning produces victory just as surely as a winning home run in the eighth or ninth. Even a home run in a late inning occurs nearly every day. The clutch hit, or lack of it, is a standard part of the game, even for the many poor teams that always dominate in baseball.

The essence of the big hit, which goes far, far beyond a winning hit, is the drama of the situation, out of which myth can arise. The hit itself is less than the context for the hit. A national audience creates the necessary atmosphere for a big hit, but mythic hits occur only on the biggest stages and in the most desperate circumstances when the hitter, always at a disadvantage, is the last best hope. Even that, which seems like everything, is not enough. There are also the imponderable elements of glamour and fashion.

In the seventh game of National League Championship Series of 1992, the Pirates led the Atlanta Braves 2 to 0 going into the last of the ninth inning. But Doug Drabek weakened, loading the bases with no one out. Stan Belinda, in relief, got the first two outs, while allowing one run to score on a sacrifice fly. The last out is always the hardest. Pinch hitter Francisco Cabrera, the last gasp for the Braves, got a two-out single to drive in the tying and winning runs. The winning run, Sid Bream, a slow runner gasping for breath and giving all the speed he had, scored just ahead of the throw.[3] Cabrera's hit came in the nature of a baseball miracle, for he was not a big hitter, or even a regular player, and had only two at-bats in the entire seven-game series. In Atlanta they remember and in Pittsburgh they try to forget, but in the land at large Cabrera's big hit has not become a mythic event. Francisco Cabrera somehow lacked the glamour of the Mighty Casey.

The biggest stage can sometimes be too small, even in the World Series, and that also happened. In 1991, the Minnesota Twins played the Atlanta Braves, and neither team represented a national market nor had developed a national fan base. The Series was even and exciting, going to the seventh game. The Braves, like the Cardinals in 1987, had won their three home games, but the Twins had won all the games played in their oddly configured home stadium, the Metrodome. Winners in 1987, the Twins were poised to do it again, being down 3 games to 2 when the Series returned to the Metrodome. In the sixth game, Kirby Puckett homered to open the home half of the eleventh inning, ending the game, 4 to 3, in favor of the Twins. Minnesota had now won seven consecutive home World Series games. The last game of the 1991 Series also went into extra innings. In the bottom of the tenth, Dan Gladden opened with a double. He was sacrificed to third, and the Braves walked Kent Hrbek and Kirby Puckett intentionally. Then Gene Larkin, not then or now a household name, singled to center field and won the game, 1 to 0, for Jack Morris, who went all the way. Larkin, in the biggest hit of his career, also won the World Series.[4]

Neither of these big hits, and hits do not come any bigger, have been elevated into a mythic moment in baseball, except in Minnesota. Perhaps that is just the way things are. If fame is fickle, myth is even more unpredictable. The triumph of glamour over reality is one of the definitions of an imperfect world. Dorothy Kilgallen, an exceptionally tough and capable newspaper woman in the thirties and forties, when journalism was not kind to women, understood about stage and setting and glam. She once commented about a critic (of her) that if he were so smart what was he doing in Perth Amboy?

Mythology suggests that some hits are bigger than big, fitting into the category of super-colossal, the Hollywood minimum for success. That describes Kirk Gibson's pinch-hit home run for the Los Angeles Dodgers to win the first game of the 1988 World Series. Bill Mazeroski hit an even bigger home run, in the ninth inning of the seventh game of the 1960 World Series, bringing victory to the Pittsburgh Pirates over the Yankees. Both were seen on television, ensuring national celebrity. Gibson's dramatic homer has steadily grown in mythic importance, and a recent (2003) fan poll voted it as the biggest and most spectacular hit of all. This is hardly surprising, as population growth, money, and leading trends in popular culture and technology increasingly find their home on the West Coast. Mazeroski's blast defeated the Yankees, the Evil Empire of baseball to those not Yankees fans. It has also given rise to a category of time, "Mazeroski moments," the fleeting joy felt when the good guys win and the world seems right. Mazeroski moments arrive infrequently, and are gone in an instant, but their memory never fades.

Super-colossal once amounted to something, but it has now given way to Immortal. In Hollywood, an environment of cynicism and hyperbole, Immortal usually means six months of good box office and thirty years of action toys, video games, clothes, stuffed animals, lunch boxes, back packs, syndication, cable television, reincarnation as an official golden oldie, and all the while a constant tsunami of money. In baseball, which is about losing as much as winning, Immortal is far less common than in Hollywood, and the biggest hits transcend mere money. They live on in myth and memory as moments of love and anguish. In the nature of things, nothing can be bigger than that.

I

In the summer of 1945, the soldiers began to come home. The war in Europe had ended, and the country simultaneously prepared for the horrific invasion of Japan and began the reconversion to civilian production. The war was coming to a close but at the same time was becoming more ferocious and violent. In that twilight time, the nation oscillated between relief and a terrible anxiety.

Part of the return-to-normalcy mode involved players rejoining to their teams after being released from national service. Hank Greenberg, the slugging star of the Detroit Tigers, now thirty-four years old, returned on July 1, after four years in the Army, where he had risen from private to captain. Hank showed he still had it by hitting a home run in his first game, and hit .311 over the last half of the season. Detroit needed his hitting, because the "nine old men" as the Tigers veterans were called were well past their prime. Outfielder Roger "Doc" Cramer, had played for the Philadelphia Athletics in the 1931 World Series, and, aged forty, he symbolized wartime baseball.

Detroit manager Steve O'Neill guided his veterans into first place on June 12, but the Tigers could never get a comfortable lead. Although the Yankees faded early in August, the Washington Senators and the St. Louis Browns continued to chase Detroit. The race went down to the last day, just as it had in 1944 when the Browns won their only pennant. On September 30, Detroit remained one game ahead of Washington; the Tigers had a record of 87 and 65 while the idle Senators were 87 and 67. Detroit had a doubleheader scheduled with the Browns. It rained in St. Louis that day, forcing an hour's delay to start the first game, which was played in a steady, gray drizzle above and increasingly sticky mud below. The Tigers needed to win that game to win the pennant, but trailed 3 to 2 in the ninth inning. Detroit loaded the bases, and Hank Greenberg hit a grand slam through the rain into the bleachers to win the pennant.[5] The war hero had resumed his role as the baseball hero.

Greenberg's clout put the Tigers into the World Series against the Chicago Cubs, and reminded fans of a similar twilight home run, this one by Cubs catcher Gabby Hartnett in 1938. The Cubs had a pretty good team in the 1930s. The country may have been mired in the Depression, and the Chicago school system might have gone bankrupt, paying teachers in script, but the Cubs stayed afloat. They won the pennant in 1929, only to lose the World Series to the Philadelphia Athletics in October, the same month as the stock market crashed on Black Tuesday. The Cubs won again in 1932, but became the victims of Babe Ruth's called home run in the World Series. Again, in 1935, the Cubs won, beating out the World Champion Cardinals by four games, but the Detroit Tigers, who had lost to the Cardinals in 1934, defeated the Cubs in the Series a year later. As the 1938 season began, the Cubs were again one of the favorites.

For most of the 1938 season the Cubs looked as if they would disappoint the fans on the North Side. Jolly Cholly Grimm, who had taken over late in the 1932 season and brought the Cubs home first, now seemed a bit shopworn. Eighty games into the season, with the Cubs only nine games over .500 and in fourth place, Grimm gave way to catcher Gabby Hartnett who became the player-manager. Perhaps that would help; after all player-manager Frankie Frisch had brought the Cardinals home first in 1934. Hartnett by 1938 had been the best catcher in the National League for a decade, and he might put a little vim and hustle into the Cubs. He did. The Cubs began to win at an accelerated pace, and entered September with the wind at their backs. Over the last month of the season the Cubs won twenty games while losing ten, slowly gaining on the first place Pittsburgh Pirates. On September 22, the Cubs visited the last place Phillies for the first of two doubleheaders. Chicago won them both, starting a ten game winning streak that carried them to the pennant.[6] The season climax began on September 27, when the Pirates came into Wrigley for a three-game series with the Cubs. The Cubs beat Pittsburgh in the first game, 2 to 1, for their eighth consecutive victory. Over 42,000 fans, standing room only, jammed into Wrigley Field to see Dizzy Dean, who had almost nothing left, pitch well enough to win, cutting the Pirates lead to only half a game.[7]

On September 28, with first place on the line, a mere 34,000 fans saw a memorable game. The Pirates went ahead in the top of the eighth inning, but the Cubs tied it with two runs in the home half of the eighth. The Pirates did not score in the top of the ninth, and enough daylight remained for one more half-inning. In the bottom of the ninth, with two men out, Cubs catcher and manager Hartnett came up. He would be the last hitter of the day. Pirates relief ace Mace Brown got two quick strikes on Hartnett. On the 0 and 2 pitch, Hartnett hit a long drive into the left field bleachers for a game-winning home run.[8] Hartnett's twilight homer not only won the game for Chicago, 6 to 5, it also put the Cubs into first place by half a game. It would become known as the "Homer in the Gloaming," giving a poetic and mythic touch to Gabby's big hit. Hartnett knew it was a big hit at the time. He told the sports writers after the game that the Homer in the Gloaming was "the greatest thing that had ever happened" to him.[9] The next day the Cubs defeated the demoralized Pirates, 10 to 1, moving a game and a half ahead with four games to go. For the Cubs one of the games with St. Louis was rained out, and the Cardinals took two of the remaining three. But the Pirates lost three out of four to the Reds, and Chicago won the pennant by two games.[10]

The Chicago Cubs were not the only ones to have a good September in 1938. As the Cubs won 11 of their last 13 games to win the National League pennant, Adolf Hitler bullied Great Britain and France into the Munich Accords. The crowds and the Party faithful in the streets of Munich, watching the officials riding to their meetings and awaiting news of war or peace, were as enthusiastic and much more numerous than the Chicago faithful who filled Wrigley for the crucial series against Pittsburgh. A fateful counterpoint to the Cubs' victory drive was Hitler's victory drive that led to the Munich crisis and delayed World War II for eleven months. *The New York Times* followed both the drama of joy and the drama of terror. On September 28,

GABBY HARTNETT. Standard hitter's pose, taken in the late thirties when Gabby became, for a time, a mythic figure. The photograph brings back the brief time of glory and greatness.

1938, the *Times* headline read: "Roosevelt Appeals Again to Hitler As Hope Wanes Reich Sets Attack For Saturday."[11] Neville Chamberlain's address was also front page center, just below the headlines. Chamberlain was appalled at the events, but unwilling to abandon efforts for peace. "How horrible, fantastic, incredible it is that we should be digging trenches and fitting gas masks because of a quarrel in a far away country.... I am going to work for peace to the last moment."[12] The Royal Navy thought the last moment had come, and called up 60,000 reservists. [13] Shooting would begin in three days.

The next day, in front page headlines as bold as those in the sports section describing Hartnett's Homer in the Gloaming, the *Times* announced the war might yet be averted: "Hitler Halts War Moves, Calls 4-Power Conference."[14] The Munich agreements were under way. Cognizant of domestic public opinion supporting peace at any price and recognizing that the Western democracies were unready for war, Chamberlain and Edouard Daladier gave Czechoslovakia to Hitler. A nervous America, sunk in economic depression, supported the Munich Accords and hoped that Hartnett's clutch performance would be a better omen for the future than Hitler's moment of dark triumph.

While the Thousand Year Reich came up 988 years short, baseball has continued to prosper. In the postwar years both leagues had close pennant races, some that went to playoffs and some that were decided on the last day of the season. In the National League in 1950, for the second year in a row, the pennant race came down to the last day of the season.[15] On October 1, 1950, the Philadelphia Phillies and the Dodgers, with the Phils on top and the Dodgers in pursuit, would decide the pennant in a single game.

The Phillies were fighting for their first pennant since 1915. The Phillies had long been one of the doormats of the National League, normally finishing in or near the cellar. They occasionally provided some gaudy entertainment in spite of a poor record. In 1930, the Phillies had a .315 team batting average, scored 944 runs in a 154-game season, had two hitters, Chuck Klein (.386) and Lefty O'Doul (.383), in the top five in the League, and had the worst ERA, at 6.71. The fans saw a lot of action at Baker Bowl. The Phillies, of course, came in last.[16]

In 1915, the Phillies had won their only other (to that time) pennant. This was due entirely to Grover Cleveland Alexander, who won thirty-one games, more than a third of the team's total ninety.[17] After that brief movement of glory, the Phils fell back to their accustomed ineptitude, which did not begin to change until 1948, when they came in sixth. In 1949, the Phillies improved to third, their highest finish since 1917, a forgotten highlight of the home front during the war to end all wars. And then, in 1950, the Phils were still in it on the last weekend of the season. Indeed, they were in first, barely. This departed dramatically from the usual Phillies season, and the Philadelphia fans, hardened to catastrophe, assumed that it was just a matter of time until the Phils blew it again. The novelty was that this year, Phillies fans would have to wait until the last day of the season for inevitable disaster.

The Philadelphia climb from the lower depths to the pennant began in 1946, when they added Del Ennis to the outfield and Andy Seminick became the regular catcher. The rest of the team were veterans of better years with better teams. In 1948, the Phils brought in three new faces, two destined for the Hall of Fame. Robin Roberts joined a shaky pitching staff, Richie Ashburn hit .333 as a rookie center fielder and Granny Hamner took over at second base. These were the core of the "Whiz Kids" as the young Philadelphia team would be called two years later. In 1949, the Phils added Willie "Puddin' Head" Jones at third base, and Curt Simmons, Russ Meyer and Jim Konstanty joined the pitching staff. A year later Eddie Waitkus took over at first, Bob Miller and Bubba Church strengthened the always shaky pitching, and Jim Konstanty, with a record of 16 and 7, and twenty-two saves in seventy-four games, became baseball's premier relief pitcher.[18]

The Whiz Kids went into first place during the last week of July, and stayed there, though they did experience moments of vertigo. In the ten days between September 19 and 29, the Phillies blew five and a half games of a seven-game lead, and had two games with the on-coming Dodgers to end the season. The Dodgers won on September 30, and the Philadelphia lead shrank down to a single game.[19]

In the last game of the season both teams pitched their best. Robin Roberts worked for the Phils against Don Newcombe of the Dodgers. Roberts was young and strong, and, as the pennant seemed to be slipping away, Phils manager Eddie Sawyer went to Roberts more and more often. By the last day of the season, Roberts was starting his third game in five days. As was usually the case, both Roberts and Newcombe were better than the hitters. The score was 1 to 1 going into the last of the ninth inning, when the Dodgers almost won. Roberts walked Cal Abrams to open the ninth and Pee Wee Reese followed with a single. Duke Snider singled to center and Richie Ashburn make a perfect throw to catcher Stan Lopata to nail Abrams at the plate by several feet. Roberts then walked Jackie Robinson to load the bases with one out, and got Carl Furillo on a foul ball pop-up and Gil Hodges on a fly ball.

In the tenth inning the Phillies won the game and the pennant. With two men on and one out, Dick Sisler, a run-of-the-mill left-handed hitting outfielder, who was having his best year in the Show, hit an opposite-field home run down the line into the left field stands. The Phils won 4 to 1, making Robin Roberts the Phils' first twenty-game winner since Grover Cleveland Alexander and making Dick Sisler an instant hero. It was a blinding moment of fame and recognition in an otherwise average career.[20]

For the Dodgers and their fans it was a sharp disappointment. Branch Rickey, the Dodgers president, lost his temper and criticized Dem Bums for being lazy and complacent, which was not true. The Brooklyn Dodgers went on to win four pennants in the 1950s, and then, transported to Los Angeles, won again in 1959. After a couple of winning years, in 1952 and 1953, the Brooklyn fans began to forget Sisler's clutch blast. Not in Philadelphia. For the Phillies fans this grew to be a moment to savor and remember, a rare moment of success in a long slog of failure. It had been thirty-five years since the Phils had won, and it would be thirty more before they won again. No one forgot Dick Sisler and the Whiz Kids. As the Phillies resumed their habit of coming in last, Sisler's home run remained a memory of triumph over all the odds and against the arrogance of success.

II

A clutch home run in the World Series can gain mythic resonance from the magnitude of the underlying event. The stage expands from local to national, especially in coverage by television. Public interest attains the cultural critical mass of general memory, constantly reinforced as the hit reappears on the warm-up shows of subsequent Series. After a few years hundreds of millions of people have seen the hit, often more than once, and sports fans look forward to seeing the hit again as part of the shared ritual of World Series lore.

One of these television-enhanced big hits came in the 1954 World Series between the Indians and the Giants, where it functioned as the counterpoint to Willie Mays' stupendous catch. The catch did not end the game; it allowed the game to continue still tied at two runs apiece. In the bottom of the tenth inning the Giants threatened. Bob Lemon, who had gone all the way for Cleveland, walked Willie Mays with one out. Mays stole second on the first pitch to Hank Thompson. Lemon walked Thompson intentionally to set up the double play. Monte Irvin, a Hall of Fame outfielder was the next hitter, but Leo Durocher, the New York manager, made a change. He brought in Dusty Rhodes, a left-handed hitting utility outfielder to hit for Irvin. Rhodes had had a good year in 1954, hitting .341 in eighty-two games, most of those as a pinch hitter. [21] Monte Irvin was much the better hitter, but Leo had a hunch. He had honored his hunches all season, and brought the Giants home five games ahead of a better team, the Brooklyn Dodgers. Now, in a World Series no one thought the Giants would win, Leo played his hunch. On Lemon's first pitch Rhodes hit a towering pop fly into short right field. The Indians' right fielder Dave Pope and second basemen Bobby Avila chased the lazy pop back toward the right field stands. The ball had just enough height so the parabola carried it into the first row of the lower deck, where it dropped in for a three-run game winning homer.[22]

In those days, homers into the short right field stands at the Polo Grounds were still called "Chinese home runs," and the sports writers honored baseball tradition and used that politically incorrect phrase. Though the origins of the name remain occluded, the reasons for comment were clear enough. The Polo Grounds, where the Giants played, was an oddly shaped park. It was 257 feet down the right field line to the stands, which was elevated behind about 12 feet of wall, and it was even a few feet shorter down the left field line into the overhanging upper deck. The oblong park dropped rapidly away, and it was 483 feet to the center-field bleachers, and more than 500 feet to the recessed clubhouse in dead center field.[23] If a player planned on hitting home runs in the Polo Grounds, he needed to pull the ball.

Rhodes, whose World Series heroics in 1954 included another home run, two pinch-hit singles, and seven RBIs, was not the only player to be accused of hitting Chinese home runs. One of the Giants' greatest and most popular players, Mel Ott, hit plenty of homers into the short right field porch, though often into the upper deck. Ott had a strange batting style, dropping his hands and raising his front leg, perching on his back leg as the pitcher threw. Everyone in baseball knew that no one could hit that way, certainly not for power and average. That observation was mostly true. No one but Ott could hit that way, but he could hit superbly. He had hit 511 home runs, at the time the National League record, had batted in 1860 runs and compiled a .304 average over a twenty-two-year career.[24]

Mel Ott came to the Giants in 1926 from Gretna, Louisiana, a small town across the river from New Orleans. He was then sixteen years old, and never played in the minors. He was recommended to John McGraw, the Giants manager, by a local lumber magnate. Scouting was rather casual in those days. Walter Johnson had been recommended to the Washington Senators by a traveling cigar salesman. Ott had been a schoolboy standout on the sandlots of Gretna, where he both caught and played the outfield. He was small for an athlete, only five feet nine inches when fully grown, but there was something about him. He could really play. Observing his unorthodox hitting style, McGraw kept him on the Giants. Exaggerated stance or not, the kid could hit, and McGraw said that he didn't want a minor league manager to tinker with it. When Ross Youngs, a Hall of Fame outfielder, died after the 1927 season, McGraw sent Ott, also a Hall of Fame outfielder, into right field as Youngs's replacement. Ott remained there through the 1945 season.

Sports writers used to kid Ott about his Chinese home runs, saying that he had mastered the technique of hitting the short homer. Ott, who was serious about baseball and worked hard on his game, put the short right field at the Polo Grounds in its proper perspective. He reminded the writers that the other hitters in the National League faced the same right field fence that he did. If hitting a home run down the line was so easy, they should be able to do it also.

Ott's biggest home run, which achieved a mythic status for a time, was not a Chinese home run, nor was it hit at the Polo Grounds. It came in Griffith

Stadium, in the tenth inning of the final game of the 1933 World Series, in which the Giants defeated the Washington Senators, 4 games to 1.

For most Americans the autumn of 1933 was a terrible and testing time. A quarter or so of the working population was unemployed, and many were on the road looking for anything in the way of work, which always seemed to be somewhere else. Others fell into the listless desperation of defeat admitted and accepted. Those still working lived in constant anxiety about their jobs and companies. Through it all, though, Americans continued to follow baseball. Attendance dropped as disposable income vanished, but people still followed the game in the papers. Newspapers in Major League cities covered the game lavishly with picture and prose, and fans could keep themselves fully informed on why their team was losing and how it happened. In the nature of the game, some team must win, and in 1933 the Washington Senators, having finished third in the American League the season before, played unexpectedly strong baseball. The Senators entered first place, passing the World Champion New York Yankees, on June 21, and, save for two days in July, stayed there for the rest of the season.[25] They finished a comfortable nine games ahead of the Yankees, who had pitching problems. The New York Giants were really a long shot. The Broadway Beauties, as they had been called in earlier and happier times, had not won the National League pennant since 1924, and in 1932 they had finished in sixth place, ten games under .500. In 1933, informed opinion held that the Giants could finish fifth, or fourth, maybe. But Bill Terry, in his first full year managing the Giants, took his club into first place on June 10, and held it for the rest of the season, beating out Pittsburgh by four games.[26] Only a single reporter on a major league paper predicted both winners.

Having handicapped the pennant races so successfully, the conventional experts on baseball, mostly sports writers, turned to the Series. Washington was the consensus choice. Position by position the Senators seemed stronger and their pitching looked to be as good as the Giants, perhaps better. The Giants were a surprise winner, and the AL was the stronger league, so the experts went with the Senators.

In life, there are few things so unimportant that they ought to be left to experts, and baseball is not one of them. But here the experts get a pass. No one could have anticipated the pitching performance of Carl Hubbell, who won games 1 and 4. Even Hubbell could not pitch every day, and on the days when he did not pitch, the Senators had a chance, or, to be more precise, a third of a chance. In the fifth and final game, the Giants started "Prince" Hal Schumacher against Alvin "General" Crowder for Washington. The Giants scored early, and knocked the General out of the box in the sixth inning. Leading 3 to 0 into the bottom on the sixth, Prince Hal gave up a three-run homer to Fred Schulte which tied the score. Bill Terry brought in Dolf Luque, "the Pride of Havana." The veteran Cuban right-hander, who had a twenty-year career in the National League, was near the end, not surprisingly since he was forty-three years old in 1933. But he still had his good stuff in short stretches, and he held the Senators at bay. In the top of the tenth inning, with two outs, Mel Ott hit a home run off Schulte's glove into the stands. It won the game, 4 to 3, and the 1933 World Series.[27] The Pride of Havana held the Senators scoreless in the bottom of the tenth, and gained his only World Series victory with 4.1 innings of scoreless relief pitching.

III

Mel Ott and Dusty Rhodes hit World Series home runs a long time ago, and the New York Giants no longer exist, so the memory of their mythic hits has faded. More recent World Series home runs have updated the mythology of the big hit, changing the details of the story but leaving the essential truth untouched. America is the land of everything "new and improved," and mythology has no exemption from the national affection for modernity. The old days and the old ways may be ritually celebrated with parades, fireworks, picnics, and political speeches of incomparable boredom, but genuine enthusiasm is usually reserved for the latest electronic technology. In baseball, the original American team sport, recent mythic home runs illustrate the American cultural practice of renewing accepted categories of entertainment through modern examples. Popular music sets the style, constantly adding "songs" while simultaneously making everything old new again.

Kirk Gibson's home run to win the first game of the 1988 World Series for the Dodgers over the Oakland Athletics has become a striking baseball moment, and its mythic importance has steadily grown over the years. Every component needed or desired for mythic awe embellished this home run. The Dodgers were decided underdogs to the powerful Athletics. Tommy Lasorda, the Dodgers manager, told the press: "We shouldn't even be on the same field with the Athletics."[28] This was, of course, the usual praise ritually lavished on the other guys, and was designed to lower their emotional intensity and induce complacency. It formed part of the ordinary warm-up to the Series. Lasorda, however, was not alone in holding these sentiments. *New York Times* sports writer Murry Chass reported: "The Athletics ... are considered a relatively heavy favorite to beat the Dodgers. But the Mets had more than their pitchers and they, too, were supposed to beat the Dodgers."[29] The sense that upsets can and do happen in a short Series also appeared in the press comment. St. Louis Cardinals manager Whitey Herzog noted: "Over 162 games form holds up; in 7 games chance may show up."[30] The air of confidence in impending victory certainly affected comments made by the Athletics. Jose Canseco, a feared slugger, gave an interview that combined eagerness with complacency. "We're on a roll; we're enthused, and we've got lots of confidence."[31] Since Oakland had just defeated the Red Sox, 4 games to 0, in the playoffs, there seemed no reason to doubt either the sentiment or the authenticity of Canseco's remarks. The sports reporters picked up the atmosphere around the Athletics locker room. A story on the eve of the Series stated baldly that the Athletics "are the favorites here, and they seem to like it."[32]

Part of the confidence exuded by Oakland seems to have come from the injury to the Dodgers' leading slugger, Kirk Gibson. A former college football player, Gibson had been a star with the Detroit Tigers before coming to Los Angeles in 1988, just in time to help the Dodgers to the pennant. But the long season took its toll on the thirty-one-year-old Gibson. He had played in increasing distress during the playoff games against the Mets, and he could not go against Oakland in the first game of the Series. Joseph Durso in the *New York Times* built most of his story of the game around Gibson's absence and presence. "Gibson hobbled by a strained ligament in his right knee, and a severely pulled hamstring in his left leg, sat and watched for nine innings." For all but the first of those nine innings, the Dodgers were behind. Mickey Hatcher had hit a two run homer in the bottom of the first, but Canseco had answered with a grand slam in the top of the second. By the last of the ninth, Los Angeles had cut the Athletics' lead to one run, but Oakland went to their ace relief pitcher, Dennis Eckersley. For a while that seemed like a good idea. Eckersley got two of the first three Dodgers he faced, and then, as a last hope, Lasorda sent the limping Gibson out to pinch-hit. Gibson couldn't run; he could hardly walk, and it was clear that anything less than a home run would see him thrown out at first. Joseph Durso described a mythic moment in mundane terms.

> And out of the dugout came Gibson, who had received a cortisone shot before the game. He had not been expected to play for perhaps a few days.
> The count rose to 3 balls and 2 strikes, and then Gibson reached and pulled a long drive to right field, where it carried into the seats for a two-run home run that electrified the crowd of 55,933 and gave the opening game to Tommy Lasorda's "team of destiny." [33]

The *New York Times* confined coverage of this triumph of competitive fire and will over debility and long odds to the sports pages. The front page described assorted matters of ordinary insignificance. There was a presidential election going on, but the Bush-Dukakis race produced mainly boredom. Civil war and starvation continued in the Sudan, but that is, apparently, the immemorial Sudanese way. Ongoing ethnic strife defaced the public life of Yugoslavia, still a state but never a nation, but civil war, atrocity, hatred, communal violence and partition are standard historical practice in the Balkans. Only in a technical sense could any of the stories dominating the front page be considered news; at most they were mere detail embellishing conditions already known, expected, and deplored. The real news, a dramatic expansion of the mythic dimension of baseball, the transformation of the momentary into the momentous, the visible personification of all that Americans like to think embodies themselves as a people, all of this strong and wondrous stuff rated only a small note in a box.

Kirk Gibson's home run won the first game of the 1988 World Series, but, now and then, someone hits a home run that wins the entire Series. In 1993, Joe Carter hit a home run to bring the Toronto Blue Jays their second consecutive Series victory and condemn the Philadelphia Phillies to their accustomed Series defeat, on the few occasions the unlucky Phils even got that far.

The Blue Jays led, 3 games to 2, when the Series returned to Toronto for the sixth game, and the seventh, too, if necessary. By the ninth inning it appeared that a seventh game might be necessary. The Phils led, 6 to 5, going into the bottom of the ninth, and they had Mitch Williams "Wild Thing" pitching in relief. Williams was erratic both of mind and arm, lacking control of his temperament as well as his pitches. When he was "in the groove," as the players used to say, Williams was a mighty effective relief pitcher. And when he was not, the Wild Thing had his troubles.

In the ninth inning of game six, Williams gave clear indication that he was going to have his troubles. Two of the first three hitters got on base, bringing up Joe Carter. Williams got the count to 2 and 2, even though only his slider was working well. For his fifth pitch, the Wild Thing tried another slider, down and in. He didn't get it far enough down or far enough in, and Carter hit it over the left field fence for a three-run homer. Phillies outfielder Pete Incaviglia watched it disappear over the wall, taking with it the game, the World Series, the ring, the fame, the money, and the opportunities that go to the victors.

Writers covering the Series compared Carter's home run to that hit by Bill Mazeroski to win the 1960 Series for the Pittsburgh Pirates over the New York Yankees, the only previous time a Series had ended on a home run. The opening of the main story on the game began with those two hits. "With Joe Carter ... reprising the act of Bill Mazeroski, the Toronto Blue Jays tonight repeated as World Champions."[34]

The national paper of record, the *New York Times,* ran a picture of the hit on the front page, but the story was confined to the sports section. The front page covered some perennial worries about health care, dealt with the mayoral campaign of the not-yet-celebrated Rudy Giuliani, and featured a town in Somalia that was, to everyone's surprise and delight, no longer a scene of dearth, death, and destruction, which are the immemorial Somali way. While the Somali story was genuine news none of the other stuff had the psychic heft of Carter's mighty belt.

The initial home run to win the World Series came in 1960, and has grown into one of the mythic moments in the history of baseball. The lordly Yankees of 1960 were one of the good teams in the history of the game. They no longer had the incomparable Joe DiMaggio, but the Yanks did have Mickey Mantle and Roger Maris, to say nothing of Yogi Berra and Whitey Ford. The rest of the team was strong as well, and Casey Stengel had become a legendary manager. The Yanks had won ten pennants in the last twelve years, and they had taken the Series eight times. The Pirates, by way of comparison, were merely a team with most of the players having good years, but no one thought of a Pittsburgh dynasty. Sports writers and fans alike agreed that the Yanks would win the Series. Winning the World Series was what the Yankees did.

For a while, it looked as if the smart money, and much of the ordinary money as well, had been right. The Pirates did win the first game, played at Forbes Field in Pittsburgh, by the score of 6 to 4, as Vern Law, the Pirates' twenty-game winner, pitched seven strong innings. But for the next two games it looked as if the Pirates' first hurrah had also been their last. In the second game the Yanks won, 16 to 3, getting nineteen hits and pounding six Pittsburgh pitchers. When the Series moved to New York, Whitey Ford pitched a four-hit shutout and the Yanks scored ten runs on sixteen hits. The Pirates' starting pitcher, Vinegar Bend Mizell, who was later elected to Congress, got only one man out of the four he faced in the first inning, when New York scored six runs, four coming on Bobby Richardson's grand slam.[35] The Yankee assault on the Pirates' pitching might be a little beyond what the New York fans expected, or even hoped, but the results were just what they had expected.

Then, after having been slaughtered twice, the upstart Pirates came back and won another game. Pittsburgh sent Vern Law back to the mound for his second Series start, and he pitched better than he had in the opener. Law again lasted into the seventh inning, giving up only two runs, and Roy Face saved the game, just as he had in the opener.[36] Pittsburgh won, 3 to 2, and the Yanks made only eight hits. The next day, to the surprise and dismay of the Yankee fans, the underdog Pirates did it again. This time Harvey Haddix pitched into the seventh inning, and again Face saved the game, his third in the Series. The Pirates won, 5 to 2, and the Yanks got only five hits. Pittsburgh had taken two of three at Yankee Stadium, and headed home with a 3 to 2 Series lead.[37]

Returning to cozy Forbes Field seemed to suit the Yankees perfectly. Stengel sent Whitey Ford to the mound again and he shut the Pirates out again. This time the Yanks got twelve runs on seventeen hits, and Bobby Richardson drove in three more runs to raise his total to a Series record of twelve.[38] For the Yankees fans, the renewed barrage on Pittsburgh pitching restored order. The overall pattern of the Series was now clear. Hitting meant the Yanks would win, and Forbes Field was a friendly place for hitters.

For the seventh game the Yankees started Bob Turley, who had won game 2, pitching into the ninth inning. This time Turley lasted one inning. After giving up a two-run two-out homer to Rocky Nelson in the first, Turley began the second by giving up a lead-off single to Smoky Burgess, the Pittsburgh catcher. Stengel had seen enough. He brought Bill Stafford in to relieve Turley, but Stafford allowed two runs of his own, and the Pirates led, 4 to 0, after two innings. The Pittsburgh pitcher, Vern Law, making his third Series start, was doing just fine. He gave up a home run to Moose Skowron in the fifth, but the Pirates still had a three-run lead when the Yanks came to bat in the top of the sixth. Then things fell apart for the Pirates. Law had given all he had. After Bobby Richardson and Tony Kubek got on to start the inning, Roy Face came in to relieve one more time. One time too many. Face could not hold the line, and the Yanks scored four runs in the sixth to take the lead, 5 to 4. New York added two more runs in the eighth, and it looked as if the powerful Yankee bats would pull it out.

In the bottom of the eighth inning the Pirates came back, thanks largely to a bad hop on a double-play ground ball. After Gino Cimoli led off the inning with a single, Bill Virdon hit a sharp bouncer to Tony Kubek at shortstop. It was a room-service double-play ball until it hit a pebble, bounced up sharply, and hit Kubek in the throat. Both runners were safe, and Kubek had to leave the game. The Pirates used the lucky break to score four runs, the last three coming on reserve catcher Hal Smith's home run. Pittsburgh now led, 9 to 7, going into the ninth. Bob Friend, the new Pittsburgh pitcher, had had a tough Series, and now he had a tough inning. He gave up two quick singles to Bobby Richardson and Dale Long. Danny Murtaugh, Pirates manager, brought in another starter, Harvey Haddix, to stop the rot, but the Yanks got two runs to tie the score at 9 apiece.

Then it happened. Ralph Terry, who had gotten the last out in the bottom of the eighth, faced Bill Mazeroski leading off in the bottom of the ninth inning. Terry survived his first pitch, but not the second. Mazeroski hit Terry's second pitch over the left field wall to win the Series in a single swing.[39] The Pittsburgh Pirates were World Champions for the first time since 1925, when America had Prohibition, no one had heard of Hitler, and the movies were silent. The crowd of 36,683, which filled Forbes Field, an old park, went into baseball delirium, and the fans in the field boxes raced onto the field to accompany Mazeroski around the bases. Victory in the Series "touched off a celebration that is sweeping through the city like a vast conflagration."[40] Mazeroski himself said that he was too happy to think, but he was not too happy to be gracious. A fourteen year old kid, Andy Jerpe, got the ball in a vacant lot, and brought it back to the hero. Mazeroski autographed the ball and handed it back. "You keep it, son. The memory is good enough for me."[41]

3

The Perfect Game, or Close Enough

Baseball, Yogi Berra tells us, is 90 percent pitching and the other half is mental. The opposite view was expressed by Gene Mauch who called the pitcher a mere initiator of the action. Yogi, one of modern America's significant social philosophers, has it right this time as he usually does. From the time of Jim Creighton, a pitcher who was baseball's first professional player, the game has revolved around pitching. Much of the evolution of baseball rules concerns the proper balance between pitching and hitting. Since 1890, the rules have almost always shifted to favor the hitters, who seem perennially in need of help.[1] In 1893, baseball moved pitchers from the box back five feet to the rubber, which increased distance and limited pitchers' lateral mobility. For a few years hitters feasted on the change, but by the first decade of the twentieth century pitching again dominated the game. Pitchers were learning to spit on the ball, scuff the ball, oil one side of the ball, drive small nails into the ball, all found to be useful techniques if you lacked the ability of Christy Mathewson or Walter Johnson, and everyone else did. By 1920, pitching had become so dominant that baseball outlawed adulterating the ball, except for seventeen designated spitball pitchers (eight in the National League and nine in the American) who could not continue if denied their primary pitch.[2] Several of the designated spitballers went to the Hall of Fame and the rest of the hurlers, formally denied outside help, developed clever and clandestine ways to massage the baseball.

Outlawing the spitball, the scuff ball, the shine ball and other imaginative competitive activity turned out to be inadequate support for hitting. Fans loved home runs, and the baseball itself became livelier. The rabbit ball certainly helped. Babe Ruth set a season record for home runs in 1919 (twenty-nine), 1920 (fifty-four), 1921 (fifty-nine) and 1927 (sixty). Hack Wilson drove in 191 runs in 1930, in spite of being hung over nearly every day of his adult life. Lou Gehrig, Mel Ott, Jimmie Foxx, Hank Greenberg slugged away, setting records and becoming fan favorites. Baseball prospered. The owners loved it.

But pitching began to change, adjusting to the rabbit ball and the batters' efforts to hit for power and distance. The last .400 hitter was Ted Williams (1941) and the last before him was Bill Terry (1930). By the postwar era hitters belted out home runs, but a .300 average became steadily less frequent. Pitchers tried new things, such as a slider, split-finger, or cut fastball. They threw harder, and ninety miles per hour became the minimum speed unless you were Greg Maddux, which no one else was, or mastered the spitter for over 300 victories, like Gaylord Perry. Relief pitching went from being a novel success to several distinct pitching categories, from closers to set-up men, and became an essential part of the game. Adjustment is the essence of baseball.

By 1968, pitchers were doing so well that the baseball moguls lowered the mound to help hitters, and by the nineties the baseball was wound so tightly that it bounced on its own with no one touching it. But perfect balance still eludes the purveyors of the game. What is wanted is clear enough. Pittsburgh pitcher Bob Veale put it in a nutshell. "Good pitching always stops good hitting and vice versa."[3] And sometimes it does.

The gold standard in stopping good hitting, as well as the much more common category of ordinary hitting, is pitching a no-hitter, and that is done every year, often by pitchers who are otherwise quite ordinary.[4] Most achieve the requisite fifteen minutes of fame, and then fall back into the ranks of workaday ball players. Their stunning individual performances fail to attain mythic status. This unkind fate occurred to the greatest pitching performance to that date in the history of the World Series, which fans and writers duly noted and soon forgot. It came during the World Series of 1945, which has passed into history but not into memory.

Claude William Passeau was a pretty good pitcher in his day. In 1940, he won twenty games, and during the pennant year of 1945 he won seventeen. It was good enough to earn him the start for the Chicago Cubs in the third game of the World Series. Since the Series was tied at a game apiece, this was a crucial start. No one then knew the Cubs, who had last won in 1908, would never again win a World Series, or even lose one. Over the years the Cubs had been a good team. Why would that not continue? There seemed to be a lot at stake.

Game 3, on October 5, 1945, was an afternoon game, played on grass at Briggs Stadium in Detroit.[5] The park was full, over 55,000 in attendance, with most rooting for the Tigers who, having won the second game of the Series, were presumed to be on their way. After all, Passeau was the Cubs' third starter, and Detroit's big hitters, who had scored only four runs in the first two games would surely open up on this guy. The Chicago fans, not entirely unreasonably, saw a different dynamic for Game 3. This was the last game in Detroit; the next four, if all were needed, would be in Chicago in friendly and historic Wrigley Field. If the Cubs could win this game, they would return home with a two-to-one advantage in the Series and with the home field in their favor. So Game 3 was not just a game, it was the pivotal game in the whole Series. Win this one, the Cubs fans reasoned, and the Cubs would win a World Series for the first time since Teddy Roosevelt ruled America and nobody had heard of Al Capone.

Passeau, third starter or not, began the game in an encouraging fashion. After the Cubs had failed to score in the top of the first inning, Passeau began in the bottom of the first by getting routine outs. Skeeter Webb, the Detroit shortstop and a .199 hitter, hit a grounder to Roy Hughes, and the Cubs shortstop threw him out. Eddie Mayo bounced to third, and Stan Hack threw him out. Roger Cramer hit a routine fly to Andy Pafko in center field. Passeau was in complete control. But that would change in the second inning. After Hank Greenberg struck out and Roy Cullenbine hit a fly ball to Peanuts Lowrey in left, Rudy York, the Detroit first baseman, hit a single to left field. O.K. thought Tiger fans; now it starts. But that would be the Tigers' big offensive threat. York was stranded at first as Jimmy Outlaw flied out to Andy Pafko in center field. But the Tigers had a hit, the first of the game.

Rudy York's single was also the Tigers' last hit of the game. Detroit did not even have another base runner until catcher Bob Swift walked to start the home half of the sixth inning. Sensing big things, Detroit manager Steve O'Neill put Red Borom in to run for the not-too-swift Swift. It made no difference. Harvey Walker, pinch-hitting for pitcher Stubby Overmire, promptly hit into a double play. That ended the Detroit offensive outburst. Passeau retired the next ten hitters. He had faced twenty-eight men, one over the minimum, and had pitched a one-hit shutout. The entire game had taken less than two hours.

Passeau had pitched in a tight ballgame. The Cubs got eight hits, scoring two runs in the fourth and an insurance run in the seventh, driven in by Passeau himself on a fly out. Detroit was never out of the game. Passeau had pitched under pressure conditions, with modest hitting support and in the World Series. It was a career game, and, after the Series, which the Cubs lost four games to three, everyone forgot about it. Even the *Baseball Guide* for 1946 treated it as just another Series game worth only a short paragraph.[6] James Mutrie, manager of the New York Giants in the 1880s, used to moan that baseball was "an uncertain game." So is memory.

The reasons why achievement leads to trivia rather than fame are often obscure, but perhaps not this time. In 1945 the headlines, the hopes, the fears and the entire attention of all America centered on war, peace and death. The stunning ferocity of the battles at Iwo Jima and Okinawa convinced Americans that Japan would not surrender, but, in view of Pearl Harbor, the war could end in no other way. The nation awaited in resigned horror for the invasion of Japan. Military and naval staffs working on Operations Coronet and Olympic estimated casualties at over a million, and some thought more, and no one had any reason to doubt it.

During the summer of 1945 the attention of America remained fixed on the mailbox and the front doorbell, as millions awaited communication from the War or Navy Department stating that a son or husband or brother had been killed or was missing in action. Then, suddenly, the terror lifted. On August 6, the United States dropped an atomic bomb on Hiroshima, and three days later, on Nagasaki. The violence and horror of a new weapon did what the greater violence and horror of standard ordinance could not. The Japanese surrendered and the war ended. Over 55 million, mostly civilians, had died in the World War, and the American dead numbered nearly 300,000.

Wrenched from anticipatory dread to sudden relief, America rejoiced in victory. But the exuberant celebrations, heartfelt though they were, lasted only a brief time. The tension of war gave way to the nagging uncertainties of peace. The nation began the process of reintegrating the boys and girls who began to come home into a civilian world that would certainly change in ways few could imagine, and would remain constant in ways many deplored. Some of those returning home were in bad shape, both physically and psychologically. Demobilization was as wrenching an experience as mobilization, indeed for most it was worse since the military life was clearly temporary and the civilian postwar world was clearly permanent. Jobs, relationships, plans, all seemed confused and uncertain, and life could not just be picked up again from having been laid down before the war. Americans worried about the returning veterans, and at the same time look forward to the end of rationing (November 23, except for sugar) and the return of normalcy. In 1920, Warren Harding had proclaimed that "America's present need is not heroics but healing; not nostrums but normalcy."[7] That prescription fit the mood in the fall of 1945 as well, along with the uncertainty in time of triumph, of foreboding in time of hope. Baseball, an icon of normalcy, still seemed faint and far away, with the national attention and the national memory turned elsewhere. Baseball had not quite yet, as Hamlet remarked, "got the tune of the time." Claude Passeau had labored and prevailed in the shadow of inattention.

Baseball also lost the center of national stage in less heroic but still troubled times, when the stakes had shrunk but passions and allegiances remained intense. In the late 1960s, America became immersed, more psychologically than militarily or economically, in the traumas and pretensions of the Vietnam War and the traumas and realities of the politics of race. Less that a quarter century separated the America of V-J Day, with its patriotism, tightly defined gender roles and racial segregation, from the vastly looser and more fluid land of Lyndon Johnson, Martin Luther King, Jr. and pharmaceuticals, both the Pill and various powders. During the troubled time — and all times seem a bit troubled to those who must cope with them — one of the best pitchers in baseball was Bob Gibson, a fire-balling right-hander who glowered at hitters individually and the world generally. He pitched the St. Louis

Cardinals to three pennants, 1964, 1967 and 1968, and he was even better in the glare of the World Series than he had been during the season.

Gibson won two games in the 1964 World Series, as the Cardinals defeated the Yanks, now fading but still able to win their fifth consecutive American League pennant. In 1967 the Cardinals won again and defeated the Red Sox in seven games, and Gibson won three of them, joining a select group (Bill Dineen and Deacon Phillippe, 1903; Christy Mathewson, 1905; Babe Adams, 1909; Jack Coombs, 1910; Smokey Joe Wood, 1912; Red Faber, 1917; Stan Coveleski, 1920; and Harry Brecheen, 1946) who had won three games in a single World Series. In 1968, the Cardinals won the National League pennant, and Bob Gibson had a season ERA of 1.12. Baseball started keeping earned run average statistics in the 1912 season, and Gibson's 1.12 was the best in League history, overcoming Grover Cleveland Alexander's mark of 1.22 in 1915, when "Old Pete" had won thirty-one games and pitched the Philadelphia Phillies to their first pennant. Gibson was close to the best of them all. In 1914 Dutch Leonard of the Red Sox had an ERA of 1.01, which seems likely to be the record for ever, similar to Old Hoss Radbourn's sixty wins in a single season (1884). The game has changed sufficiently, with relief pitching, longer rotations, the lively ball and scoring that consistently favors hitters, that Leonard's and Radbourn's records stand as benchmarks for an older version of the game and reminders of how it used to be.[8]

Gibson also pitched thirteen shutouts in 1968, second only to the single season record of Grover Cleveland Alexander's sixteen in 1916. He threw five of these in a row, in June, and completed twenty-eight of thirty-four starts, never being knocked out of the box. Completing twenty-eight games is, for a modern pitcher, a superb accomplishment, particularly when striking out as many as Gibson did, 268 in 1968. But twenty-eight complete games does not come close to a record. With the addition of relief specialists, the game has moved toward pitching as a communal activity. But in 1893, Amos Rusie of the Giants started fifty-two games and completed fifty of them. Jack Taylor, who pitched for St. Louis and Chicago from 1898 through 1907 started 286 games and completed 278. The Major League record is far in advance of this modest effort, of course. Cy Young started 816 games and completed 753, and 77 of them were shutouts. He pitched 7,356 innings, a career record for an entire modern staff. The game, like the law, is stable but never stands still.[9]

During the middle of the 1968 season, Bob Gibson was unbeatable. On June 2 he defeated the New York Mets at Shea Stadium, 6 to 3, to break a personal five-game losing streak. Then he defeated Houston, again away, to even his record at five and five. He won fifteen games in a row, and did not lose again until August 24, when Roy Face of the Pirates beat him, 6 to 4. This fell short of Carl Hubbell's winning streak of sixteen to close the 1936 season, or Tim Keefe's nineteen consecutive victories in the middle of the 1888 season.[10] It was also four short of the modern Major League record of nineteen consecutive victories, set by Rube Marquard to start the 1912 season. Still, as had Hubbell, Keefe and Marquard, Gibson pitched his team to the pennant, winning the Most Valuable Player and the Cy Young Awards in the process.

Bob Gibson was a tough man and a ferocious competitor. A quintessential power pitcher, he threw and controlled a blazing fastball. To this Gibson added a curve and a hard slider. He threw so hard that he almost fell off the mound to his left in an effort (successful) to get every last ounce of leverage from his delivery. Gibson would come inside with his hard stuff. For a right handed hitter, with that tailing fast ball boring in at ninety-five to ninety-eight miles an hour, digging in at the plate against Gibson was life-threatening. He thought as he pitched. When asked how one should pitch, Gibson replied darkly: "Bring all you got." He, himself, had plenty. There is a story about Gibson when he was a pitching coach in Atlanta. He went to the mound to talk to Rick Mahler, who led the Padres, 1 to 0, in the seventh, but had allowed the other guys to fill the bases with two outs. Gibson fixed Mahler with a gimlet glare and told him that he better get this guy because the Braves manager and pitching coach were not coming out to get him. Bolstered by a dose of reality, Mahler got his man and won the game. This may actually have happened. The participants are alive and one could check. Whether the story is factual or not has little importance. It rises to the level of existential truth, as does Gibson's lack of a nickname. The writers tried, with Gibby and Hoot, but neither really seemed to fit. When a player competes as hard as Gibson, and throws as hard inside, it might be better just to call him Mr. Gibson.

The Cardinals of 1968, though they won by nine games, had, for the most part, rather average years, and fell off a bit from their performances in 1967. The team won 101 games in 1967 and 97 in 1968. But the pitching held up well. The club ERA was a league-leading 2.49, and Gibson, who had been hurt in 1967, went from thirteen wins to twenty-two. Having pitched the Cardinals to the pennant, Gibson got the start against Detroit in the first game of the World Series.[11]

The Series opened October 2, at St. Louis. The previous year he had pitched the first game, producing a complete game victory, winning 2 to 1. This year he would do better. Facing the Tigers' ace, thirty-one-game winner Denny McLain, Gibson began the game by striking out the Detroit second baseman, Dick McAuliffe. Shortstop Mickey Stanley singled and was thrown out trying to steal second base. Then Gibson fanned Al Kaline. In the second inning Gibson struck out the side, Norm Cash, Willie Horton, and Jim Northrup. In the third, Gibson struck out Bill Freehan and pitcher McLain bunted foul on a third strike for a strikeout. Gibson had fanned seven in the first three innings.

The Cardinals went ahead with three runs in the fourth inning and Gibson continued to mow them down. Kaline took a called third strike in the fourth, as did Don Wert in the fifth. In the sixth the Tigers got two hits, but Norm Cash struck out with runners on second and third to end the inning. Gibson struck out Northrup and Freehan in the seventh, as the Cards got their fourth run on a homer by lead-off hitter Eddie Mathews, then in his last year and once a fearsome hitter for the Braves. In the ninth inning Gibson again struck out the side. After Stanley singled, Gibson fanned the heart of the Tigers order, Al Kaline for the third time, Norm Cash for the third time, and Willie Horton, who only whiffed twice. Gibson had pitched a five-hit shutout for his sixth Series victory and had struck seventeen hitters out. It was a Series record.[12] But, like Passeau's one-hitter in 1945, it was only one game. The Tigers won the 1968 Series. The previous year Bob Gibson had won three games, and the Cardinals needed him to do it again. But Gibson only won two.

Reasons beyond the passage of time or "enterprises of great pith and moment" explain the failure of moment to be remembered as myth. Cultural factors also intrude. In modern America these do not seem to include piety or beauty, those earliest Western expressions of duty and joy.[13] For Americans, whether because of or in spite of (or both) the melting pot, group identity plays a role in mythic memory. So does proximity to the cult of celebrity and the media, both centered in Los Angeles and New York. Kirk Gibson's home run to win the first game of the 1988 World Series for the Dodgers gains greater regard from the fans than Joe Carter's homer to win the 1993 Series for Toronto over Philadelphia. Of course Gibson limped to the plate, adding bathos and melodrama to his hit, but the connection to Los Angeles matters also. Memory does not always follow celebrity as form does function, but the two remain connected. Finally, myth must tap a cultural aquifer of affection and respect. This is denied to some; Billy Martin, George Steinbrenner, Charlie Finley and Albert Belle seem notably unlovely, as pitcher Sal "The Barber" Maglie did to Dodgers fans and Carl Furillo did to Maglie. Others, such as Tommy Lasorda, Ernie Banks, and Joe DiMaggio, achieve iconic status. Most players move to neither extreme, but unless some basic respect and affection undergird achievement, memory only lingers and myth seldom arrives.

If Passeau's brilliance in a World Series game was forgotten and Gibson's has become occluded, a pitching performance lasting two innings in an exhibition game became an enduring part of baseball myth and memory. It involved the All-Star Game, which, in 1934, was still a novelty with plenty of sentiment for getting rid of it as a hindrance to the pennant race. But the 1933 game had been a success, with Babe Ruth hitting a home run, and so, in 1934, baseball went ahead and scheduled a second one. It was to be held at the Polo Grounds on July 10. The fans were again asked to cast a newspaper ballot for the players and the World Series managers of the previous year, Joe Cronin of the Washington Senators and Bill Terry of the New York Giants, supplemented the fans' opinion with their own selections. The fans responded well to the ballot and the manager's selections, and about 48,000 showed up, a lot for a Depression game, enough to fill most of the seats, and more than attended either home game of the Series the year before. The whole effort convinced both leagues to play again in 1935.

The high point of the 1934 game came early. Carl Hubbell of the Giants started for the National League and he started slowly. Charlie Gehringer, Detroit's second baseman, led off with a single, and Hubbell then walked the Washington outfielder Heinie Manush. Two men on, no one out and Babe Ruth at bat — that was a good description of being in trouble. But Hubbell did not give in. He struck Babe Ruth out. Then he fanned Lou Gehrig. Jimmie Foxx came up next and Hubbell struck him out as well, ending the inning and leaving the two men on base. In the second inning Al Simmons led off and Hubbell struck him out. Joe Cronin, the Washington shortstop, became Hubbell's fifth consecutive strikeout victim. Bill Dickey, the Yankees catcher, singled, and American League pitcher Lefty Gomez, a .147 lifetime hitter, then struck out. After the game Gomez complained to his battery-mate, Bill Dickey. "Why didn't you strike out?" Gomez asked. Then the newspapers would all write that Hubbell had fanned the seven greatest hitters in the American League. Dickey's reply is lost; perhaps just as well.[14]

As it was, striking out Ruth, Gehrig, Foxx, Simmons and Cronin sufficed to gain immense newspaper interest. Both scribes and fans regarded it as one of the great pitching feats in the history of the game. No one had ever done it before, and, in the nature of things, no one could do it later. No one but Carl Hubbell could have done that, went the general opinion. Hubbell didn't need to strike out Bill Dickey. Five Hall of Fame hitters were enough. The mythic quality of that achievement appeared at an interview with seventy-six-year-old Hubbell at the 1979 All-Star Game. Could Nolan Ryan, the reigning king of strikeouts, equal Hubbell's record of striking out the five leading hitters in the American League? Hubbell replied: "Well, it would be kinda hard to answer that because Nolan Ryan won't be pitching against Ruth, Gehrig, Foxx, Simmons, and Cronin."[15] Nor against Dickey and Gomez, either.

Explanations for the mythic quality of this event, which affected the outcome of nothing in baseball, suggest themselves. It happened in New York and a New York pitcher did it. Hubbell's pitching also fit Stephen Jay Gould's requirement for a "single transcendent event to fix him permanently in memory."[16] Those five strikeouts fixed themselves in cultural memory, proof against moth, rust and thieves. They were for Hubbell the equivalent of the streak for Joe DiMaggio, though at a lesser mythic level since pitching lacks the fan esteem so lavishly assigned to hitting.

The rarity of an event also matters. No other pitcher even faced Ruth, Gehrig, Foxx, Simmons and Cronin in consecutive plate appearances, let alone struck them out. Hubbell's status as a pitcher counts as well. In the 1933 World Series he started the first and fourth games, and pitched twenty innings without giving up an earned run. In 1936, when the Giants faced the Yankees in the Series, fans of both teams wondered if the Yankees could beat Hubbell. They could, but only half the time. In the Series of 1936 and 1937, Hubbell won two games and lost two to the Yanks. Hubbell's two victories against the Yankees need to be put in perspective. From 1927 through 1939, the Yankees won seven World Series, in which they lost only three games. Carl Hubbell won two of them.

As a pitcher Hubbell seemed almost casual. He had a low leg kick and didn't seem to be working very hard. But his easy delivery was deceiving. Hubbell had good speed on all his pitches, and he had exceptional control, especially with his trademark screwball. Billy Herman, the Cubs second baseman, described Hubbell with a touch of awe.

> I'll tell you something about Hubbell. When he was pitching, you hardly ever saw the opposing team sitting back in the dugout; they were all on the top step watching him operate. He was a marvel to watch, with that screwball, fastball, curve, screwball again, change of speed, control. He didn't really have overpowering stuff, but he was an absolute master of what he did have, and he got every last ounce out of his abilities.[17]

Respect for Hubbell's mastery of the game went beyond the players and extended to the fans, even to fans not usually noted for supporting the New York Giants. Jocko Conlan, the great National League umpire, came up in 1941 and discovered that borough rivalry had its limits. Both Mel Ott and Carl Hubbell "were so popular, those two, that the fans didn't even boo them in Brooklyn."[18] That wouldn't be said about everybody, including those who played for the Dodgers.

As a person, Hubbell was quiet rather than flamboyant. When the Giants trained in Baton Rouge in the late thirties, Hubbell spent hours playing pool in a parlor at the corner of Third Street. He often ate supper with a cousin who taught at LSU. As the family supper neared its end, boys from the neighborhood would line up at the kitchen steps. People ate in the kitchen in those days. After supper, Hubbell would come out and sign autographs. He was past his prime in 1938 and 1939, but he was a legend anyway. Everyone remembered the All-Star Game in '34.

In the end, the persistence of memory about the All-Star Game seems to rest upon the sheer artistry of the moment. Here, for this one time, five of the greatest hitters in the game faced one of the greatest pitchers, and he struck them all out. Six, if you count Lefty Gomez. For the fans, then and since, it has become "the stuff that dreams are made of."[19]

Perfection remains the permanent goal in pitching because it is possible. One can retire twenty-seven hitters consecutively; it has been done before.

Of course, logic would dictate that hitters also can be perfect, going five for five and, now and then, six for six. But there is no logic in baseball lore and history, and a perfect day at the plate is overlooked and a perfect day on the mound is enshrined. For pitchers, perfection is always one start away.

A perfect game ought to be pretty cut and dried. The pitcher has his best stuff, gets everybody out, and wins the game. Not always. On June 23, 1917, Babe Ruth started for the World Champion Boston Red Sox against the Washington Senators. He walked Ray Morgan, the first hitter, and complained so bitterly that the home plate umpire threw him out of the game. Needing a new pitcher, Boston manager Jack Barry picked Ernie Shore off the bench and sent him in. Without warming up Shore went to work. The base runner was caught stealing, and Shore retired the twenty-six hitters he faced. He pitched a perfect game, getting all twenty-seven outs, but it also stands as the only perfect game with a base-runner, or with a relief pitcher who faced only twenty-six hitters.[20] At least Ernie Shore won, 4 to 0. It is also possible to pitch a perfect game and lose.

This cannot happen often and ought not to happen at all. But it did. On May 26, 1959, the Pittsburgh Pirates sent Harvey Haddix to the mound to face the Milwaukee Braves ace Lew Burdette in an ordinary game, with only 19,000 fans in the park, and no impact on the pennant race beyond any other early season game. Haddix was a good pitcher, lasting fourteen years in the Bigs. In 1953 he had his best season, winning twenty games for the Cardinals. Utterly forgotten now. In the World Series of 1960, Haddix won two games without a loss, but Bill Mazeroski's home run is what the fans remember. But for one night, Haddix transcended mere excellence, soared into the empyrean, and lost.

Both Burdette and Haddix were on their game, and at the end of nine innings the Pirates had nine singles but no runs. Haddix had retired all twenty-seven hitters he had faced. In the tenth inning, Haddix retired three men he faced. He did the same thing in the eleventh. And the twelfth. Haddix had retired thirty-six hitters in a row, something no one had ever done before and no one has done since. But Burdette hung in there, and the Pirates had not scored either. In the bottom of the thirteenth inning the Braves broke through. Felix Mantilla got on via an error, the first Milwaukee base runner. After a sacrifice and an intentional pass to Hank Aaron, Joe Adcock hit a home run. Mantilla scored, but Aaron, seeing this, thought the game was over and after touching second headed for the dugout. Adcock passed him on the base paths. Someone was out as a result of that; maybe everyone was out. The issue went to the National League president who ruled that Mantilla's run ended the game. Haddix lost, 1 to 0, on one hit after twelve perfect innings. You don't see something like that everyday. Sometimes, mere perfection is not enough.[21]

Usually, it is, and the only perfect game in a World Series followed the proper pattern. In the 1956 Series, Dem Bums were again facing the Bronx Bombers, whom they had unexpectedly defeated in 1955, after trying five times previously without success. For the Dodgers the 1956 Series started splendidly. Sal "The Barber" Maglie defeated Whitey Ford before the home folks in Ebbets Field. Jackie Robinson and Gil Hodges homered for the margin of victory. All in all, a fine Brooklyn day. Two days later it got even better. The Dodgers got off to a slow start as the Yanks scored six runs in the first two innings and shelled the Brooklyn ace, Don Newcombe. He gave up five runs in the second, four scoring on Yogi Berra's grand slam homer. But the Dodgers scored six runs in the home second, knocking out Don Larsen and then Johnny Kucks, and tying the score. Brooklyn continued to hit and won 13 to 8. The Yanks used seven pitchers, and Brooklyn had won both home games. The Yanks evened the series by winning the third and fourth games at Yankee Stadium, setting the stage for the return of Don Larsen who had lasted less than two innings in his previous Series start. New York manager Casey Stengel hoped for better this time.[22]

Larsen faced Sal Maglie, who had won the first game, and the Barber was better this time around. He surrendered only two runs and five hits, one of them a home run by Mickey Mantle. Don Larsen, however, was perfect. He threw only ninety-seven pitches, going to three balls on only one hitter, Pee Wee Reese in the first inning, who struck out on a 3-2 pitch. Only a couple of hitters came close to getting on base. Leading off the second inning Jackie Robinson hit a sharp line drive off third baseman Andy Carey's glove. Shortstop Gil McDougald grabbed the ball and nipped Robinson at first by a step. In the fifth Gil Hodges hit a long drive to center field where Mickey Mantle made a nice back-handed catch. Carey made a good play on Hodges's line drive in the eighth inning. Larsen kept mowing the Dodgers down. He struck seven men out, including the first two, Jim Gilliam and Pee Wee Reese, and the last hitter, Dale Mitchell, the only substitute in the game, batting for Sal Maglie. On a 1 and 2 pitch, Mitchell took a called third strike. Larsen had pitched the first World Series no-hitter, and it had been a perfect game.[23]

Larsen was far from a great pitcher, though for one afternoon he had the greatest day a pitcher could have. After the perfect game, which helped the Yankees win a seven game Series against the Dodgers, Larsen remained in the Show for another decade as a more or less marginal pitcher. In 1959, the Yanks traded him to Kansas City, and from there he went to the White Sox, the San Francisco Giants, the Astros, the Orioles and finished with the Cubs, pitching in three games in relief in 1967. His overall record was eighty-one wins and ninety-one losses, though in the World Series he did much better, winning four while losing only two, the same record as Carl Hubbell.[24] Larsen never pitched another perfect game, nor even a run-of-the-mill no-hitter. He didn't need to. After a perfect game in a World Series, there is nothing more can you do.

For reasons that seem obscure, a perfect game, which is the ultimate achievement in baseball, has generally failed to capture the imagination of the fans, or find a prominent place in baseball memory. Pitching does not seem to be as exciting as hitting, a fact that baseball moguls clearly realize as they tinker with the game to promote scoring. Those involved with the game rather than the business, however, have a different opinion. For managers, there is never enough pitching. Even with four twenty-game winners (Chicago in 1920 and Baltimore in 1971), managers worry constantly, as they should.

The problem with pitchers is that they are fragile. It doesn't matter how hard you throw or how strong you are. A little thing can topple you. Dizzy Dean broke a toe in 1937 and apparently came back too early. How much too early? No one knew then or knows now. The strain of adjusting to the toe injury hurt his arm. How was it hurt? No one knew then or knows now. But Ol' Diz lost about half a mile on his fastball, and his other pitches also suffered. Nothing could be done to repair the damage, whatever it was. Diz was through, victim of the always imprecise and all-too-common sore arm.

A sore arm, a generic term for losing zip on the fastball or bite on the breaking ball, has finished pitchers from the time the game started, including the third man to pitch a no-hitter in the National League, John Ward (June 17, 1880, and it was a perfect game), who had to switch to being an infielder. Ward became a major star as a position player, which showed immense athletic ability, but he could no longer pitch. Sometimes pitchers can be repaired, as was Tommy John when he tore his rotator cuff. Sometimes, like John Smoltz's tendonitis in the elbow, the soreness can be ameliorated by rest, and a change of roll from starter who goes seven or eight innings to a closer who gets three outs. Even then, with all the care that can be lavished on an All-Star pitcher, Smoltz had to go on the disabled list late in the 2003 season, and the Braves, who had been winning two out of every three games, fell back to a .500 team without him. Although Smoltz was a superb closer, saving over fifty games a season, he preferred to start, and, for the 2005 season, he was back in the rotation.

Not surprisingly, pitchers are a nervous and superstitious lot. Since disaster can come without warning and may end a lucrative career, the sympathetic magic of invariable routine can't hurt, could help, and does give the illusion of doing something useful and being in control, which provides much needed comfort. Nevertheless, the most careful attention to off-field activities cannot undo the reality that the most common cause of pitching injuries is pitching. Of course, not all pitchers are as careful off the field as they ought to be. Curt Simmons, a left-hander for the 1950 Phillies Whiz Kids, ran a lawnmower over his foot and never completely recovered from the careless domestic accident. That kind of thing was a recurrent nightmare for pitchers, and for the clubs that employ them.

Since good pitching is so scarce, clubs and teams have become even more careful to cosset and care for pitchers. Trainers hover over pitchers, who now seem to sport ice on arm, elbow or shoulder after every game. The bench coach or the pitching coach keeps careful count of pitches, and pitchers are lifted when they near the limit regarded as appropriate for their age and style of delivery. In 1959 both Haddix and Burdette went the full thirteen innings. Today, even with a no-hitter going, pitchers are pulled when they reach their limit, with 80, 90, 100, 110 being the more common numbers. The effort is all directed to get a little more quality work out of an aging arm. The end is always the same — to have the pitcher work until age, not injury, ends a career. And age always will. Even Warren Spahn, the best left-hander in the history of the game, eventually ran out of arm.

So the pitchers toil on, the center of the game as it is played, as Yogi pointed out, but at the edge of memory and myth. This is one of the major gaps in imagination between the fans who watch and those who work in the game. For the fan, apparently, pitching is just not sufficiently beautiful or sufficiently interesting or sufficiently important to move automatically into myth. Offense, not defense, describes the American dream, and in baseball, it is the defense in the person of the pitcher that holds the ball. But memory usually follows desire, and, in baseball, the fan eternally yearns for the big hit and the imperfect game.

4

Glory and Infamy

Baseball is a team game played by one individual at a time. On every pitch or play, individual skills and performance receive intense scrutiny. Instant replay is unnecessary; in baseball the tempo of the game is sufficiently measured so that each part of each play can be seen, understood, judged and scored. Baseball isolates the player in real time, and then joins him with his teammates in collective outcome. The shards of individual play, though combined into the whole of the game, remain separate always.

The result of this singular combination of tempo, team, and individual is that players can become heroes or goats. Back when Brooklyn had a team, Dodgers fans developed a litany of affectionate abuse to be heaped on players who made mistakes. "You, bum, you" was heard all over Ebbets Field when Dodger players performed at less than perfection, and before the 1940s imperfection was all the Dodgers fans ever saw. Sometimes things got so bad that abuse was expanded to the communal: "Youse bums, youse." Leading Dodger fans, such as Hilda Chester, became aficionados at loud and loving rebuke. Of course, that was in Brooklyn. Elsewhere, it was mostly just abuse. At Yankee Stadium, the home team hardly ever made a mistake; it was the visitors who did that, and they received constant abuse and denunciation. New York can be a tough town.

It is easier to be a bum than it is to become a hero, and being a bum tends to be a sticky label. This permanent designation of goat received powerful support from sports writers, who search, and need to search, endlessly for "color" and for the most vivid tags that the restless mind of man could possibly invent. Thus Fred Merkle, a first baseman who played for fifteen years for the Giants, Dodgers and Cubs, was stuck with the name Bonehead. In a crucial game between the New York Giants and the Chicago Cubs during the pennant race of 1908, Merkle was on first and failed to touch second base after the winning hit. The Giants and the Cubs were struggling for the pennant in 1908, and had the hit been allowed the Giants would have won. As it was, the game was replayed and the Cubs defeated Christy Mathewson and won the game, the pennant and later the World Series. Bonehead Merkle was in his second year with the Giants and John McGraw, the Giants manager, who did not tolerate failure well, never blamed his player and kept him on as a regular. But the fans and the writers never forgot, and Bonehead Merkle became the primary example of losing your concentration and not keeping your head in the game. Merkle carried the tag all his life. Few remember him today, but those who do know of him as Bonehead Merkle. Only the passage of time and memory, along with the existence of new gaffes, can lift the burden of *infamia* from the shade of Fred Merkle.

There always are new gaffes, of course, and none was bigger than that made Arnold Malcolm ("Mickey") Owen on October 5, 1941, at Ebbets Field in the fourth game of the World Series. The Dodgers were playing the mighty Yankees and were not given much chance of beating them. The Yanks had won seven World Series in a row, and most fans, even in Brooklyn, thought the Bronx Bombers would make it eight. But the Dodgers had won Game 2 when the Brooklyn ace Whit Wyatt had defeated Spud Chandler, 3 to 2. This was not an insignificant straw in the wind. In their last seven Series victories, the lordly Yankees had lost only three games, two of them to the incomparable Carl Hubbell. Winning even a game against the Yanks was something to savor. In the third game the Yankees restored order, though just barely. In the seventh inning of a scoreless tie Yankees pitcher Marius Russo hit a hard line drive off the leg of the Brooklyn pitcher, Freddie Fitzsimmons. The ball popped in the air to be caught for the final out of the inning, but Fitzsimmons had to be helped off the field to sustained applause from the home crowd. Brooklyn brought in Hugh Casey, who surrendered two runs in the eighth and the Dodgers lost, 2 to 1. That's the way things went when you played the Yankees.[1]

But in the fourth game, the Dodgers had scored two runs in the fourth inning and two again in the fifth, and led 4 to 3 in the top of the ninth. Hugh Casey, who had entered the game in the fifth, was working his fourth inning. Casey faced the top of the order with first baseman Johnny Sturm, who worked the count to three and two before grounding to Pete Coscarart at second base for the first out. Red Rolfe hit a bounder back to the mound and Casey threw him out. Tommy Henrich was the Yanks' last chance. When the count was three and two, Casey threw a pitch that Henrich missed by a foot. The catcher, Mickey Owen, also missed it and Henrich took first on the passed ball. Things were not yet out of control, but Casey lost his composure. Joe DiMaggio singled. With a count of two strikes Charlie Keller doubled off the right field wall, driving in Henrich and DiMaggio. Bill Dickey walked, and Joe Gordon doubled Keller and Dickey home. The Yanks had four runs and won the game, 7 to 4. Mickey Owen's dropped third strike was seen by everyone as the root cause of all the ninth inning carnage.[2]

My mother was at the game with her brother, my Uncle George, a rabid Dodgers fan. Uncle George didn't say much about the game, but my mother had a theory to explain the catastrophe. Owen had signaled for a fastball, but Casey instead threw his spitball. The pitch was (technically) illegal, but lots of pitchers threw them. Casey had a good spitter. It looked like a fast ball, but with late movement, darting down as it reached the plate. At his best, Henrich didn't miss fastballs by a foot, but he couldn't have hit a prime Casey spitter with a snow shovel. Owen, expecting a fastball, let the spitter get under his glove for an error.

I have always thought my mother was right about Owen's catastrophic miscue. She put the blame on Casey, as he did himself. After all, twice the Yankees were down to their last strike, and twice Casey let them off the hook. Casey was one of the last people whom one would have thought of as losing his composure and concentration. He was a hard case, who owned and ran a tavern in Brooklyn when it was not only the borough of homes and churches it was also the borough of saloons, a long waterfront, a flourishing culture of bar fights, Coney Island and organized crime. Casey was his own bouncer and that was a no-foolin' job. The Dodgers broadcaster, Red Barber, who knew the players well, characterized Hugh Casey as

> A mean, rough man. It's an old line in baseball, but I truly believe that if it meant something in a ball game Casey would not only knock his own mother down with a pitch, he would have hit her and in the head. He did not care for man or devil. He didn't even care for himself, as he proved several years later, after he was out of baseball, when he stuck a shotgun in his mouth, pulled the trigger, and blew himself into eternity.[3]

Barber, it must be added, was a deeply religious man with a large dose of Christian charity, and he was not inclined to accentuate the negative. He meant every word, and he meant it in a time when players did not wear helmets and the last player to get hit square on the side of the head, Ray Chapman, was killed. But in the fourth game of the 1941 World Series, Casey didn't throw at anyone.

Of course, it was not totally unexpected that given a break, the Yanks would come back. And they did. If any team but the Yankees had come back this way it would be a sign of moral courage; with the Yankees it was instead another confirmation of the tragic view of life. But the fans and the press concentrated on Owen's error. Even the rigidly impartial *Official Baseball Record Book* for 1942 had an editorial comment:

> Owen's missed third strike on Henrich cost the Dodgers a ball game and, according to their far from disheartened adherents, possibly the Series.
> Possibly minus Owen's aid, the Yankees would have won the Series, anyhow. But Mickey's error certainly helped.[4]

That became the nation's judgment.

A similar error, also in a World Series, also costing a game and perhaps the Series, was made by Boston Red Sox first baseman Bill Buckner in the sixth game of the 1986 World Series. In 1986, the Red Sox had a good chance of winning. It wasn't like facing the fearsome Bob Gibson, as Boston had done in the seventh game in 1967, and, of course, lost as Gibson pitched a three-hitter. This time the Sox faced the New York Mets, a good team but not a great one, and the Sox went into the sixth game with a 3-to-2 lead. The last two games were to be played in Shea Stadium in Queens, but the Red Sox had won both previous games played there and could certainly win again. It looked like they would. The sixth game was tied at three runs apiece at the end of ninth, and in the top of the tenth inning the Red Sox scored twice, the first on a home run by Dave Henderson. The Mets came up for the home half of the tenth. Three outs to go. Calvin Schiraldi, the Boston pitcher, got the first two with ease. After Keith Hernandez, the Mets' first baseman, flied to center field for the second out, he walked slowly back to the Mets dugout, picked up his glove, and went to the clubhouse. The scoreboard even flashed, for an instant, a message congratulating the Boston Red Sox on their Series victory. There was one out left to go.

The last out is always the hardest to get. Ask the ghost of Hugh Casey. Schiraldi went to work on Gary Carter, who got a single. The next hitter was rookie Kevin Mitchell, hitting for pitcher Rick Aguilera. Mitchell usually faced only southpaws, but here he faced a right-hander and singled. Schiraldi, like Casey before him, got two quick strikes on the next hitter. Ray Knight was a dangerous hitter, but the situation was still under control. As Charlie Keller had done in 1941, Ray Knight came through with a big hit in 1986. He got a two-out, last inning, 0-and-2 hit, singling in Carter and sending Mitchell to third. Red Sox manager John McNamara had seen enough. Schiraldi had lost it. It was time for the closer, Bob Stanley, an ungainly flame thrower who would now, in a spectacular violation of the laws of physics, throw heat to put out the fire. Stanley threw a hard sinker, and so third base coach Bud Harrelson warned Mitchell to be on the lookout for a wild pitch. Mitchell was, after all, the potential tying run.

Bob Stanley went to work on Mookie Wilson, the sixth Mets hitter in the bottom of the tenth. Mookie was a contact hitter and a tough out. The count was two and two on Stanley's seventh pitch, a hard sinker which got away from Boston catcher Rick Gedman. Mitchell, alerted by Harrelson, scooted home, as Stanley lumbered to the plate. Mitchell scored, and the game was tied 5 to 5. Ray Knight was now on second, and Mookie Wilson was still at bat. Two pitches later Wilson hit a slow bouncer down the first baseman. Buckner had aging and aching knees. As the ball bounced toward Buckner, Ray Knight headed to third and then home. Two outs, run on anything is an axiom from grade school play grounds, and Knight took off. Bob Stanley hustled to first as a pitcher must on any ball hit to the right side of the infield. Mookie Wilson tried to outrun the ball to Buckner, for that was the only way he was going to be safe. Then Buckner let Mookie's dribbler go through his legs into right field. The ball went under his glove. He had failed to obey the first rule of fielding a grounder: The glove must be lower than the ball. Ray Knight came home with the winning run. The Mets won, 6 to 5, and the series was tied at three games each.[5]

No one had any doubts what would come next. The Red Sox would lose the Series, and they did. Buckner's error, in living color on television, had finished Boston. Neither the Dodgers in 1941 nor the Red Sox in 1986 could come back from something like that. The Buckner error had an air of finality about it.

Buckner himself explained the play. In a comment for the *Washington Post* (a neutral city paper is better for these things) Buckner said: "The ball went skip, skip, and didn't come up. The ball missed my glove. I can't remember the last time I missed a ball like that, but I'll remember that one."[6] It's all there, including acceptance of responsibility. The glove is supposed to contact the ball, not the other way around. The little speech also showed a sense of destiny. Buckner already knew that this was a mythic moment that neither he nor anyone else would ever forget. There was much newspaper comment, some of it less than kind, and even more public comment, some dwelling on the miraculous and other accentuating tones of despair. Perhaps the best was from Billy Gardner: "I heard that Bill Buckner tried to commit suicide over the winter. He stepped in front of a car, but it went through his legs."[7] The Buckner error can be interpreted both more broadly and more specifically. It is frequently counted as a part of the Curse of the Bambino, which rested on the Red Sox for a generation as punishment for Red Sox owner Harry Frazee selling Babe Ruth to the New York Yankees on January 3, 1920.[8] The Curse of the Bambino, which, over the years has manifested itself in the inevitable superiority of the Yanks over the Sox, does not, however, reach beyond those two teams. While it is the fate of the Red Sox to lose the close ones to the Yankees, the Mets are outside of the curse; though they come from the Big Apple, they are not in the American League. No one sold Babe Ruth to the Mets, or the Cardinals, or the Reds, all victors over the Red Sox in the World Series.

The theology of *defixiones* (curses) is quite precise. A specific person, possessed of *infamia* for a particular reason, is bound by a specific curse to a particular misfortune. Defixiones surviving from antiquity all follow this formula, which may be regarded as standard. The Curse of the Bambino follows the ancient model. The Red Sox, for selling the Babe, are bound by the Curse of the Bambino to fail against the Yankees. Only against the Yankees, but always against them, do the Red Sox see success and surcease go to another.

Until 2004. Under the sun, nothing abides always. Curses wear down, gradually softened by the passage of time or cultural changes in the content of belief. The Curse of the Bambino has not been immune to time and attitude, and it has been further eroded by callow publicity and a shallow secularism.

During the past decade or so, the curse has become a staple on sports talk shows and has appeared with some frequency in the more serious venue of print. It has also been caught in the cultural process of demythologizing, or desanctification, removed progressively from the mysterious and wonderful and consigned to the ordinary and mundane. No curse can survive as a part of the psychological everyday. The end of the Curse of the Bambino could clearly be foreseen; what could not be known was the manner and day of its coming.

The curse ended in October 2004, nearly eighty-five years after the offense. The end came, as had the origins, dramatically and unforgettably, not with a whimper but a hell of a bang. In the League Championship series, the endlessly victorious New York Yankees took a three-game lead in a seven-game series, a lead that had historically been insurmountable. The Yanks had even rubbed salt into the psychic wound by scoring nineteen runs in the third game, played, for an even greater affront, at Fenway Park. When a curse breaks, and fortune turns against those formerly favored, present discomfort or historical discomfort have no effect. The Red Sox won the last two games in Boston, moving the series back to New York. The series would end in the House That Ruth Built, though of course most thought the Yankees would win it, as they always had. But not this time. The Red Sox won the last two games of the series, sweeping the Yanks at the stadium. There had come a new day in the continuing rivalry between the Sox and the Yanks, perhaps a better one now that the results of the rivalry are in doubt, perhaps not if the rivalry diminishes in mythic scope and intensity.

A broader definition of the Buckner error is that it represents, yet again, a manifestation of a fallen world. Certainly, this is so. The same thing can be said, however, of things even more humble, though the success of the Yankees is one of the definitions of the word *fallen*. But even Yankee victories yield in defining Original Sin to the unspeakable Walter O'Malley, who took the Dodgers and Giants West and destroyed Brooklyn by that act. This deliberate betrayal of the public weal and trust merits eternal cohabitation with Brutus, Cassius, and Judas in the mouth of Satan.[9] The Curse of the Bambino can be described by historians; Dante alone can express appropriate disgust and revulsion for Walter O'Malley.

Most comment about baseball infamia is less theological but is sometimes quite bitter, particularly in referring to the Curse of the Bambino. From Boston comes savage rage for New York and the Yankees. In the *Boston Globe Magazine* Alexander Theroux stated: "To Bostonians, New York is helltown, and the Yankees the devils who inhabit it."[10] For Bostonians, vulgarity is the essence of New York, and Red Sox fans hate everything about the Yankees. In New York, the attitude toward the Hub, the Athens of America, is condescension and contempt. "Boston — not quite Norman, Oklahoma — is still dorkville to New Yorkers ... Out of it. Provincial."[11] But this is a rabid exception. Baseball is more the emblem of life as love than life as loathing. The contretemps of baseball are to be treated with understanding rather than *menis*. Reconciliation is the dominant mode of baseball thought and feeling, as it was for Homer.[12] Baseball is usually combined with a little fun over the mishaps of another, but rarely descends to genuine hatred.

Schadenfreude never inspires and usually embarrasses, so it is a relief to switch from events that blighted lives to plays that enhanced careers. These are frequently associated with important hits, but they occur as often in the field and on the base paths. Baseball is more than brute power, in spite of the endless publicity given to home runs. In a game where distance is measured to the sixteenth or thirty-second of an inch, finesse has its place. The "little game" also wins championships, especially for the underdogs, and never more clearly than in the seventh game of the 1946 World Series between the Red Sox and the Cardinals.

In the eighth inning, with the score tied 3 to 3, Bob Klinger replaced Joe Dobson as the Boston pitcher. Enos "Country" Slaughter opened the inning with a single to center field. But Klinger settled down and got Whitey Kurowski on popup and Del Rice, the St. Louis catcher, hit a routine fly to Ted Williams. That brought up Harry "The Hat" Walker, who had not had a good year, hitting .237, but was having a much better Series, hitting .412. Walker hit a line drive over shortstop Johnny Pesky into left center field. Leon Culberson, who replaced an injured Dom DiMaggio in centerfield, fielded the ball and threw to the cut-off man, Johnny Pesky, in short left field. Pesky looked around for Slaughter, saw him past third base, and threw home to catcher Roy Partee. Partee caught the relay in front of home plate. Slaughter was off at the crack of the bat — with two outs, run on anything. By the time Pesky got the ball, Slaughter was on his way home. He slid in safely at home behind Partee with the winning run in the World Series. He had scored from first on a short double to left center field.[13]

Johnny Pesky, an exceptionally able player, heard a certain amount of criticism for holding the relay and checking on Slaughter before he threw home. But that was exactly what he should have done. Players are taught not to throw the ball around promiscuously; more throws to more bases mean more errors. The problem lay not with Pesky, the middle man in the play, but at either end. Leon Culberson had an ordinary arm and Partee caught the ball in front of the plate rather than along the third baseline where he could block the plate. Slaughter may have beaten the throw by a nanosecond, but he beat any possible tag by plenty. Beyond that, Slaughter had the whole play in front of him. He could see when Culberson got to the ball and knew that only a perfect play could get him. By rounding third he forced the Red Sox to make a perfect play, which rarely happens and did not happen this time. Slaughter became a hero, whose hustle, concentration and baseball sense won a World Series.

Slaughter was a Hall of Fame player with a lifetime .300 batting average, so a superb play was not entirely unexpected. But ordinary players (who are ordinary only in comparison with Hall of Famers) also have exceptional athletic skills and can make extraordinary plays. They do so all the time, and, to achieve celebrity, need only Aristotle's occasion of a certain magnitude. Sandy Amoros was such a player, having a modest seven-year career as a utility outfielder, only once (1955) playing (in the field and at bat) in more than 100 games, and hitting .255 for his career. But he had one movement of blinding fame, when his play was the difference between winning and losing a World Series.

In fall 1955, the Brooklyn Dodgers, having lost the Series to the Yankees in 1941, 1947, 1949, 1952, and 1953, were back to try again. In the post–Hiroshima years the Brooklyn Dodgers faced only the Yankees in the Series. Other teams— the Giants, the Cubs, the Braves, or the Cardinals— might face some other American League Club and now and then (1946, 1954) would win. But the Dodgers specialized. Only the Yanks. And only defeat. "Wait 'til next year" was the mournful chant of hope that described the Dodgers. Someday, one fine day, Dem Bums would win it all.

The Yanks were certainly expected to win in 1955, but the Dodgers did not do badly. After losing the first two games, which they also did in 1947, the Dodgers bounced back to win the next two. The Dodgers then won the crucial fifth game when rookie Roger Craig pitched six strong innings and Sandy Amoros hit a home run. But the Yanks won Game 6 when the Series returned to Yankee Stadium. The Dodgers had been in this situation before.

In the seventh game Dodgers manager Walter Alston sent Johnny Podres to the mound. Although Podres had only 9–10 season record, he had won Game 3 of the Series and was pitching well. He pitched well again and the Dodgers led two to nothing in the sixth inning. Podres began the sixth by walking Billy Martin on four pitches and Gil McDougald beat out a bunt to put runners on first and second with no one out. Yogi Berra then hit a high fly to left field. As the ball sliced toward the stands, Sandy Amoros, a defensive replacement for Junior Gilliam, raced after it. Most of these hits drop in, and Martin and McDougald were running on the hit. With less than a stride to spare, the left-handed Amoros stuck his glove out and the ball dropped in the webbing, just a foot or two from the stands. A right-hander who had to make a back-handed stab at the ball would not have made the catch. There wasn't enough room. After this stunning catch Amoros kept his concentration sufficiently to throw to Pee Wee Reese who threw to Gil Hodges at first to double up McDougald. The Yanks did not score. Although the Yankees made eight hits off Podres, he pitched well with men on base and shut them out. The Dodgers won, 2–0, and Brooklyn had finally won a World Series. It had not happened before and would never happen again. Amoros had made a catch that reminded the fans of Al Gionfriddo in 1947. Al had been spectacular, extending the Series to the seventh game. Amoros won the Series. His catch was the difference. Simple as that.[14]

Amoros's catch may have made the difference in a World Series, but his was not the best grab enshrined in baseball memory. For aficionados of the desperate, twisting, last-gasp, going-down-for-the-third-time stab at the ball, Al Gionfriddo's catch of Joe DiMaggio's blast in the 1947 Series remains the gold standard. It was luck, of course, since Gionfriddo couldn't see the ball as he caught it, but it was glorious. The catch everyone remembers and has been seen on television at least once every World Series, was made by Willie Mays in the first game of the 1954 World Series. That is the gold standard for all catches, not just the lucky ones but also the stupendous plays that derive from skill.

The 1954 season was unusual in both leagues. The Cleveland Indians, fueled by superb pitching, interrupted an epic run of Yankee pennants. The Yanks had won from 1949 through 1953, five pennants and five Series. They then won from 1955 through 1958, four pennants, but only two World Series. Interrupting the Yankee decade was the Cleveland victory in 1954. In the National League the New York Giants won to interrupt a Dodgers run. Brooklyn had won in 1952 and 1953, but had, of course, lost the Series to the Yankees. The Dodgers would win again in 1955 and 1956, and even win a Series (1955) from the loathed and respected Yanks. But in 1954, the best teams did not win, and the Indians and Giants enjoyed a rare break in the standard baseball pattern.

To capture the American League flag the Cleveland Indians had to put together a stupendous season. They won 111 games, a record for the American League, to finish 8 games ahead of the Yankees, who themselves won 103. The Indians climbed into first place during the third week of May, and never lost their grip on the lead. Pitching carried the Indians. Bob Lemon and Early Wynn each won twenty-three games, while Mike Garcia won nineteen, Art Houtteman won fifteen and Bob Feller thirteen. The Indians beat up the weaker teams, winning eighteen games (out of twenty-two) from Washington, Baltimore and Philadelphia. The Yankees could not compete with that, in spite of winning thirteen in a row in early July. The five-time World Champions settled for second.

In the National League, the Giants used another method for winning the pennant. Willie Mays got out of the army, and he had a banner year. He led the League with a .345 batting average, hit 41 home runs (which was second), and drove in 110 runs, which was sixth. Without Willie Mays the Giants had finished second in 1952 and fifth in 1953. With him they won. The other major addition to the Giants was pitcher Johnny Antonelli, who came over from the Braves. Antonelli had his best year in 1954, winning twenty-one games while losing seven. Ruben Gomez also had his best year, winning seventeen games. The stars of earlier years had mixed results. Sal "The Barber"

Maglie (fourteen and six) had a good year. Jim Hearn won eight games, still had some arm left, and would continue to pitch in the Majors, while the elegant Larry Jansen, at thirty-four, was about done. He won only twice. These three had pitched the Giants to the pennant in 1951, but by 1954, that was long, long ago.[15]

Comparing the Indians to the Giants, most experts and all fans are expert at analyzing the game and managing baseball teams (I have never met a fan who was not, and neither has anyone else) figured that the Indians would win. They had a better record in a stronger league, along with better pitching than the Giants, and everyone knows what Yogi says about pitching. The Giants had Willie Mays, of course, and he was the greatest player in the game (unless you were a Yankees fan, in which case it was Mickey Mantle, but no one I knew was a Yankees fan, though I heard they existed). But it really was Willie Mays. Joe DiMaggio himself said so, and he was the most beautiful player in the history of the game. "Always try for perfection. There's never been a perfect ball player. Willie Mays came closest. But always try."[16] DiMag should know. Still, Mays might not be enough. The smart money said the Indians, 8 to 5, and the American League would win the Series for the eighth consecutive year.

The first game of the 1954 Series was played at the Polo Grounds in New York. That stadium, venerable even in 1954, is no longer standing. It has been torn down to make room for a parking lot, or an apartment complex, or something else trashy, utilitarian, and unneeded. America has little respect for either age or beauty, defects which H. L. Mencken called a "libido for the ugly."[17] This is true enough as far as it goes, with MTV as the first exhibit, followed closely by Bauhaus architecture. But America also invented the endless beauty of baseball.

Al Lopez, the Cleveland manager, started Bob Lemon and Leo Durocher, who ran the Giants, countered with Sal Maglie. Both Sal "The Barber" and Bob Lemon pitched well. Cleveland got two runs off Maglie in the first, but the Barber was a tough competitor and shut the Tribe down after that. Lemon had a few early problems, and gave up two runs in the third. With the score tied at two apiece in the eighth inning, Maglie weakened. He walked Larry Doby to open the inning, always an ominous sign with a control pitcher. Al Rosen singled Doby to second, and Don Liddle came in to replace Maglie. Vic Wertz was the next Cleveland hitter. Liddle laid one in there and Wertz hit a tremendous blast to dead center field. In the Polo Grounds the center field bleachers were more than 480 feet from home plate. The Giants' center fielder, Willie Mays, turned his back to home plate and raced toward the bleachers. He outran Wertz's towering fly ball, and somehow without looking, he knew where the ball would come down. With his back to home plate, Mays stuck his glove out and extended his bare hand to steady it. The ball just dropped in. Wertz had hit it only 465–470 feet. That was not far enough.

Mays not only caught the Wertz drive, he then turned and made a superb throw to hold Al Rosen at first base. He made the complete play, as the perfect player always does.[18]

Jocko Conlan, who was umpiring at second base for the first game of the 1954 Series, had a perfect view of the whole play. He, too, noticed more than the catch. Jocko acknowledged that Mays made a great catch, but

> what he did *after* he caught the ball was something to behold. The score was tied 2–2, and there were two men on base and nobody out. Willie caught the ball ... and as he caught it he spun around and threw the ball, all in one motion. His hat fell off and he fell to the ground, but the ball came in to the infield on a line all the way from the center-field fence. It kept a run from scoring that would have given Cleveland the ball game.[19]

The throw impressed Jocko Conlan more than the catch. He remembered thinking to himself, "This has got to be the best throw that anyone could ever make."[20] The catch is enshrined, but the whole play, catch and throw together, changed the outcome of the Series.

The catch became an instant iconic wonder. *The Baseball Guide* called it "the most spectacular catch in Series history," and added that many analysts "regarded this catch, which prevented Cleveland from winning the first game in nine innings, as the turning point of the Series."[21] It became the symbol of Mays's entire career. The 3,283 hits, 660 home runs, and 1,903 runs batted in were all subsumed into that magnificent moment. No one else could have made that catch, and with the Polo Grounds gone, no one will have that chance. Mays's catch, as it ought, stands alone as a moment that cannot be swept away by adverse opinion. It was, for Mays, the mythic equivalent of the Joe DiMaggio's hitting streak. It is also the symbol of the greatest player of his time.

In the nature of the hero journey, for one to succeed another must fail. Odysseus' victory in the debate over Achilles' armor, described by Ovid in the *Metamorphoses*, meant death for Telemonian Ajax.[22] In the 1954 World Series, Mays made a catch that prevented Wertz from becoming the hero of a World Series in which he hit .500. Had Pesky nailed Enos Slaughter in the 1946 Series, his throw home would have become a mythic moment.

The same balance does not apply to those who merely benefit greatly, who gain from great blunders. Mookie Wilson is not a mythic hero because he hit the slow bouncer to Bill Buckner. Wilson is merely lucky, or the recipient of mysterious and unmerited grace. Tommy Henrich, who took first on Mickey Owen's passed ball, was called "Old Reliable" throughout his career, which is about as romantic as antifreeze. He, too, did not become a hero, but remained a player who kept his concentration sufficiently to benefit from an unexpected lucky break. Blunders fill Stephen Jay Gould's definition of a defining moment only on the down side. The goddess Fortuna gives unexpected bounty, including World Series rings, but she lacks the power to create a hero.

Both *infamia* and the heroic moment have a social resonance, illustrated by the iconic enlargement as emblems used as general social symbols. In his book *Iconologia*, Cesare Ripa displayed a woodcut of abundance (Abondanza) as a gracious woman holding grain and accompanied by an overflowing cornucopia of fruits and vegetables, in a quantity implied as endless, beyond production or consumption.[23] The emblem tied reality to imagination. Mays's catch underwent the same process and became the emblem of all great catches and all magnificent outfield play, while Mickey Owen's dropped strike or Bill Buckner's error summed up the mistakes that are part of baseball. Eventually, of course, imagination displaces the event itself, and the emblematic moment becomes memory and all that surrounds it fades. We still talk about bonehead plays, but Fred Merkle exists only on the edge of memory. The same is happening to Mickey Owen and will for Bill Buckner. The hero journey ends in myth, with the emblematic displacing the personal. The cultural significance outweighs the personal triumph or travail.

II

Center Stage

5

Murderers Row

Buzzy Bavasi, an official in the Dodgers front office, once commented on the insatiable need for good players, on the field, on the bench, and in the minors ready to come up to the Show. "You can never have too much talent. Even the 1927 Yankees didn't win every year."[1] They did win in 1927, however, which was thought to be pretty good at the time, and is still considered to be the best year in the glorious history of America's team.

When fans and sports writers discuss baseball's greatest teams, the Yankees of 1927 invariably land on top of the list. In 1927, the Yankees won 110 games and lost only 44, for a .713 winning percentage. Only the Chicago Cubs of 1906 (.763) and Cleveland Indians in 1954 (.721) would have a better record. The Yankees finished nineteen games ahead of the second-place Philadelphia Athletics, a pretty good team in its own right having Lefty Grove, Jimmie Foxx, Al Simmons and an aging Ty Cobb who hit a mediocre (for him) .357.

But pretty good was not good enough in 1927 because the Yankees were genuinely superb. They were in first place the first week of the season and every day thereafter. Lou Gehrig played first base, for every game as usual, and he hit .373, with 47 home runs and the huge total of 175 runs batted in. Tony Lazzeri at second base hit 18 home runs and drove in 102. Both Mark Koenig at shortstop and Jumping Joe Dugan at third base had good years, while Babe Ruth hit .356, drove in 164 runs and hit 60 home runs, breaking his own record of 59 (1921) and setting a season standard that lasted until 1961 when Roger Maris hit 61. Bob Meusel in left field had one of his best years, hitting .337 and driving in 103 runs. In center field Earle Combs had his best year, hitting .356 and leading the league with 231 hits. The team batting average was .307, the best in the majors that year but not the best ever. In 1894, the Phillies had hit .349 as a team and came in fourth. They lacked pitching. But the 1927 Yankees had pitching. Waite Charles Hoyt, who, like so many great Yankee players, had come from Boston, won twenty-two games, a league leading total. Wilcy Moore, a rookie, had his career year in 1927, winning nineteen games. Herb Pennock also won nineteen games, Urban Shocker won eighteen, while Dutch Ruether won thirteen and George Pipgras won ten. Moore also saved thirteen games, a league-leading total. When they needed it, as they sometimes did in the days of doubleheaders, the Yankees could send a six man rotation to the mound, and they were all good pitchers.[2]

Although the Yankee pitching led the league with a 3.20 ERA, the hitting drew the attention of the writers and fans. The middle of the New York lineup, Ruth, Gehrig, Meusel, and Lazzeri, hit so well that the sports writers called them Murderers Row, a tribute to one of the more celebrated business activities of organized gangs during Prohibition. By 1927, gangland murders had become routine, the funerals were gaudy and immense, often attended by cops, judges and politicians, and the papers covered them thoroughly. Since Prohibition had became unpopular in urban America by 1927, and gangsters were good copy, the newspapers' use of the term Murderers Row did not imply disapproval. It seemed both breezy and appropriate, as the 1927 Yankees banged out 158 home runs, almost three times as many as their nearest competitor. When Donie Bush, manager of the National League Champion Pittsburgh Pirates, was asked about the World Series, he replied in the spirit of it all, "Let's go out to the ball field and hope we all don't get killed."[3]

THE 1927 YANKEES. "Murders Row" plus the rest of the cast of what is usually thought of as the best team in the history of baseball. In 1927, the best players on the Yankees had outstanding years, giving that team its special aura.

Donie Bush did not manage a bad team. The Pirates had a good outfield, with rookie Lloyd Waner hitting .355 and his older brother Paul, now in his second year with the Pirates, hitting .380. Kiki Cuyler and Clyde Barnhart shared the other outfield post, and both hit over .300. The infield was also pretty good. Anchored at third by Pie Traynor, who hit .342, the infield included Glenn Wright at shortstop, George Grantham at second base and Joe Harris at first. All were good players and had good years, but Harris, who hit .326, was hurt much of the year and played through it as best he could. The pitching was also strong, starting with the astonishing season of Carmen Hill, who won twenty-two games. In only one other year (1928) would he win more than three games, but in 1927 he was the ace of the staff and pitched Pittsburgh to the pennant. Lee Meadows and Ray Kremer each won nineteen games and Vic Aldridge won fifteen. Former star pitcher Jughandle Johnny Morrison was nearing the end of his career, and won only three games. Without Carmen Hill's unexpected career year, the Pirates would not have won.[4]

Pittsburgh had a .305 team batting average, but the Pirates did not dominate the National League as the Yankees did the American. Pittsburgh was not in first place to stay until Labor Day, and even then both the Giants and the Cardinals stayed close. Pittsburgh won on the last weekend of the season, finishing a game and a half ahead of the Cardinals and two games ahead of the Giants. Donie Bush and his troops had done a fine job, winning a tight race against strong competition, but no one thought of the Pirates as a Murderers Row. They were just another team which would be murdered by the invincible Yankees.

I

In 1927, America was at the height of a postwar craze for organized entertainment of all sorts. New York theater was at its zenith, with more plays and more theaters during the years from 1925 to 1928 than in any period before or since. Florenz Ziegfeld put on his annual *Follies*, which opened August 16 at his own Ziegfeld Theatre, and starred Eddie Cantor. Irving Berlin wrote the music. The *Follies* ran for 167 performances, but this was far eclipsed by the musical *Good News*, which included the signature song for the era, "Flaming Youth," and ran for 551 performances. Prefer Richard Rodgers and Lorenz Hart? They had a hit musical, *A Connecticut Yankee*, drawn from Mark Twain, which ran for 418 shows. George and Ira Gershwin put on *Funny Face* at the Alvin Theater, but it was only a huge hit, not a super-colossal mega-hit, and closed after 244 performances. The biggest hit of all, which became a movie (1936) and part of the general culture, was *Show Boat*, which opened at the Ziegfeld Theatre during the Christmas season, on December 27, 1927. Jerome Kern wrote the music, Oscar Hammerstein II did the lyrics and Edna Ferber wrote the book. The songs included "Ol' Man River," a vehicle for Paul Robeson. This American almost-opera ran for 527 performances, even though it dealt with race, which was a socially touchy topic, and which baseball still avoided.

A banner year for musical theater was matched by Hollywood. In 1928, Hollywood gave out the first Academy Awards, which were designed more to promote the product than to recognize excellence. The golden statuette for Best Picture went to *Wings*, starring Clara Bow, the "it girl," Buddy Rogers, Richard Arlen and Gary Cooper. It was not the most memorable movie of 1927, of course. Abel Gance produced *Bonaparte*, which was silent in French, while Sergei Eisenstein's *The Ten Days That Shook the World* had no sound in Russian. So they didn't count. Buster Keaton starred in *The General*, which was silent in English, but the Hollywood politics were never quite right for the incomparable Buster. After all, he had nothing but talent, and who in a position of administrative power is interested in that? The really big movie was none of the above. It was the semi-talkie, *The Jazz Singer*, produced by Darryl F. Zanuck for Warner Bros. It starred the vaudeville headliner Al Jolson, and it had sound, only brief bits of song and dialogue. The picture opened in New York on October 6, the second day of the Series. People in New York lined up and down the block to see the movie, and every showing played to standing room only.

Big as the Yankees, or *Show Boat* or *The Jazz Singer* were, there were things that might have been even bigger. Henry Ford introduced the Model A to replace the twenty-year-old Model T. This new Ford came in colors other than black, including "Arabian Sand." The public was delighted, and the Model A sold at a furious rate, making Ford again the largest producer and seller of automobiles. Also in the general area of transportation, Charles Lindbergh landed the *Spirit of St. Louis* in Paris at 10:24 in the evening of May 21, having flown solo across the Atlantic from Roosevelt Field in Long Island to Le Bourget. He navigated by dead reckoning, had so much weight in fuel that he almost hit a power line on take-off, and stayed (mostly) awake for thirty-three hours and twenty-nine minutes. Lindbergh's flight was an absolute sensation. He became a national hero and received a ticker-tape parade in New York, the biggest one yet.

Along with entertainment, of which baseball, airplane barnstorming, and "automobiling" were a part, there was also the ongoing story of American business. Much business was routine — manufacturing, invention, retailing, and advertising — but one growing American industry was far from established national norms. It was the business of providing Americans with illegal booze and beer, some imported but much produced locally. Bootleggers, though technically in the transportation and delivery end of the business, became a generic term for the entire industry. Booticians, as H. L. Mencken called them to impart dignity to their profession, worked around the clock in their socially useful labors to brew, import, and supply thirsty New Yorkers, and others as well, who by 1927 had discarded even the pretense of supporting Prohibition. Because illegal booze and beer was such a huge business, it needed rationalization, and substantial criminal organizations emerged rather quickly to manage the business from manufacturing and import all the way down to retail. The two most important New York mobs, and there were several, were those of Salvatore Maranzano and Joe "The Boss" Mezzeria, and they enjoyed a certain public approval, their activities being vital to enjoying a spacious and diversified urban life. They also employed thousands, killed a few dozen, and more or less supported the New York municipal government. They were absolutely necessary for smooth functioning of the speakeasies, including the posh and prominent like the joint owned by Texas Guinan, who greeted customers with a cheery and doubtless heartfelt "Hello, sucker." Her prices were mighty high, but probably worth it. She served the good stuff, not booze whose base ingredient was paint thinner, Sterno, or sheep dip.

There were, of course, those who supported Prohibition, including the usual suspects of small towns, Evangelical religions, and female reformers who regarded Prohibition as equal in importance to suffrage. These tended toward the censorious and a dismal self-righteousness which newspapers found to be bad copy and unappetizing generally. But none of these defects attached themselves to two colorful New Yorkers, Izzy Einstein and Moe Smith. Both were middle-aged. Izzy was short, round, balding, and bespectacled, and Moe was taller, less round, had more hair and could see. They became Prohibition agents in 1920, largely because they were available and did not look like detectives. Izzy and Moe brought to law enforcement an artistic flair, which, then as now, was almost unknown in the routine of copping. Working as a team, they donned elaborate disguises and infiltrated breweries, booze warehouses, and speaks. As they knocked over this joint and then that, the papers covered their activity. Izzy and Moe fooled even the cops who were in the speakeasies to have a quiet snort. They announced their busts as the work of Izzy and Moe. Those arrested often smiled. Being busted by Izzy and Moe acquired a certain cachet, and few really minded, since the cops, juries, judges and pols were all bought off. Most Prohibition agents were in it for the grease, of course, but Izzy and Moe were incorruptible. They were in it for the fun, the theater, the artistry. By 1925 they had made nearly 5,000 arrests, had confiscated over a million gallons of bootleg booze, and were constant and growing newspaper copy, not as defenders of the dry faith but as a comedy team reminiscent of Weber and Fields or Gallegher and Sheen.

But the bosses in the Prohibition Bureau became irritable, and then jealous. Like administrators everywhere, particularly in universities, they utterly lacked a sense of humor, but they made up for it with an exaggerated sense of self-importance. In 1925, they fired Izzy and Moe for bringing the bureau into disrepute. Thereafter, enforcement in New York came slowly almost to a halt, a great relief to the hardworking tars of the rum fleet. And the newspapers stopped treating Prohibition as a comic turn and began to look at it as a growing social problem that increased crime. That earnest tone was fine as far as it went, but, taking one thing with another, New York missed Izzy and Moe.

There was a lot going on in New York in those days, much of it outsized and larger than life, and very little was gaudier or of more general interest than the doings of the Bambino and the games of the New York Yankees.

II

The World Series of 1927 began out of town, sort of like a tryout in New Haven. The first game was on October 5, and Miller Huggins, manager of the mighty Yankees, sent his ace, Waite Hoyt, to the mound. Donie Bush countered with the veteran Ray Kremer. Neither pitcher was especially sharp. After getting Earle Combs and Mark Koenig out in the first inning, Kremer had his first look at Murderers Row. Babe Ruth singled and Lou Gehrig hit a line drive to Paul Waner, who tried to make a shoe-top catch and missed it. The hit went for a triple, scoring Ruth with the first run of the Series. Hoyt began the bottom of the first by hitting Lloyd Waner, who was doubled home by his brother Paul. After an inning the game was tied at one.

Kremer got through the second inning but in the third, going through the Yankee order for the second time, he ran into trouble. With one out George Grantham booted Mark Koenig's easy grounder. Ruth then singled and Gehrig drew a walk. With the bases loaded Kremer walked Bob Meusel and forced Koenig home. Tony Lazzeri hit a ground ball to Glenn Wright, who threw to Grantham forcing Meusel at second, but the relay to first was too late. Babe Ruth scored on the fielder's choice. The Yankees then pulled a double steal, and Gehrig scored when Pirate's catcher Earl Smith dropped the ball. The longest hit was a single and there was only one of those, but sloppy Pittsburgh play had given the Yankees three runs, none of them earned. The Pirates got one run back in the home half of the third inning when Kremer doubled and scored on Paul Waner's single. The Pirates were down 4 to 2 after three innings.

In the fifth inning the Yanks added another run when Koenig doubled to right field, moved to third on Ruth's infield out and scored on Gehrig's sacrifice fly. In the bottom of the fifth, Pittsburgh got the run back when Lloyd Waner doubled and Clyde Barnhart singled him home. When Tony Lazzeri opened the Yankee sixth inning with a double, Donie Bush lifted Kremer and brought in Johnny Miljus, who promptly shut down the Yankees, both in the sixth inning and for the rest of the game. The Pirates got a run in the eighth when Glenn Wright, Pie Traynor and Joe Harris singled, but it was not enough. Wilcy Moore replaced a tiring Waite Hoyt in the eighth inning. The thirty-year-old rookie ended the rally and the Yanks had won the first game, 5 to 4. The Murderers Row had hit no home runs. Koenig had a double and Gehrig hit a lucky triple. Errors and walks, not the power game, had done the Pirates in.[5]

In the second game Miller Huggins sent a surprise starter, George Pipgras, to the mound. Pipgras had gone ten and three during the regular season, his first full year in the majors, and a start in a World Series, especially an away game, put a lot of pressure on inexperienced shoulders. But Pipgras was up to the challenge. He gave up a run in the first inning, when Lloyd Waner tripled and scored on Barnhart's sacrifice fly, and another in the eighth when Paul Waner drove Lloyd home with a sacrifice fly. The Yanks, however, scored six runs off Vic Aldridge. The second time through the batting order, again in the third inning, proved to be a tough assignment. Combs and Koenig singled and Gehrig doubled to center, scoring Combs and sending Koenig to third. Meusel singled Koenig home and Lazzeri scored Gehrig with a sacrifice fly. Aldridge then righted the ship and held the Yanks scoreless for the next four innings, benefiting from a great catch in center field by Lloyd Waner on what looked like a certain triple by Earle Combs. By the eighth inning Aldridge had run out of gas. Meusel singled, went to third on Lazzeri's single, and scored on Aldridge's wild pitch. Jumping Joe Dugan tried to bunt Lazzeri to third but Pittsburgh catcher Johnny Gooch threw Lazzeri out. Then Aldridge walked Yankees catcher Pat Collins and pitcher George Pipgras. Mike Cvengros came in to pitch for Pittsburgh and walked Combs, forcing Dugan home. Koenig then singled home Benny Bengough, running for Pat Collins, with the last Yankee run. With a 6 to 2 victory, the Yanks had swept the Pirates at home. Again pitching had dominated. Pipgras threw a complete game and the Yanks had only one extra base hit, a double by Gehrig.[6]

The general consensus of fans and writers alike was that the Pirates would be lucky to win even a single game in New York. With the victory by Pipgras, the Yankees still had Herb Pennock and Urban Shocker, both veteran front-line pitchers, had only used Wilcy Moore in relief and could go back to Waite Hoyt. The Pirates still had Lee Meadows and Carmen Hill, and the New York fans thought they would hardly be capable of stopping Ruth, Gehrig, Meusel and Lazzeri. But again, the story of the Series would be pitching.

Herb Pennock, the Knight of Kennett Square, had come from Boston (1923) like many of the great Yankee players of that era. He was established as one of the best pitchers in the American League by 1927, when he won nineteen games and lost only six. In Game 3, Pennock pitched superbly. He walked no one and retired the first twenty-two hitters he faced. Not until Pie Traynor singled with one out in the top of the eighth inning did the Pirates have a base runner. Barnhart doubled Traynor home, but that was Pittsburgh's only run. Lloyd Waner got a single in the ninth, but Pennock got the next two Pirates and finished with a three hitter, one of the better games in World Series history.

Lee Meadows, the Pittsburgh pitcher, also pitched well. In the first inning, after Combs and Koenig had singled, they were driven home by Gehrig's triple. After that Meadows settled down and held the Yanks scoreless for the next five innings. In the seventh inning, Meadows weakened. Lazzeri led off with a single, went to second on Dugan's bunt single and third when pinch-hitter Cedric Durst grounded out. Pennock hit a grounder to second baseman Hal Rhyne, who threw home. Lazzeri beat the throw. Combs then singled pinch runner Bengough and Pennock home, and Koenig doubled to right. Cvengros came in to pitch for Pittsburgh and Babe Ruth hit a three-run homer to right field. The Yanks had scored six runs, had their first home run, along with two doubles and a triple, and won in standard Yankee fashion.[7]

The fourth game produced the most remarkable play of the Series. The Yankees went to their rookie sensation, Wilcy Moore, and Donie Bush started Carmen Hill, for this year alone, the Pirate ace. Both pitched pretty well. Pittsburgh got a run in the top of the first inning. Lloyd Waner, who hit .400 for the Series, opened with a single to left, advanced on a fielder's choice, and scored when Glenn Wright got a two out single to right. The Yanks tied it in the bottom of the first when Combs, Koenig and Babe Ruth singled. One run home, two men on, no one out, and Gehrig, Meusel and Lazzeri were coming up. Hill looked finished. He was not, promptly striking Gehrig, Meusel, and Lazzeri out. The Yanks got only one run. They added two more in the fifth. Combs again led off with a single and Babe Ruth homered into the right field stands. The game looked won already. But Hill shut the Yankees down through the sixth inning and the Pirates tied the game with two runs in the seventh. Pirates catcher Earl Smith was safe when Wilcy Moore, covering first base, dropped Gehrig's toss. Fred Brickell, pinch-hitting for Carmen Hill, was safe on Lazzeri's error. Lloyd Waner sacrificed the two runners along. Clyde Barnhart singled Smith home, and Paul Waner drove Brickell in with a sacrifice fly. The score was tied, 3 to 3.

By the ninth inning, Johnny Miljus was again pitching for the Pirates. He had done well in the first game, and Donie Bush hoped he could hold the fort here. But things started to go downhill at once. Combs drew a base on balls from Miljus. Koenig singled and Miljus wild pitched the runners to second and third. Miljus walked Ruth and the bases were loaded with no one out in the ninth inning of a World Series game. But Miljus did not fold under the pressure. He struck out Gehrig. He struck out Meusel. Lazzeri then hit a foul drive, and Miljus tried a curve to fool the Yankee second baseman. The ball slipped and Miljus threw it over the catcher's head for a wild pitch. Combs came home with the winning run of the game and the Series. The crowd and the players were stunned by the unexpected play. The crowd filed out with only a smattering of cheers, and the players left the field silently as well. The World Series had ended on a wild pitch, "not with a bang but a whimper."[8]

The Yankees had won the game, 4 to 3, and the World Series, four games straight. This matched the success of the 1914 Miracle Boston Braves who had beaten the Philadelphia Athletics in four games. But the Murderers Row hardly lived up to their billing. Babe Ruth hit two home runs, and Lou Gehrig had two triples, but the sustained slugging that had marked the Yankees during the regular season, and which the fans confidently expected, never occurred. Nonetheless, even if the Yanks wound up with a mediocre .279 Series batting average, there was no doubt which was the better team. Indeed, there was every reason for the fans in 1927 to suppose that they were watching the best team in contemporary baseball and in the history of baseball. Subsequent opinion tended to confirm that judgment. It was also the beginning of a Yankee dominance that created legends. Before 1927, the Yanks had been in four Series and lost three of them. Beginning in 1927, the Yanks rarely lost a game, never mind a Series. It began the aura of invincibility that could justify Waite Hoyt's remark while being harassed by opponents when pitching for Pittsburgh in the twilight of his Hall of Fame career: "Shut up, you guys, or I'll put on a Yankee uniform and scare the — — out of all of you."[9]

III

The 1928 Yankees are never thought of as being Murderers Row. They are remembered as a lesser team, on the few occasions when they are remembered, though they were, for the most part, the same players who wore the pinstripes in 1927. They won the American League pennant, though by only two and a half games, down from nineteen the year before, over the second place Philadelphia Athletics. They led the American League in home runs, at 133, down from 158 the year before, but even that lower total sufficed to lead the majors in 1928. Babe Ruth did not hit sixty home runs again, but he did hit fifty-four, which is not bad, though Lou Gehrig dropped off from forty-seven in 1927 to twenty-seven in 1928. The Yanks also won the World Series in 1928, and hit nine home runs in the process, far better than the mere two, both hit by Babe Ruth, against the Pirates in 1927. But the 1928 Yanks are not the Murderers Row, nor even the equally lethal but less felonious Bronx Bombers. Memory and myth has left the 1928 Yankees in the shade of afterthought. Buzzy Bavasi had nothing to say about the 1928 Yankees not winning every year, though Miller Huggins's boys did at least win in 1928, which is almost as good.

The Yankees in 1928 were, in fact as well as myth, not quite as good as they had been the year before. Changes do occur from year to year. The 1963 Mets did not lose quite as many games as the 1962 Mets (111 as opposed to 120), though they were, of course, still the worst team in baseball, and, while everyone remembers the dreadful 1962 Mets, everyone has mercifully forgotten the inept crew from 1963. The 1928 Yankees have suffered the same fate, largely, looking back on it, because of pitching. Wilcy Moore had won nineteen games as an antique rookie in 1927, but he sank to four and four in 1928. Dutch Ruether, who had won thirteen games in 1927, was no longer in the Majors. Urban Shocker, who had won eighteen games in 1927, only pitched two innings in 1928 and died during the season. But the Yanks added Hank Johnson, who won fourteen games and Al Shealy, who won all eight games in his brief Major League career for the 1928 Yankees. Moreover George Pipgras won twenty-four games, his career year, up from the ten of the year before. This was a big help, and with Waite Hoyt winning twenty-three and Herb Pennock winning seventeen, the Yanks did win 101 games. But it was not 110, the team did not win by 19 games, and it did not have about it that aura of invincibility.[10]

For the rest, the team was about the same. Gehrig improved his batting average to .374 (from .373 the year before) and drove in 142 runs. Babe Ruth, who hit .323 (down from .356), led the league with fifty-four home runs. Lazzeri hit .332 and Mark Koenig .319, but the team batting average slipped to .296, though that was good enough to lead the league. The Yanks did add a rookie second baseman, Leo Durocher, who combined modest talent with a huge ego, a massive will to win, and a world-class dollop of chutzpah. He became known as Leo the Lip, because of caustic comments about his numerous enemies, but in 1928 those rhubarbs were still in the future. Not in the future was a dust-up with the ferocious and legendary Ty Cobb, who combined a bad temper with a vicious streak and was the most feared player in baseball. When Leo Durocher spiked Cobb on a play at second, Cobb sprang up in fury and began to berate the rookie. Durocher yelled back and Cobb said he would see Leo under the stands after the game. Leo said he would be there, but Babe Ruth intervened, telling Durocher that Cobb would kill him. Ruth went instead and smoothed things over. Ruth was right. Cobb would have killed Leo the Lip just as he killed a mugger in Washington in 1912. Cobb was stabbed in this attempted robbery, but, roaring with rage and dripping blood, he chased the mugger up an alley and beat him to death. Everyone knew the story. Babe Ruth, who was a kindly man, prevented a similar occurrence in 1928, and the Lip lived through his ill-advised encounter with Cobb.

Even with the addition of Durocher, whose .270 batting average did nothing to strengthen the Yankee attack, the Yanks seemed generally less fearsome. The team ERA slipped to 3.74 from 3.20 the year before. The Yanks no longer led the league in hitting and pitching. There were those who thought the Philadelphia Athletics, stronger in 1928 than a year before, might win the pennant. In 1929 they would. A bit of the gilt had rubbed off the gingerbread.

The St. Louis Cardinals won the National League pennant in 1928 by two games over the New York Giants. The Cardinals had won in 1926 and had defeated the Yankees in a seven-game Series by winning the last game, when a hung-over Grover Cleveland Alexander came in from the bullpen to strike out Tony Lazzeri with the bases loaded in the last of the seventh.[11] Maybe they could do it again, or at least improve on the Pirates' performance of 1927. After all, the Cards had a lot of the same team from 1926. Sunny Jim Bottomley still played first base, while Frankie Frisch replaced Rogers Hornsby at second. Rabbit Maranville shared shortstop duties with the 1926 regular, Tommy Thevenow. Wattie Holm replaced Les Bell at third base, but none could say that this was an improvement. The Cardinals' outfield also showed more continuity than change. Taylor Douthit and Chick Hafey remained, while George Harper and Wally Roettger replaced the hard-hitting Billy Southworth. The pitching was about the same. The starting rotation consisted of Billy Sherdel, Flint Rhem, Jesse Haines and Grover Cleveland Alexander, while, among the supporting staff, Art Reinhart remained from 1926. All in all, the Series did not look too one-sided. St. Louis had won ninety-five games, and their pitching was second in the National League only to Brooklyn. The Cards seemed to have a decent chance against the former Murderers Row.

But the former 1927 Yankees, now demoted to just a good team, pounded the Cardinals. They hit nine home runs, rather than the two of the year before. Only in the first game, when Waite Hoyt defeated Billy Sherdel, 4 to 1, did the Yanks score fewer than seven runs. The Yanks won the game on a two-run homer by Bob Meusel in the fourth inning, and Hoyt, like Pennock the year before, gave up one run on three hits. In the second game the Yanks faced Alexander, who had defeated them twice in 1926 and had saved the final game of the Series. This time "Ole Pete" didn't have it. He gave up a three-run homer to Lou Gehrig in the first inning. The Cardinals came back to score three runs in the second inning, but Pipgras survived and shut the Cardinals out the rest of the way. Alexander was knocked out of the box in the third inning as the Yankees won, 9 to 3. The Series now shifted to St. Louis, where the somewhat discouraged fans still hoped for the best.

In the third game, Miller Huggins started left-hander Tom Zachary. The Washington Senators had traded Zachary to the Yanks in midseason 1928, and Zachary had gone three and three in seven games with his new team. He was a most unlikely starter. But Huggins had a hunch. Zachary had been in two World Series with Washington and had won two games in 1924. Perhaps he could do it again. Tom Zachary could do it again. In his last World Series appearance, Zachary was not overpowering, scattering nine hits, but Gehrig supported him with two home runs. Jesse Haines, who had won two games in 1926, lost this one, 7 to 3. The Yanks were up by three games.

In the final game of the 1928 World Series both Bill McKechnie of the Cardinals and Miller Huggins of the Yanks went back to their opening game pitchers. Again Waite Hoyt pitched a complete game and defeated Billy Sherdel. Here the Yanks hit in reality like the Murderers Row of myth and imagination. Babe Ruth hit three home runs as he had in the fourth game in the 1926 World Series. Lou Gehrig hit his fourth homer of the series and reserve outfielder Cedric Durst hit his only World Series home run. Five home runs in a single game was, at the time, a Series record. The Yankees won the game, 7 to 3, and swept their second straight World Series. Murderers Row had appeared, a year late perhaps, but only in fact, which always is and always ought to remain subordinate to myth. After all, the myth celebrates the 1927 Yankees, which didn't lose in 1928 either.[12]

IV

The final appearance of Murderers Row of the 1927 Yankees came in the World Series of 1932. But while the Yankees retained many similarities to the team of 1927, the country had changed radically. The gaudy urban prosperity of the 1920s had vanished, and the ersatz champagne in the speakeasy had gone flat. Booze made from bug spray no longer seemed a romantic defiance of Prohibition in particular and conventional bourgeois social standards in general. Organized crime did not seem to be as entertaining as it had once been, and corruption of cops and courts were now viewed as a problem and not a comedic and cynical lark. Gangster killings, from St. Valentine's Day in 1929 to the Castelmare war in April 1931 between the New York gangs of Joe "the Boss" Mezzeria and Salvatore Maranzano, were now viewed as symptomatic of a breakdown of social order rather than survival of the fittest, who, in this case, was Lucky Luciano. Banditry in the Mid-West, symbolized by John Dillinger, Pretty Boy Floyd, Baby Face Nelson, Bonnie and Clyde, et al., required the intervention of the FBI, and the bandits were gunned down as they were found. Crooks had become bad guys, and the speakeasies had changed from fashionable venues of entertainment into the grubby haunts of drunks. The Yankees still hit home runs, but no one called them Murderers Row.

The Great Depression had changed everything, from social attitudes about crime to the social reality of joblessness or the threat of joblessness. When the stock market crash came, on October 29, 1929, the economy slipped, slowly at first, and then with terrifying speed into Depression.[13] Things were really serious. Even the speakeasies started to close. For much of America, fear had replaced optimism. No one knew what to do. It was worse than anyone had ever seen, heard of, or even imagined, and no one could explain how it happened or when it would end.

In these straightened circumstances baseball soldiered on, playing to smaller crowds, though the game on the field was as good as it would ever get. As the economy contracted baseball made less money. In Philadelphia, Connie Mack was forced to sell off many of the stars from the 1929–1931 Athletics powerhouse teams. Mickey Cochrane went to Detroit, and Jimmie Foxx and Lefty Grove went to the Red Sox. Connie had bills to pay. Other teams nearly went broke. The Phillies sold their best hitter, Chuck Klein, to the Cubs in 1934, got him back and sold him to the Pirates in 1939. The Phils owner, Gerry Nugent, had bills to pay.

The Yankees, however, continued to do pretty well. They were a big draw everywhere in American League, and made additional money from barnstorming in the spring. Everyone wanted to see the Babe. The Chicago Cubs, who won the National League pennant in 1932, lacked the mighty Babe, the premier sports attraction in the land, but they had a loyal fan base on the north side of Chicago and a millionaire owner in Philip Wrigley. Moreover, before free agency, when the reserve clause was in full force, it was easier to keep a good team together. Consequently, the Yankees in 1932 still had the core of the 1927 team; though the players were a bit older, they were still pretty good. Gehrig, who played every game as always, hit .349 with 34 home runs and 151 runs batted in. This did not lead the league as Jimmie Foxx of the Athletics hit 58 homers and drove in 169 runs. Even so, Gehrig had a good year. So did Babe Ruth, now somewhat out of shape and much slower than he had been. But the Babe hit .341, with 41 homers and drove in 137 runs. Once again, he had a better year than Herbert Hoover. Tony Lazzeri still played second base, he hit .300, and he drove in more than 100 runs. So did Ben Chapman, the new left fielder who replaced the retired "Long Bob" Meusel. Adding to the Yankees power was catcher Bill Dickey, who hit .310 and drove in eighty-four runs. The Yanks still had a Murderers Row. They hit 160 home runs, 2 more than they had hit in 1927. Frank Crosetti had replaced Mark Koenig at shortstop and Joe Sewell, who was traded to the Yanks by Cleveland in 1931, played third base. In 1932, he had over 560 plate appearances, and struck out three times. Sewell always got wood on the ball, and had a clear idea of the strike zone. He also had a lifetime .312 batting average. At third base the Yanks were better than ever. Finally, Earle Combs played center field, and hit over .300. In the field the Yanks had more continuity than change.

The pitching showed the changes. Herb Pennock (9–5) and George Pipgras (16–9) were still in New York and were still front-line pitchers. But they were nearing the end of their careers. In 1933, Pipgras would be traded to Boston for his last full year in the Show. Herb Pennock would go to Boston in 1934 for his last year. The Yanks had added some new arms. Red Ruffing had come over from the Red Sox in 1930. He had been one of the best pitchers in the American League for a couple of years before the trade, and after the trade he became a consistent winner as well. In 1932, he won eighteen and lost seven, and his earned run average, 3.09, was second only to Lefty Grove.

The leading Yankee pitcher in 1932 was Vernon Louis "Lefty" Gomez. In 1931, his first full season with the Yanks, he had won twenty-one games, and in 1932 he led the league with twenty-four wins. Lefty Gomez was a wit and a free spirit as well as a great pitcher, and there were many times when the staid and humorless Yankees front office shook their heads over the latest Gomez comment. But if you wanted to win ballgames rather than imitate bankers, Gomez was your guy. The five man Yankee rotation also included Johnny Allen, who won seventeen and lost four. A rookie in 1932, Allen was rumored to throw an excellent spitball, and would have several good years with the Yanks before being sent to Cleveland where, in 1937, he won fifteen games and lost only one, on the last day of the season. With some new pitching the still-slugging Yankees won 107 games in 1932, and finished 13 ahead of the second place Athletics.[14]

In the World Series, the last that would feature Babe Ruth and Lou Gehrig, the sometime Murderers Row faced the Chicago Cubs, which had lost the 1929 series to the Philadelphia Athletics and were back to try again. The Cubs had a good team, one first put together in 1929 by Joe McCarthy, now manager of the Yankees. The veteran Jolly Cholly Grimm played first base and hit .307. Billy Herman hit .314 and played second, Billy Jurges was at shortstop and Woody English played third. The Cubs had a good outfield with Kiki Cuyler, Riggs Stephenson (whose .336 lifetime is the highest for any player *not* in the Hall of Fame), and Johnny Moore. Gabby Hartnett was the catcher. The Cubs were good, but except for Hartnett, who was the best catcher in the National League, no one would confuse the Cubs with the Yanks.

The strength of the Chicago team was its pitching. The staff ace in 1932 was Lon Warneke, "The Arkansas Hummingbird." He won twenty-two games while losing only six, and led the league with 2.37 ERA. Warneke was in his first full year with the Cubs, and his improvement from two wins the year before was the difference between third place in 1931 and the pennant in 1932. Just behind Warneke was veteran Guy Bush, "The Mississippi Mudcat," who won nineteen games. Charley Root and Pat Malone each won fifteen games, and veteran Burleigh Grimes, "Ol' Stubblebeard," who was at the end of a Hall of Fame career, won six. Grimes had been around since 1916, when he broke in with the Pirates, and the Cubs were his sixth National League team. Burleigh Grimes was one of a handful of legal spitball pitchers in the Majors. Ol' Stubblebeard had been a good pitcher for a long time, and, as the Cubs only won by four games, they needed his six victories.[15]

The World Series, last for the Babe, began in New York on September 28. Guy Bush started against Red Ruffing, and the Mississippi Mudcat seemed to have his best stuff. He got the first nine men out, but the Yanks scored three runs in the fourth inning and five in the fifth. Going through the lineup for the second time was always a problem for pitchers who faced the Yankees. Red Ruffing was far from perfect, giving up six runs on ten hits, but the Yanks scored twelve runs, including a home run by Gehrig, to support him. The second game was much tighter. Gomez went up against Lon Warneke, and was the better pitcher. In a game with no home runs, Ben Chapman's two-run single in the third inning was the decisive blow. The Yanks won, 5 to 2, and departed for Chicago with a two-game lead.

In cozy Wrigley Field, the Series again featured the Murderers Row. Both Ruth and Gehrig hit two home runs, one of them Babe's called shot against Charlie Root. Kiki Cuyler and Gabby Hartnett homered for Chicago, but it was not enough and George Pipgras beat Charlie Root, 7 to 5. The fourth game was an even bigger offensive show. The Yanks started Johnny Allen and the Cubs chased him in the first with a four-run inning. Allen lasted two-thirds of an inning. Guy Bush did not pitch that long. After one-third of an inning the Mississippi Mudcat was replaced by the Arkansas Hummingbird. Warneke lasted through the third inning. Jackie May, in his last year in the Majors, pitched into the seventh inning when the Yanks knocked him out of the box with a four-run rally. Bud Tinning followed, lasted the eighth, and Burleigh Grimes gave up four runs in the ninth. For the Yanks Wilcy Moore pitched five innings for the win, giving up no earned runs, and Herb Pennock finished up. Tony Lazzeri hit two home runs and Earle Combs one, giving the Yanks eight homers in all, one fewer than in 1928 and six more than the Murderers Row in 1927. The Yanks won the game, 13 to 6, and swept their third straight Series. The Yanks had won twelve straight World Series games, which remains the record. Chicago pitching had a 9.26 ERA as a result of the assault by the Murderers Row. Poor Burleigh Grimes had a 73.63 ERA and Guy Bush gave up 14.92 earned runs on a nine-inning basis. The Cubs scored nineteen runs, not bad at all for four games, but the Yanks tallied thirty-seven, or nine a game, fourteen more than in 1927 and ten more than in 1928.[16] Buzzy Bavasi was right. Those 1927 Yankees were hard to beat.

The 1932 World Series was the end of Murderers Row, or whatever name might be used to describe the mighty Yankees in the twilight of Babe Ruth and before Joe DiMaggio. Part of the problem was pitching, but for the Yankees, and this would have been true for no other team, pitching was serious but secondary. The aging Babe Ruth was the problem. Players have short careers, and Ruth, with the most varied and stupendous natural abilities in the history of the game, was no longer the best player in baseball, though his iconic status continued to grow in spite of deteriorating skills. He could no longer carry the Yankees, freezing opponents with fear and awe. It was the immense psychological size of the Bambino, compared to the image and shadow cast by other good players, that separated the Yankees of 1927–1932 from other good teams. The Philadelphia Athletics from 1929 through 1931 were as good as the Yanks at most positions and were better at some, and won three pennants in a row, beating out the Yankees each time. Yet their renown has faded with time, while the Yankees' fame continued to grow. The Babe made the difference when he was the best player in baseball, and he made the difference when he was not. Babe Ruth had turned a great team into *the* great team. As his skills faded, the aura of the Yankees faded with him. The days of 1927 seemed farther away and impossible to recapture. That had been another time.

6

Subway Series

In 1947, the Brooklyn Bridge was more than transportation. It was still "The Bridge" in New York, in spite of newer and longer spans. It was also the only bridge to have supported its own full-time bunco artist, George Parker. Parker sold the Brooklyn Bridge to eager and greedy tourists to New York. His first sale came in 1883, shortly after the bridge opened. What had begun as a casual con of opportunity became a calling, and Parker made selling the Brooklyn Bridge his life's occupation. He sold the bridge hundreds of times over the years, prospering in his profession and always perfecting his art. In 1928, he was unexpectedly arrested on the (for New Yorkers) preposterous charge of running a swindle. Astoundingly, he was actually convicted of conning the rubes, and went to Sing Sing Prison where the other inmates treated him with awe and respect. Parker's legend lived on, and buying the Brooklyn Bridge has entered the culture as a synonym for naive stupidity. The bridge, incidentally, in spite of Parker's socially useful efforts, remains public property and, in part because of Parker, has retained its iconic quality. The old New York newspaper phrase "Across the Big Bridge," used to acknowledge the boundary between the gaudy business activities of Manhattan's stock exchange, brothels and Tammany Hall politics and the families living in Brooklyn, "The City of Homes and Churches." Those phrases have now vanished, along with Brooklyn's hometown newspaper, *The Brooklyn Eagle*. But in 1947 this all survived, Parker was fondly remembered, and Brooklyn was more than a place. Crossing the Brooklyn Bridge then was not merely a commute; it was also a journey.

The World Series of 1947 brought together again two different local worlds which had not played each other since 1941. The Series of 1947 was widely considered, in New York and Brooklyn at least, to be the biggest national event since World War II, which also had been in all the papers, and was itself the biggest thing since the 1941 season, when Joe had hit in fifty-six straight games and Ted had hit .406, and Mickey Owen had dropped the third strike in the Series. Now baseball had reclaimed the biggest stage in the biggest city with the biggest media coverage (barring World War II) since 1941. Fans looked forward to a Series that matched the setting.

A subway series, of course, meant the mighty New York Yankees, the Bronx Bombers who had won nine of their last ten World Series, five of them in four games. Since their first pennant in 1921, the Yanks had led the American League fifteen times, while the rest of the league combined had won only twelve pennants. The Yankees were also the basic means of economic support for the American League, drawing fans to games with even the poorest teams in the league. The mighty Yankees dominated the collective memory of baseball, having had the most spectacular players, the ones that everyone knew, from Babe Ruth and Lou Gehrig to Joe DiMaggio. The Yanks had a huge national fan base, reaching far beyond New York into the provincial cities and remote hinterlands of the republic. Radio increased the Yankees' celebrity, bringing a rooting interest, from rabid to occasional, to fans who would never see them play. The Yankees had become part of American popular culture.

To some extent, therefore, it hardly mattered whom the Yankees played in the Series. Since the days of Silent Cal Coolidge the Yanks had only lost one World Series, so it was just a question of who would be the designated sacrificial victim for this year. But the Dodgers were different. In Brooklyn, the Dodgers were an alternate religion. They were a reminder of Brooklyn as an independent city before consolidation (1898), and there were people in 1947 who could remember that. For those who were younger, rooting for the Dodgers was a culturally inherited form of civic pride and piety. In the ethnic middle- and working-class neighborhoods that spread south and east of Brooklyn Heights, love and loyalty for the Dodgers ran deep in the soul, combining borough distinctiveness with the virtues of rooting for the underdog. In Brooklyn, the faithful loathed the Yanks as the privileged bullies they were; the Giants they merely regarded with contempt, and the rest of the nation, beyond the Bridge, was the sticks and people who rooted for teams in tank towns like Cleveland or St. Louis were deluded rubes. Brooklyn, borough and team, was the home of the world, and Dodgers fans rooted with a grim and joyful intensity that could hardly be imagined in the more placid reaches of this favored land.

In 1947, Brooklyn looked, sounded, felt and smelled very much as it had in 1937 or 1927. Legal beer and booze was about the only difference between the Roaring Twenties, when Brooklyn was the on-shore address of a vital segment of the rum fleet, and the immediate post–Hiroshima period. The great migration from Southern field and town to Northern city had just started, and the migration from city to suburbs was still a thing of dream and desire. The great building boom, symbolized by William Levitt who did for housing what Henry Ford did for cars, was in its infancy, and the road-building that would complete urban transformation did not even exist in the planning stage. The Depression and the war may have ended, but their effects lingered on in a cityscape and an urban demographic image that by now was a generation old in Brooklyn.

The Roman Catholic Church, which in Brooklyn rivaled the Dodgers, the Mob, the cops, the Navy Yard and ethnicity in importance, was still firmly Irish, run in a determined manner by Bishop Molloy. The same was true of the cops. Nineteenth-century police inspector Alexander "Clubber" Williams, famously remarked that "There is more law in the end of a policeman's nightstick than in a decision of the Supreme Court."[1] This was still unquestionably true, and most people in Brooklyn thought this was a good idea. Street justice was entirely appropriate for street crime; indeed, it was to be preferred, since the young miscreant did not go into the system and so still had a chance to turn his life around. It was equally true that more authority resided in a pronouncement or a pastoral from Bishop Molloy than in anything the mere government might have to say. Although the Irish had lost control over the Brooklyn waterfront to Tony Uale in the 1920s, this did not end Irish clout in the borough of home and churches.

It was still possible in the Brooklyn of 1947 to experience life as continuity. Small stores placed newspapers on a wooden stand on the sidewalk, and people would throw down change and take a paper. Bakery trucks delivered bread and Danish. Joe's at Borough Hall served Italian cuisine, presented by tuxedoed waiters to diners sitting at tables stretching in neat straight rows across the tile floor. The Brooklyn Heights Casino hosted the borough's debs. The Dodgers offices were on Montague Street in Brooklyn Heights. You could walk to Ebingers for pie or coffee cake, or get a haircut at the barbershop one flight up on Montague. Had not things always been this way?

Brooklyn was still a borough where layers of community feelings and obligations enveloped the residents, particularly the adults. The church and the Dodgers were community writ large, embracing family, friend, and stranger in borough life. There were categories of extended identification; to live in Brooklyn was to inhabit a recognized segment of the metropolitan area, and religion, though currently politically incorrect, was then a mark of cultural heritage. Below this level of generality came the ethnic neighborhood, which had been established a generation or two ago by hacking out living space in a hostile city, and which, while duplicated elsewhere (the Bronx or Queens) was thought (in Brooklyn) to have been done better in Brooklyn. Within the neighborhoods were families, extended back over generations and horizontally outward to uncles and cousins and aunts. For some, it seemed a narrow and restricted world; for others, such a life was abundant and rich in the things that mattered: love, memory and identity.

Change was coming to the ethnic neighborhoods of Brooklyn, brought on, of course, by the universal American solvent: money. In America, in things physical as much as social, hard times preserve while prosperity destroys. In a decade the unthinkable, and unspeakable, would occur and the Dodgers would be wrenched from their roots and taken to an alien place, and the Brooklyn they represented would be going quickly as well. But in the beautiful autumn weather of 1947, prelude to a record winter blizzard that December, the old borough persisted and seemed immensely different from the frenetic activity across the Bridge. Brooklyn still looked inward and lived locally. But just for now.

I

The New York Yankees won the American League pennant in lordly fashion by twelve games over the Detroit Tigers. The Yankees record stood at 97 and 57, forty games over .500 and the best record in baseball. This was right and proper for the most successful team (now as well as then) in all American sport. In major American sporting events, only Franklin Roosevelt had a better record than the Yanks.

The Yankees had put the pennant away by winning nineteen games in a row during June and July, thus equaling the winning streak of the Chicago White Sox in 1906 and tying the American League record for sustained group excellence. The streak began on June 29, when the Yankees were already in first place, with a 3-to-1 victory over the hapless Washington Senators who were transiently in sixth before sinking further down another rung of disappointing performance into seventh where they finished the season. The winning pitcher of this otherwise ordinary game was Don Johnson, who won four games and lost three in 1947, but won three against Washington in his only season with the Yankees. The next day rookie Spec Shea, fourteen and five for the year, defeated the Red Sox, also by 3 to 1. On July 2, the Yanks returned home for an Independence Day series with the Senators, and won all three games, followed by three more against the fourth-place Philadelphia Athletics. When the Yanks went on the road again on July 10 for a swing though the Western cities of St. Louis, Chicago, Cleveland, and Detroit they had already won eight games in a row, a respectable streak in itself. On the road the Yanks became unbeatable. They swept four games from the last-place St. Louis Browns, took a July 13 doubleheader from the Chicago White Sox, won five straight games from the Cleveland Indians and came into Detroit on July 18 to play the second place Tigers. Randy Gumpert, a spot starter who went four and one for the year, pitched for the Yanks against dour Fred Hutchinson, a ferocious competitor who won eighteen games in 1947. Among them was this game. Detroit got eighteen hits and Hutchinson shut out the Yanks on two hits, 8 to 0. The streak was over, having lasted most of a month, and the Yankee broadcaster Mel Allen, who had stopped shaving so as not to jinx the team, could look respectable again. I heard the game on radio and rooted hard with youthful vim against the Yankees. But I knew, Fred Hutchinson or no Fred Hutchinson, that the Yanks were going to win the pennant and much else besides. The essence of myth is specific joy rooted in general sorrow. As

John Donne wrote in "A Lecture Upon the Shadow": "And his short minute, after noon, is night."[2]

The Yankee team that put together the remarkable winning streak (thirteen of the games were won on the road) was a transition unit. It combined prewar Yankee stars, players obtained from other teams, Yankee wartime players, and rising Yankee stars into an improbable mix ably managed by veteran Bucky Harris. In 1924, Harris had won the pennant and the Series with Washington in his first year managing, and in 1947, he won both again in his first year managing the Yankees.

Harris made good use of the various players that president and general manager Larry MacPhail entrusted to him. At first base Harris plugged in veteran George McQuinn, acquired from the Philadelphia Athletics. McQuinn responded by hitting .304 and having his best year since 1939. Snuffy Stirnweiss, a wartime Yankees star continued at second base, but no longer hit .300 as he had against wartime pitching. Phil Rizzuto was the shortstop, returned from the war and showing prewar stardom. Billy Johnson, also back from the war, played third base, and had his best year in 1947. In the outfield the Yanks used three prewar stars, headed, of course, by the incomparable Joe DiMaggio who led the team in hitting at .315. He was flanked by Tommy Henrich in right field and Johnny Lindell, a wartime star, and Charlie Keller in left field. The catching was divided between Aaron Robinson, to be traded in 1948 to the White Sox, and Yogi Berra who was correctly judged to be the catcher of the future for the Yanks.

Like all teams, the Yanks used a lot of pitchers, not all of them effective. The best was Allie Reynolds, acquired after the 1946 season from the Cleveland Indians. Spec Shea came up from the minors and won fourteen games in his rookie year. Joe Page, who in 1947 became a relief pitcher, also won fourteen games and led the league in saves with seventeen. Spud Chandler, who had pitched with the Yanks through the war, went nine and five in his last year. The irrepressible veteran Bobo Newsom, who was something of a free spirit, came to New York in midseason from the Senators, and won seven games as a Yankee, while Bill Bevens, who had come up with the Yanks in 1944, had a disappointing year, winning seven and losing thirteen for a pennant winner. It would be Bevens's last year in the Show. The Yanks also brought Vic Raschi up from Portland in midseason, and the future star responded by winning seven games and losing only two. The pitching was not overpowering, but it was good enough. The 1947 Yankees were not the machine they had been from 1936 to 1942, nor the machine they would become under Casey Stengel in the 1950s. But no team, even one with a couple of shreds and a few patches, that wins the pennant by a dozen games plays poorly, and Bucky Harris clearly got the most out of his players.

The Brooklyn Dodgers were also a pretty good team. Like the Yankees they had a first-year manager who was a surprise appointment. Burt Shotton, summoned from Florida retirement by Brooklyn owner Branch Rickey three days after the season opened, took over in the second game from coach Clyde Sukeforth, who himself had been managing for less than ten days after the regular Dodgers skipper, Leo Durocher, had been suspended for a year for "conduct detrimental to baseball" by new commissioner A. B. "Happy" Chandler. The suspension arose from a hearing in late March, involving charges and countercharges by MacPhail, president of the Yankees and former president of the Dodgers, and by assorted Brooklyn officials. The charges were never clear, but the animus was, and Chandler hoped that the Durocher suspension would quiet things down a bit. Leo was not known as Leo the Lip for nothing. From his encounter with Ty Cobb in 1928, the Lip had insulted everyone. After a loss in the first game of a doubleheader to the last place Giants, a sports writer needled Leo by telling him to be a nice guy, like the Giants manager, Mel Ott. The nice guys are all in the other dugout, Leo snarled, and they are in last place. Leo avoided both of those things. Since Chandler could not suspend an owner, why not suspend the snotty and

JACKIE ROBINSON. **Caught in an instance of action, Jackie Robinson extended the intensity, the concentration and the competitiveness that always marked his game.**

volatile Durocher, who if not at fault in starting things was certainly at fault for continuing them. As for Leo himself, he used the leisure to marry actress Laraine Day.

Most years, the Durocher brouhaha would have been big news. But the spring of 1947 saw really big news. The Dodgers brought Jackie Robinson up from Montreal and broke the Major League color line which had existed since the 1880s. The actual moment was on April 10, a couple of days before the start of the 1947 season. The announcement was terse. "The Brooklyn Dodgers today purchased the contract of Jackie Robinson from the Montreal Royals. He will report immediately."[3] Branch Rickey, turgid of speech, arrogant, hypocritical and self-righteous as Puritans invariably are, this time stood aside and let the moment speak for itself.

Others, of course, had plenty to say, much of it vicious and some of it millenarian. But those who concentrated on the rightness of the move and the burden borne by Jackie Robinson got the story right. The Robinson saga, and it was nothing less than a saga, changed baseball forever. Along with the National Agreement (1883) and free agency (1975), the signing of Jackie Robinson to a Major League contract was one of the three most important events in the history of baseball and the most important moral moment baseball contributed to the broader national history.

It was not just Branch Rickey, the architect of the Robinson signing, who made racial integration work in a segregated game in a segregated land that had whites-only neighborhood covenants and separate public accommodations, schools, and armed forces. Pee Wee Reese, from Kentucky, accepted Robinson as a teammate, thus helping to snuff out possible trouble

PEE WEE REESE. The Kentucky Colonel was more than a Hall of Fame player, he was also the player most responsible for seeing that the Dodgers accepted Jackie Robinson as a teammate in 1947.

from other Southern players. Thinking about it later, Reese paid tribute to Robinson's courage, self-control and sense of history.

> You saw how he stood there at the plate and dared them to hit him with the ball and you began to put yourself in his shoes. You'd think of yourself trying to break into the black leagues maybe, and what it would be like — and I know I couldn't have done it. In a word: he was winning respect.[4]

That was the simple truth. As the season wore on and Robinson contributed on the field again and again, the Dodgers who had opposed him became less hostile. Eddie Stanky, from Mobile, Alabama, knew class and courage when he saw it. In a game against the Philadelphia Phillies, a lousy team with expert bench jockeys who rode Robinson hard, Stanky yelled at them: "Why don't you guys go to work on somebody who can fight back? There isn't one of you has the guts of a louse."[5] It may be doubted that these were Stanky's exact words, and it may equally be supposed that Stanky added gesture to comment. He was not known (at least by Giants fans) as stinky Stanky for nothing. His comment helped in Brooklyn, but didn't affect the Phillies much.

The story has oft been told, and it ought to be, because it is mythic in significance. It helped change America along with American habits of thought and ideas about right social order. If baseball integrated successfully, and it did, then America would integrate, less successfully than baseball, of course, because America is less innocent than baseball. With Jackie Robinson, baseball, for once, rose above the petty squabbles among owners and the routine disregard of the players by the clubs that owned their contracts, and, taking the high moral ground, made America not just a happier but also a better place. Something like this doesn't happen often, even in baseball, which is a metaphor for life, but not for perfection.

As for the Dodgers, Robinson made the difference between winning the pennant and finishing back in the pack. Burt Shotton, who managed in the role of an understanding and inspirational father, plugged Robinson in at first base where he hit .297, led the team in home runs, stole twenty-nine bases to lead the league, and was named rookie of the year, which he certainly was. During the season Robinson endured snubs, racial slurs, relentless razzing, separate housing, isolation and efforts on the field to spike him and throw at him. But he endured and became not just a regular but a star.

At second base Stanky remained and Pee Wee Reese was a fixture at shortstop. Spider Jorgensen took over from the aging Cookie Lavagetto as the regular third baseman. The outfield remained the same as it had been in 1946. Dixie Walker, "The Peepul's Cherce" continued in right field. A native of Villa Rica, Georgia, the same hometown as Asa Candler of Coca-Cola, Dixie Walker spoke an exotic tongue (for Brooklyn), was a superb player, and was a huge favorite with the Brooklyn fans. Carl Furillo was in center field and Pete Reiser played in right. Arky Vaughan came back from the service and hit .325 in a utility role, and Gene Hermanski, in his third season with the Dodgers, filled in when needed in the outfield.

The eight men on the field comprised a good team, but Bruce Edwards caught a very shaky pitching staff. Ralph Branca won twenty-one games and had a 2.67 ERA. He was dependable, but the rest were often question marks. Hugh Casey won ten games, saved eighteen to lead the league, and appeared in forty-six games, about 30 percent of the total played. Joe Hatten was good most of the time and won seventeen, Vic Lombardi went twelve and eleven, Harry Taylor won ten, Hall Gregg won four, Clyde King won six and Hank Behrman and Rex Barney each won five. Neither Barney nor Behrman completed a game. The Dodgers never did establish a firm rotation, and Burt Shotton juggled his on-again off-again pitchers to the pennant. By the end of the season, everyone in baseball agreed that Rickey's surprise nomination of Shotton as manager had been pure genius.

II

The Series began on September 30 at Yankee Stadium in front of a packed house, 73,365 fans, the largest crowd to date in Series history. It was a pleasant day, the teams were introduced in the appropriate manner and bunting decorated the stadium. The two managers posed for the customary pregame photograph, Burt Shotton in street clothes. All was as it ought to be. The crowd settled back to watch an expected Yankees win; the Yanks, after all, had lost only nine games in ten Series during all the years since the invention of talking pictures. The past is prologue.

The Yankees started rookie Spec Shea (fourteen and five), who ran into trouble in the first inning. After Eddie Stanky flied out to Johnny Lindell in left field, Shea walked Jackie Robinson. Robinson promptly stole second. The next hitter, Pete Reiser, hit a grounder back to the box. Shea threw to Phil Rizzuto and Robinson was trapped in a run-down between second and third. He eluded the tag long enough for Reiser to reach second. Dixie Walker then singled Reiser home. The Dodgers had the early lead.

Ralph Branca (twenty-one and twelve), the only twenty-game winner on either team, did not have early difficulties. He retired the first twelve hitters he faced and took a one-run lead into the fifth inning. But Branca found the second time through the Yankees batting order a bit troublesome. After getting everyone out in the first four innings, Branca got no one out in the fifth. DiMaggio, always a clutch hitter, began the Yankees rally with an infield single. Branca then walked George McQuinn and hit Billy Johnson. Bases loaded, no one out. The Yankees had a habit of taking advantage of these situations, and did so again. Johnny Lindell doubled to left scoring DiMaggio and McQuinn. Branca, who was losing control of his pitches and the game, walked

Phil Rizzuto, again filling the bases, again with no one out. When Bobby Brown, batting for Shea, got two straight balls from Branca, it was time for a pitching change. Shotton lifted Branca and brought in Hank Behrman, who finished walking Brown and forcing in Billy Johnson with the third Yankees run. Behrman got Snuffy Stirnweiss to bounce to Robinson who forced Lindell at the plate. The bases were still loaded. Then Tommy Henrich unloaded them, singling to right driving in Rizzuto and Brown. Berra and DiMaggio flied out, but the damage was done. The Yanks had scored five runs and led 5 to 1. Thereafter, Hank Behrman and Hugh Casey stopped the rot, holding the Yankees scoreless the rest of the way. Joe Page, who replaced Shea, was not quite as effective, but he was good enough. The Dodgers got a run on three singles in the sixth inning when Carl Furillo drove in Jackie Robinson. But Bruce Edwards, the Dodgers catcher, could not get the two-out hit with men on base.

The Dodgers kept pecking away. In the seventh inning Pee Wee Reese singled to right field, then stole second base, and scored from there when Joe Page threw a wild pitch into the spacious area behind home plate. The score was now 5 to 3. But that was it. No Dodgers reached base in the eighth or ninth innings. The Yankees had, to no one's real surprise though to the disappointment of many, won the first game of the Series.[6]

The second game, also played in Yankee stadium, drew only 70,000 fans, a significant crowd but not a full house. The first game had fallen quietly into the standard Yankee practice of nothing spectacular, just victory. The second game would likely follow the formula. The Dodgers, whose starting pitching defined the words *thin* and *questionable*, sent the left hander, Vic Lombardi (12–11), to the mound. Lombardi had a reputation for always being able to beat the Giants, not an unimportant talent for a Brooklyn pitcher. But the Giants had finished fourth, fifth and last during Lombardi's Dodgers years, and beating Mel Ott's mediocre bunch was not the same thing as facing the Yanks. For their part, the Yankees sent their best pitcher, Allie Reynolds (19–8), to clinch the Series advantage by sweeping the two home games. Reynolds had pitched for Cleveland during the war, but unlike most wartime pitchers (Boo Ferriss comes to mind), Reynolds pitched better in the stronger competition of postwar ball. He pitched well in the second game of the Series.

This time the Yanks got off to an early start with a run in the bottom of the first inning. Snuffy Stirnweiss and Tommy Henrich opened the game against Vic Lombardi by hitting singles. First and third, and no one out. Lombardi righted ship by getting Johnny Lindell to hit a ground ball to Spider Jorgensen at third, who turned it into a double play. Stirnweiss scored, and the Yanks led. "Dem Bums" fought back. In the top of the third Pee Wee Reese walked. After two outs, Reese stole second and went to third on Eddie Stanky's infield hit. Jackie Robinson singled Reese home. A couple of two-out hits, the hardest kind to get, and the Dodgers were back in the game. The

Yanks untied the game at once. In the bottom of the third Stirnweiss tripled to the gap in right center, and scored when Lindell got a two-out triple to dead center field. The Yanks had regained the lead. Not for long. In the top of the fourth inning Dixie Walker hit Reynolds's first pitch into the short right field stands originally designed for Babe Ruth. The Dodgers had tied it up again.

But Walker's only Series home run was to be the high point for Brooklyn. In the bottom of the fourth inning the Yanks went ahead for the third time when Billy Johnson tripled and Phil Rizzuto doubled him home. The Yanks increased their lead with two runs in the bottom of the fifth. Tommy Henrich led off with a home run into the right field bleachers and Johnny Lindell followed this with a double. Burt Shotton had seen enough and brought Hall Gregg in to pitch. Like Branca before him, Vic Lombardi had failed to finish the fifth inning. Gregg had no easy task. His first hitter was Joe DiMaggio, who hit a ground ball to Jorgensen at third and was thrown out. But George McQuinn singled, driving in Lindell. The score was now 5 to 2, a comfortable lead with only four innings to go.

But the Yanks kept scoring. In the sixth Allie Reynolds led off with a single and Gregg then walked Snuffy Stirnweiss. Henrich sacrificed them to second and third and Lindell brought Reynolds home with a sacrifice fly. In the seventh the Yanks broke the game open. Hank Behrman

DIXIE WALKER. In the 1940s, Brooklyn, the most un–Southern place in America, had a large number of Southerners associated with the team, notably Red Barber in the broadcast booth and Dixie Walker on the field. As they had fifteen years earlier with Babe Herman, the intensely parochial Dodgers fans took the "Peepul's Cherce" to their collective hearts. Dixie Walker came to symbolize a land so different from Brooklyn that even with movies the prewar South could only be dimly imagined.

replaced Hal Gregg, and had immediate problems. George McQuinn greeted Behrman with a single and then went to second on a wild pitch. Billy Johnson singled, driving in McQuinn. After Rizzuto popped out Yogi Berra was walked intentionally to get to Allie Reynolds. It was a standard strategy but the odds, while they may be favorable, are never absolute. Reynolds got his second hit of the game, driving in Johnson. Rex Barney replaced Hank Behrman, becoming the fourth Dodgers pitcher. Barney promptly gave up a single to Stirnweiss, scoring Berra, and Reynolds came home on a Barney wild pitch. The Yanks had scored four runs. A single Dodgers run in the top of the ninth inning fell short of what was needed. The Bronx Bombers won 10 to 3, and now led the Series two games to none.[7]

The Series moved to Brooklyn for the next three games. Many predicted that baseball in Yankee Stadium had ended for the year. Dem Bums might win one in Ebbets Field; few denied that was possible, but the Series looked pretty much over. After all, except for 1921, and that was a nine-game Series, no team in history of the Series had come back to win after losing the first two games.

Things were different in Brooklyn, in those days. Looking back over the course of half a century it is no longer easy to explain just why this was, but then no one anywhere in the country, which for New Yorkers ran from the Hudson Tubes to about Huntington out on the Island, would have doubted the mythical, psychic or spiritual truth of that observation. By way of proving that difference, the Dodgers, back home among the faithful, promptly won a World Series game. Joe Hatten started for Brooklyn against the venerable Bobo Newsom, nearing the end of a long career in which he had pitched for nine teams, two of them twice (the Athletics and Dodgers), one of them thrice (the Browns) and one four times (the Senators). In the course of his peregrinations, which never saw him with the same team three years, Ole Bobo won 211 games, including 2 in the 1940 World Series. But this game was in Brooklyn and Bobo did not get through the second inning. The Dodgers began their six-run rally, the biggest inning in the Series with Dixie Walker grounding out from Rizzuto to McQuinn. Then Bobo walked Gene Hermanski and Bruce Edwards doubled, driving in Hermanski with the first run of the game. Pee Wee Reese singled, driving Edwards home. After Spider Jorgensen flied out to DiMaggio, Joe Hatten singled, and both Reese and Hatten scored on Eddie Stanley's double. That was it for Ole Bobo. Vic Raschi was sent to the box but could not contain the damage. Jackie Robinson got his second single of the game and Carl Furillo doubled home both Stanky and Robinson. The Dodgers were ahead, 6 to nothing.

A six-run lead is a nice thing to have, but it is better in the ninth inning than in the second, when the other guys have time to catch up. The Yanks began to catch up at once. In the top of the third inning New York catcher Sherm Lollar singled and Joe Hatten walked Allie Clark who hit for the pitcher Vic

Raschi. After two outs, Lindell and DiMaggio got clutch hits driving in Lollar and Clark. The Yanks had cut the lead to four runs. But the Dodgers came back. In their half of the third Gene Hermanski was hit by the new Yankees pitcher Karl Drews and then took second on a wild pitch. Jorgensen drove Hermanski in with a two-out single. The Dodgers lead had inched up. In the top of the fourth inning it inched back down. Hatten walked Billy Johnson to open the inning and Sherm Lollar doubled him home. Snuffy Stirnweiss drove Lollar in with a single. The Dodgers lead had been cut to three runs. Not for long. In the home half of the fourth inning the new Yankees pitcher Spud Chandler began his efforts by walking Eddie Stanky. After Jackie Robinson's sacrifice, Chandler walked Carl Furillo. Dixie Walker got a hit scoring Stanley and Gene Hermanski followed with another single scoring Furillo. The Brooklyn lead was back to five runs. Only temporarily. In the top of the fifth, Hatten walked Lindell and DiMaggio homered. That was it for Joe Hatten. Shotton lifted him for Ralph Branca, who got the side out without further problems. For the third straight game the Brooklyn starter had failed to last through the fifth inning.

Branca, through far from perfect, proved to be an improvement over Hatten. The Yanks got only one run, not two, in the top of the sixth inning. Bobby Brown, hitting for Spud Chandler, doubled to right field and scored on Tommy Henrich's double. Branca then walked DiMaggio and McQuinn to load the bases before getting Billy Johnson on a pop fly to Stanky. In the top of the seventh inning Branca surrendered another run. Yogi Berra slammed a pinch-hit home run, the first in World Series history. That "Ballentine Blast," to use the commercial phrase of the beer that sponsored the Yankees radio broadcasts, finished Branca, who was replaced by Hugh Casey. Casey inherited a one-run lead and he preserved it. The Dodgers held on to win Game 3, 9 to 8.[8]

Game 4 was the most remarkable contest in Series history, from the beginning of the Pleistocene to now and beyond. The Yankees, who were running out of pitching, sent Bill Bevens to the mound. Bevens had gone seven and thirteen with a pennant winner, and Brooklyn started Harry Taylor (ten and five), more out of hope than expectation. It looked like a high-scoring and big-hitting game, and it certainly started that way. Taylor gave up singles to Stirnweiss and Henrich to start the game, and was then a victim of misfortune. Berra hit a ground ball to Robinson who threw to Pee Wee Reese at second to start a double play. Reese dropped the ball and the bases were loaded on the error. Taylor promptly walked Joe DiMaggio to force Stirnweiss in with the game's first run. The bases were still loaded and no one was yet out. Shotton, seeing the whole Series slipping away, yanked Harry Taylor and brought in Hal Gregg. Gregg was up to the task. He got McQuinn on an infield pop fly and Billy Johnson hit into a double play. The Yanks got only one run out of all that.

Bevens had his difficulties in the home first, walking Eddie Stanky and Dixie Walker, but he kept the Dodgers off the scoreboard. He was having control problems, but he also had his best stuff. When Bevens was around the plate the Dodgers found him very hard to hit. In the second inning Spider Jorgensen drew a walk, but was left at first as Hal Gregg struck out. In the third inning Stanky walked and went to second on a wild pitch, but was left there by Robinson and Walker. Bevens was throwing a lot of pitches, but was protecting that one-run lead. In the fourth inning Bevens got some help. Billy Johnson tripled to deep center field and scored on Lindell's double. The Yanks were now up by two runs, and Bevens looked like he was beginning to settle in. He retired the side in order in the bottom of the fourth.

The Dodgers finally broke through against Bevens in the fifth inning, when they scored a run without benefit of a hit. Jorgensen and Gregg walked to begin the inning and were sacrificed to second and third by Stanky. Jorgensen then scored on a fielders choice, but Jackie Robinson struck out to end the inning. Bevens pitched on, walking Dixie Walker in the sixth inning and Arky Vaughan, hitting for Hal Gregg, in the seventh. Hank Behrman came on for Brooklyn in the eighth inning and held the fort. Bevens retired the side in order in the Brooklyn eighth. In the top of the ninth inning, Behrman allowed the Yanks to load the bases with only one out. Hugh Casey came on in relief. On his first pitch Tommy Henrich hit into a double play when he bounced back to Casey, who threw home, forcing Rizzuto at home with Bruce Edwards throwing Henrich out at first. The score was still 2 to 1 as the Dodgers came up in the last of the ninth.

Bruce Edwards gave the Brooklyn crowd a moment of wild hope when he hit a long drive to left which Lindell caught at the fence. Carl Furillo walked and Al Gionfriddo ran for him. After Jorgensen fouled out to McQuinn, Gionfriddo stole second. Bucky Harris ordered an intentional pass for Pete Reiser, who was hitting for Hugh Casey. It was Bevens's tenth walk, a World Series record. Shotton sent Eddie Miksis in to run for Reiser, and Cookie Lavagetto in to hit for Stanky. Cookie was a lifetime .269 hitter, and was now at the end of a respectable ten-year career in the National League, which had been interrupted by four years (1942–45) in military service. He had yet to have a hit in the 1947 Series. It looked like Shotton was down to the bottom of the barrel. As for Bill Bevens, he had one not-terribly-difficult out to get. It was one out too many. Lavagetto hit a long double off the right field wall beyond Henrich's desperate leap, driving in Miksis and Gionfriddo. On the wall was an advertisement for *The Secret Life of Walter Mitty*, a movie made from James Thurber's short story about daydreams of glory. Life had imitated art. It was the first Dodgers hit; Bevens had pitched a World Series one-hitter and had lost, 3 to 2.[9] No one had ever done that. It seems unlikely that anyone will do it in the future.

That ninth inning, two-out double was Cookie Lavagetto's last Major

League hit, as well as incomparably his most important. No one had ever had a hit like that. Lavagetto broke up a no-hitter, won a game, did it in a World Series in front of a hysterical home crowd, and defeated the Yankees. He had, in one plate appearance, become a baseball immortal. So did Bill Bevens. No one had ever lost a one-hitter in the World Series, and few anywhere had pitched a more difficult one-hitter. The two previous Series one-hitters (Claude Passeau in 1945 and Ed Reulbach in 1906) had not been broken up in the ninth inning with the game on the line. It had been a gritty performance by a pitcher at the end of his career; this World Series loss would be his last decision. As for the fans, those rooting desperately for the Dodgers just lost their minds. Whether "strook with horror" or bewildered by the unexpected wonder of it all, the few who saw and the many who heard knew they had participated in an unforgettable moment. The memory of that moment would be cherished, embellished and passed down. It became part of the shared American culture.

After that game, the 1947 Series would have been a classic even if there were nothing more that could be called exceptional. But there was more, and it happened in the very next game, the last Brooklyn home game for the season. No one had come back from a two-game-to-none deficit to win a seven-game series, and to give the Dodgers a good chance to do that Burt Shotton started Rex Barney (five and two). Barney had a terrific fastball and problems with control. Had high been in the strike zone and outside been over the plate, Barney would have had a much better career. Here he was, on the big stage in a big game, and he needed to be at his elusive best. Bucky Harris went back to Spec Shea, who had won the first game. In ordinary circumstances, the objective fan would have to like the Yankees' chances in this matchup. But the 1947 Series had not been ordinary.

Rex Barney had difficulty from the start. He walked Snuffy Stirnweiss to start the game, gave up a double to Tommy Henrich and walked Johnny Lindell. Bases loaded and no one out. Barney pulled himself together. He struck Joe DiMaggio out. George McQuinn bounced back to Barney who threw home for the force out on Stirnweiss. Then he struck Billy Johnson out. The Yanks did not score. In the second inning Barney walked Phil Rizzuto, and in the third he walked Henrich and Lindell. But the Yanks had nothing to show for five walks and a hit in three innings. The Dodgers, meanwhile, had not managed a base runner in three innings.

In the fourth inning the Yanks finally took advantage of Barney's wildness. With two outs Barney walked Aaron Robinson and Phil Rizzuto. Shea then singled, driving in Robinson with the first run of the game. Barney then walked Stirnweiss to fill the bases. But Barney was tough with the bases loaded and he got Henrich out on a routine grounder. In the fifth inning Joe DiMaggio hit a home run into the left field stands, giving the Yankees a two-run lead. When Billy Johnson walked with two outs, Shotton figured Barney had done all he could. Joe Hatten came in for Brooklyn and got the final out. Rex Barney was the fifth Brooklyn starter to leave the game before the end of the fifth inning.

Rex Barney had not done badly. He had given up only three hits. He had also thrown a wild pitch and had walked nine men in just over four innings. At that rate, had Shotton left him in, he would have walked seventeen men in the full nine innings, far surpassing Bevens's paltry total of ten. But if Barney put them on, he also kept them on. Twice he had the bases loaded and no one scored, and only two of the twelve hits and walks came home. With a little help from his friends Rex Barney could have been as strange a winning pitcher as Bill Bevens was a losing pitcher.

But the Dodgers could not hit Shea. Although he gave up five hits and five walks, Brooklyn got only one run. In the sixth inning Al Gionfriddo, hitting for Joe Hatten, walked, as did Pee Wee Reese. Jackie Robinson singled Gionfriddo home, cutting the Yankees' lead to a single run. Shea protected it. In the ninth inning, with two out and Vic Lombardi on second, Shotton sent Cookie Lavagetto up to do it again. But not this time. Frank Shea struck Cookie out. Sic transit ... The Yanks won Game 5, 2 to 1, led the Series three games to two, and the Series returned to the Bronx.[10]

But the Dodgers had one more stunning play in their locker. For Game 6 the Series returned to Yankee Stadium, and the Dodgers started Vic Lombardi against Allie Reynolds. It looked like the Yanks would end it here. But Brooklyn got two runs in the first inning on a bases-loaded double play and a passed ball. They got two more in the third on three consecutive doubles by Pee Wee Reese, Jackie Robinson and Dixie Walker, knocking Reynolds out of the box and leading by four runs. Not for long. In the home half of the third inning the Yanks got four runs to tie the game and knock Vic Lombardi out, who became the sixth Brooklyn pitcher to leave before the end of the fifth inning. Ralph Branca replaced him, but the Yanks got two-out singles from Johnny Lindell, Joe DiMaggio, Billy Johnson and Bobby Brown to score three of their four runs. Getting another run on two out singles by Tommy Henrich and Yogi Berra, the Yankees now led 5 to 4. But the Dodgers came back with four runs in the top of the sixth inning to lead, 8 to 5. In the bottom of the sixth inning the Yanks threatened. With two outs and two men on base, DiMaggio hit a titanic drive to left field. Long and high, it seemed to be a sure home run to tie the game. Al Gionfriddo, the Brooklyn defensive replacement who had come in that very inning, raced back to the 415 marker. Twisting at the last second to field the ball on his forehand side, Gionfriddo caught the ball chest high with his glove a few inches over and behind the low fence, supporting himself with his left hand on the fence. He could not see the ball as it entered his glove. DiMaggio kicked the infield dirt at second base in frustration and disappointment. The Dodgers still led by three runs, and a Yankee tally in the bottom of the ninth was not enough. Gionfriddo's magical catch had sent the Series to the seventh game.[11]

For the last game of the Series, Bucky Harris went back to Spec Shea, who had won the first and fifth Series games. The Dodgers tried Hal Gregg who had done well in relief. Shea was ineffective on two days' rest. He got by the first inning, but in the second Shea ran into trouble. With one out, Gene Hermanski tripled and scored on a single by Bruce Edwards. When Carl Furillo singled, Bucky Harris brought Bill Bevens in to pitch. Bevens gave up a double to Spider Jorgensen, scoring Edwards and putting runners on second and third. This was the Dodgers' chance for a big inning, without which they were not going to win. But Hall Gregg bounced to Rizzuto who threw Furillo out at home, and Eddie Stanky popped out. Brooklyn had two runs, but their pitching was not going to be able to hold a lead that slim. In the home half of the second inning Phil Rizzuto singled with two outs to score George McQuinn. The Dodgers lead was cut in half.

In the fourth inning the Yanks won the Series. With one out Gregg walked Billy Johnson, and an out later, Phil Rizzuto singled. Bobby Brown, hitting for Bill Bevens, doubled the tying run home, getting his third pinch hit and giving him a gaudy 1.000 World Series batting average. Hank Behrman came in for Hal Gregg, who became the seventh Brooklyn starting pitcher who failed to finish the fifth inning. Behrman walked Snuffy Stirnweiss and Tommy Henrich singled to score Rizzuto, putting the Yanks ahead 3 to 2, and driving in what would prove to be the winning run of the Series. Although the Yanks scored insurance runs in the seventh and eighth inning, Joe Page did not need them. He held the Dodgers to one hit, a ninth-inning single, over the last five innings. The last game, like the first, was an ordinary contest, with the Yankees firmly in control. The Dodgers had run out of miracles, and the Yanks were the World Champions for the eleventh time, against only four losses. As for the Dodgers, well, they still hadn't won.[12]

III

The Series of 1947 ended on October 6, with the expected New York triumph. The fans, however, continued to discuss the Series into the winter and beyond. So much had happened that it took some time to put it all in perspective. There had never been a Series game like Game 4 and there never would be again. Cookie Lavagetto's last Major League hit had created two baseball immortals, himself and Bill Bevens. They had been part of a unique American event. Decent high schools broadcast the World Series over the PA system; it was before the days of portable transistor radios. Gionfriddo's catch, also heard, was harder to visualize, particularly since I had only been to the stadium a couple of times. We were National League fans in my family. But the newsreels showed it and the *New York Daily News* had a photo of it, so you could appreciate what an incredible twisting lucky grab it was.

Dodgers fans, and there were many of them in New York in those days, convinced themselves that these miracles were in the realm of the routine for Dem Bums. Why, the Dodgers were just as good as the aristocratic Yankees. One more good bounce, another couple of two-out hits, and Dem Bums could have won it all. Why, next time they would win it all. Wait 'til next year, or in this case, the year after. But in 1949, when the Dodgers and Yankees met again in the World Series, the Yanks again won, as they had in 1941, four games to one. Only those two miracles had prevented 1947 from being like '41 and '49. The Dodgers were not better than the Yankees. It was a hard lesson to learn, and baseball, as opposed to war or marriage, is a good place to learn it. Love does not create excellence. Love magnifies what is there, but it does not create what is absent.

Beyond lessons learned, the energy, excitement, the simplicity and purity, of that spectacle long ago remains with all who were there. The drama fixed public attention. But the times also mattered. America had not yet made the adjustment from wartime shortages to post–Hiroshima consumption. A housing shortage plagued much of the country and a shortage of cars plagued it all. The spring and summer of 1947 also saw the firm establishment of the Cold War, and the recognition that communism and communists were the enemy. Having longed for peace since the late thirties, Americans had gotten Pearl Harbor, World War II and now a new form of conflict, Cold War. It was not a comfortable nor an easy time in America, and the World Series of 1947 provided an interlude of drama and joy that was comprehensible, entertaining, and a reaffirmation that at least something was normal and connected to the past. This is what baseball does. It connects people to time. In the words of Rolfe Humphries in "Polo Grounds," the best single piece of literature on baseball,

> Time is of the essence. The crowd and the players
> Are the same age always, but the man in the crowd
> Is older every season. Come on, play ball![13]

7

Playoff

In the normal course of human events, a 154- or 162-game season suffices to determine a pennant winner. The long season, and they are all long, operates like a forced march across the veldt, producing casualties along way who end up on the disabled list, while the survivors suffer from exhaustion, both mental and physical. As the season proceeds, teams fall out of contention, as often through inconvenient injuries as through poor play by poor players, while the better and luckier teams fight it out during September for the flag. But in baseball, as in astronomy, the unusual, indeed the abnormal, is also normal, and now and then the length and stress of the regular season is inadequate to produce a champion. The pennant race tightens up and two teams stagger toward home a game or so apart. The race goes down to the last week, then the last weekend, and the season ends with the first two teams in a tie. This cannot be the final result since the league champions must meet in the World Series, so the regular season continues, for a single game in the American League and a three game series in the National League. Already drained by a pennant race that has been a little too exciting, the players and fans brace for the playoffs that now must decide what the entire season could not.

I

The first of these playoffs extending the regular season came in 1946, the first postwar year, when the Cardinals and the Dodgers ended in a tie, each with a record of ninety-six wins and fifty-eight losses. The pennant race of 1946 had settled early, in the second week of the season, into a two team struggle between the Dodgers and the Cardinals. Each team had ups and downs, but for the bulk of the season the Dodgers were in first place. On July 2, Dem Bums led the Cardinals by seven and one half games, and were comfortably in first place on July 4, the traditional day of prediction. The team in first place on July 4, will, the old wisdom goes, win the pennant. But the Cards hung in there, gaining slowly, though not until August 28 did they grab the lead. The Cardinals held on grimly with a margin ranging from a single percentage point to a couple of games until September 27, when the two teams were finally tied on the last Friday of the season. Both the Dodgers and the Cards won on Saturday and lost on Sunday, the last day of the season. The ex–Cardinal Mort Cooper, now with the Boston Braves and about through, deflated the Dodgers 4 to 0 while the Cubs beat the Cards 8 to 3.[1]

The National League constitution provided for a three-game series should a tie make one necessary, and in 1946, it became necessary. The Cardinals lost the coin flip and so the first game was scheduled for St. Louis with the last two in Brooklyn. On October 1, a sunny Tuesday afternoon in Sportsman's Park, Cardinals manager Eddie Dyer sent his best pitcher, southpaw Howie Pollet, to the hill for the biggest game of the year, so far. Pollet, a twenty-game winner, was not in good shape. He had a torn muscle in his throwing shoulder, but the Cardinals were thin on the mound and needed him. Brooklyn countered with young right-hander Ralph Branca, who had won only three games that season. It was a strange decision by Leo Durocher, the Dodgers skipper, who didn't have a strong pitching staff, even with four starters who won in double figures. But Leo played a hunch. On September 14, Branca had shut the Cardinals out at a time when every game mattered. Perhaps ... and perhaps not. The Cardinals got a run in the bottom of the first, driven in by Joe Garagiola who went three for four, with two runs driven in. It is hard to think of Garagiola as a hitting star, but he was in that game. Dem Bums tied the score on a home run by first baseman Howie Schultz in the top of the third, but the Cardinals won the game with two in the home third, knocking Branca out of the game. Kirby Higbe replaced Branca and held the fort for five outs, to be replaced by Hal Gregg who pitched two scoreless innings. In the top of the seventh Howie Schultz drove in his second run as the Dodgers pulled within a run. But Vic Lombardi, the fourth Brooklyn pitcher, gave up a Cardinals insurance run in the bottom of the seventh. St. Louis won the first Major League playoff game, 4 to 2, as an injured Howie Pollet pitched a complete game.[2]

The playoff switched to Brooklyn for the second game, to be played on October 3. The Cardinals started Murry Dickson against the Dodgers left-hander Joe Hatten. Dickson had had a good year, winning fourteen games, including three against Brooklyn. Hatten had also won fourteen games, but he was only two and four against St. Louis. Hatten had trouble again. He gave up two runs in the second inning and was knocked out in the three-run Cardinals fifth. Hank Behrman, Vic Lombardi, Kirby Higbe, Rube Melton and Harry Taylor followed in that order, but the Cardinals entered the last of the ninth inning with an 8 to 1 lead. Murry Dickson had given up a first inning run, but since then he had shut the Dodgers down.

In the last of the ninth, with the home crowd faithful reduced to prayerful petition and promises of postgame reformation in the event of victory,

Dem Bums came alive. Third baseman Augie Galan led off with a double, only the fourth hit that Murry Dickson had allowed. Dixie Walker then flied out, but Ed Stevens tripled, scoring Galan with the Dodgers' first run of the inning. Carl Furillo singled Stevens home, and the crowd buzz grew into a roar. Dickson, who was tiring, threw a wild pitch and Furillo went to second. Pee Wee Reese walked. The crowd ascended into frenzy. St. Louis manager Eddie Dyer yanked Dickson and brought in Harry "The Cat" Brecheen. Bruce Edwards, the Dodgers catcher, singled, driving in Furillo with the third run, and Brecheen walked pinch-hitter Cookie Lavagetto to fill the bases. The score was now 8 to 4, with the tying run at the plate. The Brooklyn crowd moved well past frenzy and lost its collective mind. The moment had come. Dem Bums would rise from the grave. But the Cat struck Eddie Stanky out on a three and two pitch. Howie Schultz, batting for left fielder Dick Whitman, also worked the count to three balls and two strikes. Then Brecheen struck him out. There would be no miracle. The Brooklyn Dodgers had lost the first play-off in the history of Major League Baseball.[3]

The first season playoff had been quite surprising. There had been close races before, particularly in 1890 when most of the positions in the final standing had been decided on the last day of the season. But this was the first time that teams had finished tied, and what had been a contingency plan became the order of the day. That this should happen in the National rather than the American League was not so surprising. The American League had had close pennant races in 1940 and again in 1944 and 1945. These were the odd years when the Yankees did not win the pennant, as they usually did and would continue to do, frequently by quite respectable margins. But the National League did not have a dominant team that won most years, the talent was spread more evenly, and three or four teams usually had an outside chance. In 1946, after nearly seventy-five years of baseball, contingency caught up with the National League and a playoff decided the winner.[4] At the time, most people thought the playoff an event they might not ever see again.

As is often the case, things once rare can become common, and the wave of postwar pennant playoffs fits that phenomenon. World War II had altered the competitive balance in baseball by taking players into the National Service, more and better players from this team, fewer and less talented men from that. The New York Yankees, though they won in 1942 and 1943, suffered from the loss of good players, especially Joe DiMaggio who was in the service from 1943 through 1945. With the Yankees weakened, other teams, with less to lose, improved comparatively. The years from 1944 through 1948 saw the Yankees as merely another good team, and the American League had some good pennant races. In 1944 and 1945 the race came down to the last day, and in 1948, beyond the last day.

The 1948 pennant race in the American League involved four teams for most of the season. On August 3, Philadelphia, New York, Boston and Cleveland were separated by only three percentage points. The Athletics dropped back, but the Indians, Red Sox and Yankees kept winning. For most of September Boston hung on to first place. On the next to last day of the season Boston, in a transient suspension of the Curse of the Bambino, had the ecstatic joy of defeating the Yankees and eliminating them from the race. On the last day of the season the Red Sox again beat the Yanks, 10 to 5, while Cleveland, with a one-game lead, lost to Detroit and Hal Newhouser, 7 to 1. The Red Sox and Indians ended in a tie, with ninety-six wins and fifty-eight losses each. The fans loved it. Four teams in the American League set new attendance records, with Cleveland going over two million for the first time, drawing a million fans more than their previous year.[5] There was nothing like winning baseball to gather the crowds and make money, at least in the days before television.

While the National League held a three-game series to determine the pennant winners, the American League had a single-game playoff. On October 4, the Indians and Red Sox met before a capacity crowd at Fenway Park for the first American League playoff. Cleveland manager Lou Boudreau gambled on the nineteen-game winner, rookie Gene Bearden, who would go on one day's rest. Joe McCarthy, the Red Sox manager, also had a pitching problem, and used Denny Galehouse, a veteran with an eight and seven record, since Boston's three best pitchers, Joe Dobson, Jack Kramer and Mel Parnell, had pitched the last three games of the season. The other possibility was Ellis Kinder, who had a ten and seven record in 1948. After the event, this became a controversial decision, though McCarthy, who had already managed the Cubs and the Yankees to nine pennants, was a master of his craft. Kinder was the better pitcher, the critics claimed, but Galehouse had a proven record in the postseason play. The decision could have gone either way, and the pennant seemed to hang on it, at least in retrospect, which is infallible.

For three innings both Lou Boudreau and Joe McCarthy looked like geniuses. Boudreau homered in the top of the first inning, but Vern Stephens singled Johnny Pesky home with the tying run in the home half of the first. In the top of the fourth the Indians took control of the game. Ken Keltner hit a three-run homer to knock Galehouse out of the box. McCarthy brought in Kinder, who gave up another run in the fourth inning and a second solo home to Boudreau in the fifth. Boston got two runs back in the sixth when Bobby Doerr hit a two-run homer, scoring Ted Williams in front of him, but that was as close as Boston could get. Cleveland got an insurance run in the eighth and another in the ninth. Gene Bearden went the distance, scattered five hits, and won the game, 8 to 3.[6] As it turned out, both Galehouse and Kinder gave up four runs, enough for Cleveland to win, so McCarthy's decision to pitch Galehouse, much criticized then and since, was hardly the appropriate target for the wrath of the Boston sports writers. Their major complaint, looking back on it, seems to have been that McCarthy was tainted by association, having once managed the unspeakable Yankees.

The year of 1948, however, belonged to Gene Bearden. The rookie left-hander won twenty games, including the playoff against Boston. In the World Series, Bearden pitched a five-hit shutout in the third game and saved the sixth game in relief of Bob Lemon as the Indians won the Series, four games to two. He allowed no earned runs in his two Series appearances. This was Gene Bearden's career year; he was never a great pitcher again and by 1954 he was out of the Show. But for one year, for one playoff, for one Series, he was the brief best in the game, he was destiny's darling. If Bearden pitched, how could Boston win?[7]

II

There are players of destiny and there are teams of destiny. What Gene Bearden was in 1948, the New York Giants were in 1951. The gods of baseball loved them. In matters of myth, it is important to recognize outside help, and no explanation, other than the favor of the fates, lavishly expressed, fits what happened that season. There had never been a season like 1951, as those who lived through it tell anyone who will listen. And there has not been one like it since. The National League season of 1951 has passed as myth into memory, with the ending of the season one of those moments where people remember where they were.

Rivalry between Brooklyn and New York, symbolized by the Dodgers and the Giants, went back into the nineteenth century as far as anyone could remember, back to the days when Brooklyn had been an independent city separate from New York. Among the first generation of fans, those rooting for New York had all the better of it, as the Giants were the premier team in the National League after 1902, and the Dodgers usually trailed badly. This only intensified the ardor and loyalty of Dodgers fans, who, like any believer, lived on hope and suffered for their faith. Then, over the short span of three years, from 1938 to 1941, the tide turned. The Giants went downhill and the Dodgers became the leading team in the league. They won the pennant in 1941, again in 1947, again in 1949, and all the while the Giants were in or near the cellar. By 1951, however, the Giants were again pretty good, and the competition between the two teams became even more intense. Doris Kearns Goodwin remembered that year.

> The rivalry between the Dodgers and the Giants was unlike any other in baseball. Even in years when the two were not contending for the pennant, every meeting was regarded as a separate war, to be fought with implacable hostility....
> But in 1951, this historic rivalry entered a new dimension, reached a level of hostility never before attained and never to be surpassed.[8]

Never far from the center of attention in the greater New York of those days, baseball dominated the municipal psyche as the season came down to the last week, then the last weekend, then the playoffs, then a single game, then to an inning, and finally to one hitter and a single hit.[9]

In the spring of 1951, pundits and sports writers had thought that the National League would be a race between the Giants and the Dodgers, the first since 1924. The St. Louis Cardinals, Brooklyn's main rival for the past decade, seemed to be fading. Few had much respect for the Whiz Kids from Philadelphia, who had won the year before. The Phils might have won the pennant on the last day of the season in 1950, but that was mostly luck. No, it would be the Giants' turn to challenge Brooklyn.

Even in those days, New York had television, though much of the rest of the nation did not. It was television of a paleolithic variety, black and white, grainy and indistinct, viewed often on sets with nine- or eleven-inch screens, and brought home via aerials that lost the signal with dispiriting regularity. Still, it was television, which was new and exciting, and New York had enough stations to broadcast the games of all three teams. Beer and tobacco sponsored New York baseball, but beer was thought to be good for you, while tobacco was not really that bad. Besides, anything associated with baseball, the undisputed national pastime, must have redeeming social value, since sponsoring baseball was in the nature of a public service.

In addition to television New York had radio, where Red Barber (Dodgers), Russ Hodges (Giants), and Mel Allen (Yankees) described the games with verve and sympathy. You could follow the game on radio better than on television; the announcers were that good, the pictures were that bad, and the beauty of baseball increased in the imagination. Beyond radio, New York still possessed newspapers, both morning and evening. An older form of mass communication, the newspapers had less immediacy but more memory than electronic media, and they carried an immense amount of detail about the game. Only the papers had the box scores, which the real fan read with meticulous care to glean every fact and statistic of the game. One might hear the game, or see it, even keep score, but the box score was still mandatory study in the morning papers. From print to voice to television, the New York fan had access to every detail of the day's game, the season to date, prospects for the future, and gossip, speculation and prediction about the players. Awash in information and punditry, fans could follow the pennant race with total immersion.

There was never any need to build up the importance of the Giants and the Dodgers to the local fans, particularly so in a year when both promised to be good. But the Giants' manager, Leo the Lip Durocher, who had raised obnoxiousness, hostility, and insult to an art form, adroitly inflamed emotions and expectations. Durocher had managed the Dodgers for nearly a decade, including the 1941 pennant year, and when he switched to manage the Giants in 1948, some Brooklyn fans thought in terms of treason, though another was heard to exclaim: "Jeez, it's Poil Harbor for da Jints." Now, in the spring of 1951, Leo the Lip talked to the numerous New York sports writers about how good the Giants were and how the Dodgers were overrated. As the Giants had a better spring than the Dodgers, Durocher increased the tempo of insult, something he always found easy to do. By the time the season started, the rivalry more than matched the comment from Andy Pafko, an outfielder who had come over from the Chicago Cubs to the Dodgers. Becoming part of the borough rivalry and the intensity of feeling accompanying baseball in greater New York, Pafko remarked: "Those Dodgers-Giants games weren't baseball. They were civil war."[10]

When the season started, and life at its fullest could begin again, the Giants started off well by winning on Opening Day against Boston, just as they had done in their inaugural season in 1883.[11] The Giants split the next two games with the Braves and then lost eleven consecutive games. By the second week of the season they were in the cellar. They hadn't started the season as the chosen of the *Moirae*.

Other teams, meanwhile, were doing better. The Boston Braves and the St. Louis Cardinals spent time in first place during the early going. The wretched Chicago Cubs, destined for the cellar, were in second place for a day at the end of the first week of the season. The Phillies justified the skepticism of the pundits by ending the first week of the season in fifth place, their eventual finish. The Giants began to right the ship on April 30, when they defeated Brooklyn, 8 to 5, breaking their eleven-game losing streak. The Giants then went on to win eleven of the next fourteen games, but only on May 27 did the Polo Grounders go over the .500 mark, when they won their twentieth game against nineteen losses. By the end of May the Giants were in third place.

The Brooklyn Dodgers, who had won in 1949 and lost in 1950 on the last day of the season, were swimming smoothly along in first place. On May 13, Dem Bums had taken over the lead and steadily put distance between themselves and the rest of the pack. No one seemed surprised by this. The Dodgers were the best team in the National League in the postwar years and were always near the top. After the All-Star Game in Detroit on July 10, which the National League won for the second year in a row, the Dodgers began to win at an accelerated rate. By the middle of July only the Giants were left in the race. On July 20, through the first game of a double-header against Boston on August 11, Dem Bums won seventeen of twenty games to stretch their lead over the second-place Giants to thirteen and one half games. Brooklyn had won two-thirds of their first 105 games, with a record of 70 wins and 35 defeats.[12] It looked as if Dodgers manager Chuck Dressen had been right when he remarked after a July 4–5 three-game sweep over the Giants: "We knocked them out; they'll never bother us again."[13] Just over six weeks of the season remained, and, down by thirteen and a half games, the Giants would have to pick up two games a week to catch up. It seemed to be over. But as the great American philosopher Yogi Berra says: "It ain't over till it's over."

The next day, August 12, the Giants won a doubleheader from the fading Phillies. The scores were close, 3 to 2 in the first game and 2 to 1 in the second, but with these two games the Giants began to win at a hyper-accelerated pace, winning sixteen games in a row.[14] When the Pittsburgh left-hander, Howie Pollet, beat the Giants 2 to 0 on August 28, ending the winning streak, New York had cut eight and a half games from the Brooklyn lead, which was now a much less comfortable five games. The Giants then lost ground, and were seven games behind the Dodgers when the two teams met at the Polo Grounds on September 1 for a two-game series. The Giants won them both, and split a two game series at Ebbets Field the next week.

By the last Western trip for both teams, which began on September 11, the Dodgers lead was five and a half games. Three weeks to go. At the end of the trip, during which the Giants won six and lost three, the Brooklyn lead was four and a half. On September 20, Dem Bums had a record of ninety-two and fifty-two, while the Giants stood at eighty-nine and fifty-eight. The Giants had six more losses than the Dodgers, and had only seven games left to play while Brooklyn had ten. The race seemed to be over. It looked as if the Giants had made it close, but thirteen and one half games had been too big a hill to climb.

In the last ten days of the season the Giants kept winning. The Giants took three in a row from the Braves, while the Dodgers lost two of three to the Phils. On September 25, the Giants beat the Phillies, 5 to 1, behind Jim Hearn, while the Dodgers lost two to Boston, 6 to 3 and 14 to 2. Brooklyn now led by one game. Both teams won on September 26, but the Dodgers' victory over the Braves, 15 to 5, ended on a sour note. In the ninth inning of a blowout, Jackie Robinson stole home. Jocko Conlan was one of the umpires that day, and he noted the effect this had on the Braves. "That riled the Braves. They thought he was trying to show them up. I don't think that. He was a competitor. He played to win, all the time. He wanted every run he could get. But the Braves felt he was pushing it down their throats."[15]

The next day, on September 27, the Giants had an open date while Brooklyn wound up their four-game series with Boston. The game turned on an eighth inning play at the plate. Bob Addis slid in under Roy Campanella's tag, and Frank Dascoli, perfectly positioned to call the play, said Addis was safe. The Dodgers reacted adversely to this call.

> The Dodgers screamed. They were jumping all over Dascoli, and Campanella was so mad he threw his catcher's glove at least twenty-five feet in the air....
> That day in Boston the whole Brooklyn club went berserk. The ball game didn't end on that disputed run — but it was the winning run.[16]

The Brooklyn lead was down to half a game.

On September 28, with the Giants again idle, the Dodgers lost to the Phillies, 4 to 3, when Andy Seminick hit a home run in the ninth inning. The two teams were now tied, both having won ninety-four games and lost fifty-eight. Over the next two days both the Giants and Dodgers won out. Sal Maglie defeated Boston, 3 to 0, on September 29, while Don Newcombe shut the Phillies out, 5 to 0. On the last day of the season Larry Jansen won his twenty-second game for the Giants, 3 to 2, over the Braves. The Brooklyn game on September 30 was what they used to call a barn-burner. The Dodgers fell behind the Phillies, 6 to 1 in the third inning, but fought back, scoring three runs in the eighth inning to tie to score at eight apiece. The game went into extra innings. In the fourteenth, Jackie Robinson hit a pennant-tying home run off Robin Roberts, and the Dodgers won, 9 to 8, to tie the Giants at ninety-six and fifty-eight. This was a mighty big hit, fully the equivalent of the clouts made by Hartnett, Greenberg, or Sisler, but iconic remembrance did not transform the hit into myth. The problem was timing, as it so often is. In 1951, and only then, Robinson's clutch blast was destined to become, and has remained, a footnote.[17] Myth can be comparative, not just absolute, reflecting not only what happened but also what else happened.

The *New York Times* carried this story on the front page. The sports pages elaborated on the basic narrative with detail, quotes, and commentary. Brooklyn outfielder Andy Pafko, always good copy, clearly enjoyed it all, and remarked that "this kind of baseball brings ulcers, but what wonderful ulcers."[18]

Arthur Daley, the columnist who wrote the "Sports of the Times," concentrated on the improbable drama, both extended over the weeks after August 11 and confined to the Dodgers victory on the last day of the season.

> The New York Giants achieved the "impossible" by coming from a thirteen-and-a-half game deficit on August 11 to a photo finish with the seemingly invincible Dodgers. And the Brooks achieved an even greater "impossibility" by winning yesterday's ball game in Philadelphia in the fourteenth inning.[19]

With the two teams tied at the end of the season on September 30, fans and sports writers alike either cheered the Giants' climb or lamented the Dodgers' decline. On one point all agreed. The Dodgers had collapsed in the last month and a half of the season. Conventional wisdom often proves false, and it did here as well. The Dodgers did fall off a bit, but they did not collapse. Until August 12, the Dodgers had won two-thirds of their games, while the Giants were winning at a 54 percent pace. Beginning on August 12, the Giants began to win at 84 percent, while the Dodgers sagged slightly to 60 percent, still a pennant-winning pace.[20] Dem Bums continued to win, but the Giants began to win at a rate beyond any pennant winner in the history of the National League.[21] The Dodgers played well the entire season; the Giants suddenly began to play at a level of success that eludes rational explanation.

In spite of that, everyone had an explanation. Some said that bringing up Willie Mays from Minneapolis on May 24 turned the Giants into winners.

But Mays came up in May and the Giants started to win in August. Others said that putting Bobby Thomson at third base on July 20 was the key decision. Perhaps, but it took nearly a month for this to sink in on the rest of the team. A better place to look is always pitching. Al Corwin, five and one for the season, won three of his five games during the sixteen-game winning streak, and George Spencer, ten and four on the year, won four of his games during the streak. Improvement at the back of the rotation surely helped. But in the end, nicked up and worn out, the Giants simply kept on winning, somehow.

New York was utterly caught up in the drama. The *Times*, and other papers as well, covered the games as closely as politicians watch money. Front page and sports page began to overlap. Taverns, which had air conditioning and television sets, were reported to be selling only bottled beer, at the monstrous price of thirty-five cents, to their thirsty patrons whose lunch hours suddenly stretched until the end of the game. The Dow Jones ticker tape carried details of the games, half-inning by half-inning, to those inexorably trapped in the cogs of commerce. General Electric took out full-page advertisements touting their seventeen-inch television sets, now reduced from $379 to a paltry $299.[22] New York area schools allowed radios, and some put the playoffs on the public address system. As for the lordly Yankees, Arthur Daley wrote in the "Sports of the Times" that they "had a workout at the Stadium yesterday, as relaxed as a big cat waiting to see which mouse will pop out of the hole."[23]

A coin flip decided the location of the playoff games, and, since Brooklyn lost the toss, the first game was in Ebbets Field. The Giants came into Brooklyn like an express train. Jim Hearn, who had won sixteen games for the Giants, faced Ralph Branca, who had won thirteen for Brooklyn. Hearn gave up a home run to Andy Pafko in the second inning, but that was all the damage the Dodgers could do. In the fourth, Branca hit Monte Irvin and Bobby Thomson homered, giving the Giants a 2-to-1 lead. Irvin hit an insurance homer in the eighth, and Hearn went all the way for his seventeenth victory, 3 to 1, pitching a five-hit game. Branca took the loss, his second in playoff games.[24]

Taking a one-game lead into the Polo Grounds on October 2 for the second game, the Giants looked to be in pretty good shape, and their fans thought this would be it. Although the Giants had lost the season series to the Dodgers, nine games to thirteen, Durocher's team had done better late in the season. Now they faced a rookie, Clem Labine, who had won only four games all season. The Giants had Sheldon "Available" Jones, who had been in forty-one games, mostly in relief, though he had an ERA of 4.28 and a record of six and ten. Still, Jones was a veteran pitcher, and in a big game, surely that counted at least for something.

October 2 was a cloudy day with rain threatening in the early innings and rain falling in the sixth, requiring a forty-one-minute delay. Perhaps it was the weather, but Available Jones didn't have it. Jackie Robinson hit a two-run, two-out homer in the first. The Dodgers hit Jones hard, and with one out in the third, Durocher lifted him for George Spencer. Spencer got out of the third with no damage, but he gave up a run in the fifth before the rain came. In the sixth Spencer gave up three more runs, one on a home run by Gil Hodges. Al Corwin took Spencer's place with the score 6 to 0, and did not hold the Dodgers down. Andy Pafko had a homer in the seventh for one of two more Brooklyn runs and Rube Walker had a two-run insurance homer in the ninth, giving Dem Bums ten runs, six of them on four homers. Clem Labine, meanwhile, a risky choice for starting pitcher by Dodgers manager Chuck Dressen, pitched a six-hit shutout. The rain delay didn't bother him at all. He was better afterward. The Giants had five hits in the first four innings, but Labine was tough with men on base. The Dodgers won, 10 to 0, and Dressen looked like a managerial genius.[25]

The *Times*, with due regard for its journalistic responsibility to all of greater New York, began its account with the way things looked in Brooklyn. "Great was the rejoicing in Flatbush last night. For not only is Brooklyn still in the National League, but just as much so in the fight for the pennant."[26] The reference to Giants manager Bill Terry's remark in 1934, "Is Brooklyn still in the League?" was not lost on fans in Brooklyn, who combined intensity of devotion with long memories.

It all had come down to one game. After the defeat in Game 2, Leo Durocher put the best face he could on it all. These things happen in baseball, but not every day. The next game would be different, Leo said, and, returning to his accustomed truculence, he told the sports writers: "But tomorrow Sal the Barber will be shaving. It'll be a different day and a different game."[27]

Rain had held attendance at the second game to 38,000, but the third game, with the pennant at stake and better weather, still drew only 34,320, less than two-thirds of the Polo Grounds capacity of 56,000, though at least half a million fans later claimed to have been there. Chuck Dressen sent Don Newcombe to the mound. He had beaten the Giants five times during the season, one quarter of his twenty wins. Leo Durocher had Sal Maglie ready. Sal "The Barber" had won twenty-two games, five of them against Brooklyn. It looked to be a great game, even if the stands where hardly more than half full.

Brooklyn got a run in the first when Maglie walked Pee Wee Reese and Duke Snider with one out and Jackie Robinson singled Reese home. After that early lapse Maglie settled down. He held Brooklyn scoreless through the seventh inning. Don Newcombe was also sharp. He made that one run stand up until the seventh when Monte Irvin doubled, went to third on Whitey Lockman's sacrifice, and Bobby Thomson drove him home with a long fly ball. In the eighth, having pitched 297 innings, Sal Maglie wore down. With one out,

Reese and Snider singled. Facing Jackie Robinson, Maglie threw a wild pitch, allowing Reese to score while Snider went to third. Maglie then walked Robinson, and Andy Pafko and Billy Cox each singled in a run. Brooklyn had scored three times, and led, 4 to 1. The Giants did not score in the bottom of the eighth inning, and Durocher sent out Larry Jansen, a twenty-two-game winner, to pitch the ninth. Jansen set the Dodgers down in order in the top of the ninth, but Brooklyn led by three runs with three outs to go. Newcombe still looked strong, having given up only four hits over eight innings. The game, the playoffs, the season, all had come down to the last of the ninth.

Alvin Dark, the Giants' shortstop, opened the bottom of the ninth with an infield single, and Don Mueller singled Dark to third. Monte Irvin popped out. Two outs to go. The next hitter, Whitey Lockman, the New York first baseman, doubled Dark home, sending Mueller to third. The Giants were now down by two runs, and "had something going." Newcombe seemed to be faltering, with the tying runs in scoring positions and the winning run at the plate. Chuck Dressen, the Brooklyn manager, went out to the mound to change pitchers.

The hinge of the season came with this ninth inning pitching change. Don Newcombe had clearly weakened, and Dressen had Clem Labine and Carl Erskine, both good breaking ball pitchers, in the bullpen, along with Ralph Branca, who threw hard. As Dressen went to the mound he was joined by umpire Jocko Conlan, who came to see what Dressen was going to do. Conlan asked Dressen: "Who are you bringing in?" "Branca." "Branca! A fastball pitcher?" "Yes, Branca." In spite of his surprise, Conlan waved to the Dodgers bullpen and called for Branca, who started in toward the most important pitching assignment of his career.[28]

Among the (literally) millions of fans riveted to the moment, Conlan was not the only one surprised by Dressen's decision to bring in Branca. Watching in the living room with her mother and sisters, nine-year-old Doris Kearns was horrified to see Branca heading for the mound. One sister was reassuring; Branca could do it, but the other and oldest spoke with the iron voice of fate. Thomson, she stated, was going to hit a home run.[29] Charlotte Kearns knew what she was talking about.

Branca got a quick strike on Bobby Thomson. His second pitch was a good one, high and inside and hard to hit safely. But Thomson swung and hit a line drive into left field with just enough height and distance to sink into the lower deck for a three-run homer. Russ Hodges, the Giants' announcer, yelled into the mike: "The Giants win the pennant! The Giants win the pennant! The Giants win the pennant!"[30] And they had. The inning, the game, the playoff, the season, it all came down to a single swing, a single hit, and a single run. Thomson's homer had decided it all.

A home run of that magnitude, involving the Giants and the Dodgers, was likely to inspire comment, and this one did. The *Times* carried the story on the front page, where it belonged, along with a picture of Thomson and Leo Durocher, the Giants' manager. The *Times* reportage ran a bit to clichés and superlatives, though in the event it's hard to see what else would have served.

> In an electrifying finish to what will be remembered as the most thrilling pennant campaign in history, Leo Durocher and his astounding never-say-die Giants wrenched victory from the jaws of defeat yesterday vanquishing the Dodgers, 5 to 4, with a four-run splurge in the last half of the ninth.[31]

Thomson's own comments emphasized the intersection of fortune and circumstance. "What a finish! Imagine being lucky enough to win a ball game that way. And, it wasn't a good pitch. It was high and inside, the kind they've been getting me out on all season."[32] This was exactly the right tone. Unlike Babe Ruth, the epic hero incarnate, Bobby Thomson was an ordinary ball player, indistinguishable from the hundreds of others who played for a decade and then passed beyond the penumbra of cultural memory. He was one of the "warriors for the working day," transformed in that instant into the subject of myth. The *Moirae* only seem to lack a sense of antic humor.

In "The Sports of the Times" column, Arthur Daley dealt with Thomson's home run in terms usually reserved for the supernatural, again just the right tone.

> It was incredible. It couldn't happen and yet it did happen. In an insane and as improbable an ending as any ball game could have, the Giants' indomitable burst past the Dodgers and into the World Series yesterday by winning the third playoff fray. To win it, Bobby Thomson had to hit a three run homer in the ninth. So he hit it.[33]

Comment in Brooklyn ran from the stunned to the censorious. More than one Dodgers fan voiced incredulity, echoing a plaintive remark heard over and over: "I can't believe it. I can't believe it." The *Times* also caught up with fans who *could* believe it, all right, and were not happy about it.

> The long-faced fans rehashing the sour mess outside the Dodgers' office at Court and Montague streets, near Borough Hall, heaped their bitterness upon Chuck Dressen, the Brooklyn manager. It was the consensus of the sidewalk coaches that Dressen lost the pennant by substituting Ralph Branca for Don Newcombe in the crucial moment of the last inning.
> "Thomson had hit six homers off Branca already this season," an irate lawyer in a blue suit and with a briefcase under his arm lectured the fans clustered before the Dodgers' office windows. "As soon as Branca walked out to the box, I said, 'Get the crepe.'"[34]

As soon as the homer was recorded in baseball journalism, it was christened "the shot heard round the world." The phrase came from the monument at Concord Bridge, and celebrates the musket fire that is generally regarded as beginning the American Revolution. After 1951, the shot heard round the world had another meaning, one of time, not space. The Thomson home run echoed through memory, across years of living, to mark a moment that none who lived through it could ever forget.

This was the playoff to end all playoffs, and the third such event in five years. Timing is everything, as they say in love, comedy, and sports, all variant expressions of the human condition. The playoffs in 1951 came at the right time and in the right place, the golden age of baseball in New York, the media center of this vast republic, and no other sport challenged baseball's ascendancy. Every fan, whether rabid or casual, had a favorite team and player, and baseball was a continuing topic of conversation in shop, office, tavern or living room. Everyone had an expert opinion on every aspect of the game. Should this guy have been lifted, should that guy have come in from the bullpen, should Stengel, Dressen, or the Lip have used a pinch-hitter in the seventh rather than the ninth? Some expert opinion was seasoned, comparing Newcombe to Dazzy Vance, or Sal Maglie to Carl Hubbell, others substituted the enthusiasm of youth for the perspective of experience. But in those years, from World War II to the Great Desertion in 1957, everyone in New York knew baseball and talked baseball.

For fans of the New York game, interest was stimulated by excellence. All three teams were good, and there was a New York team, usually two, in every World Series but one (1948) from 1947 to the O'Malley betrayal a decade later. In the National League, the Dodgers won in 1947, 1949, 1952–53, and 1955–56, while the Giants won twice, in 1951 and 1954. In the American League, beginning in 1949, the Yanks would win fourteen pennants in sixteen years, losing only in 1954 and again in 1959. Although the Dodgers had less of an edge than the Yanks, Brooklyn was always the team to beat. The better managed organizations had pulled ahead of their less effective rivals. Within the closed and monopolistic system of organized ball, talent at the top, which the Dodgers and Yankees had, would inevitably manifest itself on the field.[35] The playoff in 1951 seemed to symbolize the extraordinary quality of New York baseball.

III

Baseball, like Hamlet, knows not "seems," and the playoffs returned as the New York game was broken up. The Dodgers, after 1957 transplanted to Los Angeles, were only a half a step or so ahead of the rest. In the National League, the team to beat could be beat. Late in the 1950s, the Milwaukee Braves, powered by Hank Aaron and Eddie Mathews, and with Lew Burdette and Warren Spahn pitching, overtook the Dodgers. In 1958, the newly transplanted Dodgers actually came in seventh place, twenty-one games behind the pennant-winning Braves. But the Dodgers had just had a bad year. They were still a good team with a great manager, Walter Alston, and 1958 would only be an exception. The next year, 1959, the Dodgers bounced back and played as they had in Brooklyn. The stretch run of the pennant chase was, as they used to say, a doozie. On September 19, the San Francisco Giants and the Los Angeles Dodgers were tied for the lead at eighty-two and sixty-six with the Milwaukee Braves half a game back at eighty-one and sixty-six. For the last nine days of the season, the three transplanted teams traded the lead on seven of them. By Sunday, September 27, the last day of the season, both the Dodgers and the Braves won, ending in a tie at eighty-six and sixty-eight, while the Giants, losing a doubleheader to St. Louis, fell back to third at eighty-three and seventy-one. The Dodgers and the Braves, with their 86 wins, only 18 games over .500, had the lowest victory total for any National League pennant winner since the adoption of the 154-game season, and was the lowest winning percentage in the history of the league.[36]

In 1959, therefore, for the third time since the end of World War II, there would be a playoff in the National League, and for the third time, the Dodgers would be involved. The pennant race had been so furious that by the playoffs both teams had exhausted their pitching staffs. The Dodgers had the deeper staff, with Don Drysdale, Johnny Podres, Roger Craig, Danny McDevitt, Sandy Koufax and Larry Sherry as possible starters. The Braves had Lew Burdette and Warren Spahn each winning twenty-one games, and Bob Buhl who won fifteen. Then the staff tailed off. Bob Rush (five and six) was near the end, having had some pretty good years for the lowly Cubs, and Joey Jay (six and eleven) had a couple of strong years ahead of him for Cincinnati, while Juan Pizzaro (six and two) would have a good career with the Chicago White Sox. The Braves also had a strong relief pitcher, Don McMahon (seven and two, all in relief), who had appeared in sixty games, about 40 percent of the season's total.[37]

The playoff began on September at County Stadium, Milwaukee. Only a few more than 18,000 fans ignored the rain, which delayed the game for forty-seven minutes, and showed up to cheer on the Braves. So depleted was Milwaukee pitching that manager Roy Haney started Carl Willey, who had gone five and eight during the season and could only be regarded as second (or third) line pitching. Walter Alston of the Dodgers was in no better shape. He started Danny McDevitt (ten and eight). Both starters justified expectations. The Dodgers scored a run off Willey in the top of the first, and the Braves rallied in the home half of the second inning. McDevitt walked Johnny Logan, the Braves shortstop and then gave up singles to catcher Del Crandall and outfielder Bill Bruton. When McDevitt threw two balls to pitcher Willey, Walter Alston had seen enough. He brought in rookie power pitcher Larry Sherry. Sherry allowed Crandall to score, but shut the Braves down for the rest of the game, giving up only four hits in seven and two-thirds innings. The Dodgers got a run in the third to tie the score and another in the sixth off Willey who had settled down after a slow start. But Sherry made that one run lead stand up, and the Dodgers won the first game, 3 to 2.[38]

The second game was played the next day, September 29, in Memorial Coliseum in Los Angeles. The new park at Chavez Ravine was not yet finished, so the Dodgers played in a football stadium, the Memorial Coliseum, which resembled nothing so much as the old Polo Grounds. From home plate to the center field fence measured 420 feet, a long drive, no doubt, but between 60 and 100 feet (bleachers and club house) shorter than the Polo Grounds. Down the right field line the distance to the wall was 300 feet, and in left it was 251 with a 42-foot-high screen to cut down the number of short homers. The seating capacity of the cavernous bleachers-only Memorial Coliseum was 92,500, but for the second playoff game only 36,853 fans showed up. Los Angeles was not a baseball town, and the Dodgers were not yet fashionable, which meant Hollywood stars coming to the games and being seen there. Without the stars there was no one to see, and, much worse, there was no one to see you.

An extra day of rest allowed both teams to start their leading pitchers, Lew Burdette (twenty-one and fifteen) for the Braves and Don Drysdale (seventeen and thirteen) for the Dodgers. Burdette was the better pitcher that day. The Braves got him a two run lead in the top of the first inning. Eddie Mathews walked, Hank Aaron doubled and Frank Torre drove both home with a single. The Dodgers cut the lead in half in the bottom of the first as Wally Moon drove Charley Neal home, but the Braves got that run back in the top of the second as shortstop Johnny Logan scored on Duke Snider's throwing error. In the fourth, Charlie Neal homered off Burdette, but the Braves got that run back when Del Crandall homered of Drysdale in the fifth. That finished Drysdale. Walter Alston brought in Johnny Podres, who held the fort until the eighth, when Chuck Churn took the mound and gave up a triple to Del Crandall, who scoured on Felix Mantilla's sacrifice fly. Meanwhile, Lew Burdette had held the Dodgers scoreless since Neal's home run, and entered the ninth leading, 5 to 2. In the bottom of the ninth inning, however, the long season, with 39 starts and 290 innings pitched, got to Burdette. Wally Moon led off with a single, Duke Snider followed with a hit, and Gil Hodges got a third single to load the bases with nobody out. Fred Haney, Braves manager, immediately brought in his relief ace Don McMahon, who gave up a two run single to Norm Larker. Haney brought in Warren Spahn, the best southpaw in the history of the game. Spahn got an out, but Carl Furillo tied the game at five runs apiece with a sacrifice fly scoring Gil Hodges. The game went to extra innings.

By the twelfth inning, the Braves were running out of pitching. Haney brought in veteran Bob Rush, who was near the end of a thirteen-year career as a fixture in the starting rotation; mostly for the Chicago Cubs. Rush got the first two outs, but the last out, like the last strike, is always the highest hill to climb. Trying to be careful with a dangerous hitter, Rush walked Gil

Hodges. It was downhill from there. Catcher Joe Pignatano singled Hodges to second. Carl Furillo got a second two-out hit, a high bouncer back of second base. Felix Mantilla, playing shortstop after an injury to Johnny Logan, fielded the ball and made a hurried, off-balance throw to first in a desperate effort to get Furillo. He bounced the throw and it skipped past Frank Torre. Gil Hodges scored on Mantilla's error, and the Dodgers had won the second playoff game, 6 to 5.[39] Announcing for the Dodgers, Vin Scully, always cool, understated, and professional, simply said: "And we go to Chicago." That was the Dodgers. The Braves went home.

The playoffs of 1959 were a swan song for a good Milwaukee Braves team which had won the National League pennant in 1957 and 1958, and defeated the Yankees in the Series of 1957. By 1959 the team was beginning to fray around the edges, particularly with pitching, always the most fragile aspect of baseball. The Braves would not win again until 1969, when the team had been entirely refashioned (except only Hank Aaron), and they would lose the League Championship Series to the improbable New York Mets. For the Dodgers, triumph in 1959 was a prologue to a period of exceptional success, winning the pennant in 1963, 1965 and 1966, along with the Series in 1959, 1963 and 1965.

In the post–Jackie Robinson, Duke Snider and Roy Campanella era, Dodgers success would be built on pitching. Leading the staff was Sandy Koufax, Don Drysdale, Johnny Podres and Claude Osteen, along with relief pitchers Larry Sherry and Ron Perranoski. Pitching rarely holds up for a half decade or more, but for the new Dodgers on the West Coast it did. After 1959, although they won both the playoff and the Series, the Dodgers would continue to improve. In 1961, they finished second to Cincinnati and, in 1962, the Dodgers ended the regular season in a tie with their transplant partners, the San Francisco Giants. Each team won 101 games.[40]

Before the 1961 season, the National League expanded from eight to ten teams, adding a new franchise in New York, the Mets, and in Houston, the Colt .45s, later the Astros. Moving fiscally ailing (or not) franchises was now complemented by expansion into new and abandoned markets. The expansion teams, composed of ageing veterans and minor league hopefuls, did not play competitive baseball. While the Giants and Dodgers won 101 preplayoff games, the New York Mets in their first year (1962) were the worst team in the twentieth century, losing 120 games.[41] The gap between top and bottom was more than sixty games. While the Mets remained consistently in the cellar of the league, falling into tenth place during the last week of May and burrowing ever deeper thereafter, at the top of the Giants and Dodgers fought it out for the flag. The Giants slipped out of first during the first week of July, replaced by Los Angeles, which remained there until the very end. On Labor Day the Dodgers held a three and a half game lead over the Giants. Over the Labor Day weekend the visiting Giants took three out of four games in Los

Angeles to cut the Dodgers' lead to one an a half games. By September 12, when the two West Coast teams left on their final Eastern road trip, the Dodgers' lead was down to a half a game. Early in the trip the Dodgers pulled ahead. On September 16 they were four games in the lead with only thirteen games left to play, a comfortable lead that rapidly grew less comfortable. In the last two weeks of the season the Dodgers lost ten out of thirteen games. For Los Angeles the last four days of the season were a nightmare. On September 27, the Dodgers lost to expansion Houston, and the next day the Cardinals beat the fading Dodgers. On September 29, the Cards defeated Los Angeles again, and on September 30 the Redbirds swept the Dodgers, 1 to 0, as the veteran Curt Simmons beat Johnny Podres. Los Angeles had lost their last four games. The Giants, on the other hand, only lost two of the last four, one to Houston and another to St. Louis. On the last day of the season Willie Mays hit an eighth-inning home run and the Giants beat Houston, 2 to 1, to tie for the pennant. The Giants had won seven of their last thirteen, to catch Los Angeles on the last day of the season.[42]

The playoff series, the fourth in the National League history, also marked the fourth time the Dodgers, twice in Brooklyn and twice in L.A., had been part of the playoffs. The Giants, the Cardinals or the Braves participated as opponents, but the Dodgers were always there. Since the war, the Dodgers had won more than anyone else, but not more than everyone else. When the Dodgers didn't win they usually came close, sometimes close enough to tie. In 1962, in spite of their collapse at the end of season, the Dodgers were a good team and would be hard to beat. The Giants were not too bad either. They led the National League in hitting, .278, and in runs scored, 878, and their pitching compared well with the Dodgers. And, of course, the Giants still had Willie Mays. He had made the difference before and might do so again.

The playoff series began on October 1 at Candlestick Park, the Giants' windy stadium by the bay. The Giants started Billy Pierce, who had come over from the White Sox after the 1961 season and had won fifteen games in 1962. He was another in a long list of smallish left-handed pitchers, going back to Eddie Plank and including Harry Brecheen, Harvey "Kitten" Haddix, and Bobby Shantz, who combined great control with an assortment of outstanding breaking balls and deceptive speed. Going for his sixteenth win, Billy Pierce was at his best. He pitched a three-hit shutout, allowing one walk, to Junior Gilliam, a pinch-hit double to Doug Camilli, and harmless singles to Andy Carey and Ken McMullen. For the Dodgers pitchers, six of them, the game did not go so well. Sandy Koufax started and ran into immediate trouble. With two outs in the first inning, Felipe Alou doubled and Willie Mays homered. The Giants added a run in the second when Jim Davenport led off with a home run. Koufax then gave up a single to Giants catcher Ed Bailey. Walter Alston had seen enough. He lifted Koufax for Ed Roebuck, who held the Giants scoreless for the four innings he worked. In the sixth inning Alston sent Larry Sherry to the mound, and he gave up two runs on homers by Willie Mays and Orlando Cepeda, to make the score 5 to 0. In the eighth inning, Phil Ortega, the fifth of the Dodgers six pitchers, gave up three insurance runs on three walks, Jose Pagan's two-run double and an error. Billy Pierce went all the way and won an 8 to 0 shutout. Willie Mays also had a pretty good day. He went three for three, hit two homers and drove in three runs.[43] The Dodgers had lost their fifth consecutive game, and the Giants had gone ahead in the playoffs.

The second game, also in the afternoon despite the needs of television, was played the next day in the Dodgers' new stadium at Chavez Ravine. Only about 25,000 fans showed up for the game, a comment on West Coast baseball that few in Brooklyn failed to make. The Giants, hoping to close it out, started their ace, Jack Sanford, who had won twenty-four games that year, and the Dodgers, backs to the wall, countered with their best, Don Drysdale, who had led the league with twenty-five victories. It was a tight game for five innings, with the only run being a San Francisco tally in the second. In the sixth inning both Sanford and Drysdale ran out of gas. The Giants scored four times in the top of the sixth, and the Dodgers got seven runs in the home half of the inning. The Giants tied the score at seven all with two runs in the top of the eighth inning, and the Dodgers scored the winning run in the last of the ninth when Ron Fairly had a sacrifice fly to score Maurie Wills from third. The Dodgers' 8 to 7 victory had tied the playoff series at a game each, just like 1951.[44]

The final game, also at Chavez Ravine, drew over 45,000 fans to see the hometown heroes do it again. Both teams were exhausted from the 162-game season, then in its first year for the National League, and the playoff games that followed. Los Angeles started Johnny Podres on two days' rest while the Giants tried Juan Marichal, an eighteen-game winner. Marichal did pretty well. Staked to a two-run lead in the second inning, he pitched into the eighth, giving up four runs, three of them earned. Podres hung on until the sixth inning, when, losing 2 to 1, he allowed the Giants to load the bases with no one out. Walter Alston went to Ed Roebuck, for the sixth time in the last seven games, to put out the fire. Roebuck did. Jose Pagan forced Orlando Cepeda at the plate, and Juan Marichal hit into a double play. The Dodgers went ahead with two runs in the seventh, and Maurie Wills came home with an insurance run in the bottom of the eighth when Giants catcher Ed Bailey threw wildly trying to catch Wills on a steal of third. In the top of the ninth the Dodgers led 4 to 2, and the Giants had one last chance, just as in 1951. Ed Roebuck, till then the hero of the playoffs, was simply too tired to get the last three outs. Matty Alou singled, and Willie McCovey and Felipe Alou walked, filling the bases. Willie Mays got an infield single off Roebuck's hand, scoring Matty Alou. Walter Alston then brought in Stan Williams to pitch to

Orlando Cepeda, whose sacrifice fly brought in McCovey with the tying run. Williams walked Ed Bailey intentionally to fill the bases, and then walked Jim Davenport to force in Felipe Alou with the lead run. An error by Larry Burright, allowed the fourth Giants run to score. San Francisco led, 6 to 4, going into the bottom of the ninth. Al Dark, the Giants manager, then brought in Billy Pierce, who retired the Dodgers in order in the bottom of the ninth. The Giants won the pennant in the last inning of the last playoff game, just as in 1951.[45] And, as in 1951, the Giants faced the Yankees in the World Series. Yet again, the Yankees won.[46] The Giants and Dodgers had been there before.

The 1962 playoff series between Los Angeles and San Francisco was, in existential terms, the last of its kind. It was possible for two teams to end in a tie in the future as they had in the past, but organizational structure of Major League Baseball changed, merging such playoffs into the general category of postseason, and depriving them of their previous condition as unusual and dramatic events that monopolized, for a few days, all of baseball attention. In 1969, after admitting two new expansion teams to each league, the baseball moguls confronted the problem that had afflicted Major League ball in the 1890s: the lack of competition up and down the league. The twelve teams in the National League in the 1890s provided too great a spread in talent between Boston, Baltimore and Brooklyn at the top and the woeful Cleveland Spiders (20 wins, 134 loses, .130 baseball and 84 games off the pace in 1899) at the bottom. Most of the also-rans drifted out of contention by the second month of the season, some by the first month, while the worst team settled inexorably into the primordial ooze of sub .400 baseball in eleventh and twelfth place. The players became discouraged, the fans disinterested and the owners flirted with ruin. Even the better clubs lost money, as they played before crowds of a couple hundred in the cities of the baseball damned and could not recoup the costs of the trip. The Temple Cup series after the end of the season between the first- and second-place clubs did not generate enough fan or newspaper interest to establish an appropriate climax to the season. None of this could be thought of as a good thing.[47]

In 1969, facing two twelve-team leagues, the magnates made changes before the previous problems reoccurred. They divided both leagues into two six-team divisions, imaginatively labeled East and West. At the end of the season a League Championship Series between the eastern and western winners added two more teams to postseason play as well as doubling the number of pennant races. The reasoning was simple. More champions, now two to a league, mean more championships games, more contenders to play in those games, more fan interest, more people at the games, more television viewers, and, crucially, more money for the owners. This time around, the baseball magnates could avoid the mistakes, and the financial reverses, of the previous century. And they did.

In the new environment of postseason, every series but the World Series is called a playoff, in spite of baseball's best and official efforts to have intraleague postseason play called the League Championship Series and more recently, with three divisions and a wild card added, the Division Championship Series.[48] But the fans, unlike announcers and writers, cannot be brought to heel completely concerning baseball's political correctness, persist in using the outlawed term of *playoff*.

Nonetheless, in post–1969 baseball, one playoff, neither a League nor a Division Championship Series, but the result of a tie at the end of the season, was remarkable at the time and has entered baseball myth and memory since. On October 3, 1978, the Boston Red Sox and the New York Yankees had a single-game playoff, the American League format, at Fenway Park, to see who would go on to the League Championship playoff for the American League pennant.

The 1978 season for Boston and New York had been a study in contrasts. The 1975 American League champions, the Boston Red Sox, started out with a roar. In the first half of the season Boston won fifty-two games and lost only twenty-two to climb thirty games over .500 and opening up a fourteen-game lead over the Yankees, who had won in 1976 and 1977. This looked like Boston's year. Unfortunately for the Red Sox, the season had a second half. Boston began to lose. In early September the Sox went four and fourteen, and by September 17, the Yanks were three and a half games ahead of fading Beantown. But the Yanks, who won fifty-two and lost twenty-one in the second half of the season, could not hold the lead. Boston had a last gasp spurt, and on October 1 both teams had won ninety-nine games. [49]

Both teams could point to factors in their favor to get into the playoffs. Boston had the home field advantage, which in Fenway, with its odd configuration and the rabid Sox fans, really meant something. The Yankees had Ron Guidry, a southpaw from Carencro, Louisiana, who had a slider that broke late, hard, down, and in to luckless right-handed hitters. In 1978 Guidry had a record of twenty-five and three, along with a 1.74 earned run average, indicative of overpowering stuff.[50] The game, played in the afternoon, began well for the Red Sox. Carl Yastrzemski had a second inning home run, and the Sox scored again in the sixth to carry a two-run lead into the seventh inning. Then it began to come apart. The Yanks scored four runs, three of them on a two-out home run by shortstop Bucky Dent. Dent's shot cleared the Green Monster in left field, barely. Dent later said: "I heard it but I didn't see it. When it left the bat I thought it had a chance to hit the wall. I just ran hard to first. I didn't think it would clear the fence. I heard the silence of the crowd as I got to first. I knew it was a homer."[51] The Yanks, now ahead 4 to 2, added what seemed to be a meaningless insurance run in the top of the eighth when Reggie Jackson hit a home run. But that run would be the difference. Down 5 to 2, the Red Sox scored twice in the bottom of the eighth to close the gap to one run. In the bottom of the ninth the Sox rallied again.

With two on, the tying run on third, and two out, Carl Yastrzemski came up for a last plate appearance. This time he could not do it. Yastrzemski popped up to third. Yankee third baseman Graig Nettles later said he had been hoping for a popup, but "not to me." Nettles, an exceptional fielder, made the routine play, and the Yanks were the American League eastern division champions, having been one out better than the Sox, over the course of the entire season.[52]

The New York playoff victory, which most fans and sports writers more or less expected, resonated beyond a tight pennant race and a tied finish, indeed, beyond baseball and into the general culture. It was part of the rivalry between the Apple and the Hub, emblematic of two different visions of America in the nineteenth century, an emphasis on moral culture for the Boston elite and commerce and economic growth for New York. More recently, the rivalry has descended into the popular culture of entertainment, with the Yanks and the Red Sox as emblems of the different cities.

The history of the baseball rivalry has greatly favored New York. For Boston fans, the playoff loss in 1978 brought back painful memories of 1949, when the Yanks had also defeated the Red Sox with the pennant on the line. In 1949, the Red Sox led the Bronx Bombers by one game with two games to play. Both would be in Yankee Stadium, but Boston only had to win once. Boston had a superb team, the best in baseball or very close to it, with Ted Williams, Don DiMaggio and All Zarilla in the outfield and Johnny Pesky, Vern Stephens, Bobby Doerr and Billy Goodman in the infield. At Fenway Park, the Sox had won sixty-one games and lost only sixteen.[53] But the Yanks had Joe DiMaggio, who was sick and hit only .346, and deeper pitching than Boston, and they had been in first place for all but a couple days the whole season. The Sox made a strong run for the pennant, going twenty-four and eight in August, climbing into second place. On September 18, they were two and a half games behind the Yanks, and by September 26, the Sox were in first place, for two days. On September 30, the Sox regained the lead by one game. Just the two left at the Stadium, and if Boston could split the series they would win the pennant.[54]

October 1 was Joe DiMaggio Day, and to honor the event, the Bronx Bombers came back from a four-run deficit to win, 5 to 4, on Johnny Lindell's eighth-inning homer. Joe Page pitched six innings of scoreless relief. For the last game, on October 2, the Yanks sent twenty-game winner Vic Raschi against Ellis Kinder, who had won twenty-three games for Boston. New York got a run in the first, and the score was 1 to 0 until the eighth inning. After lifting Kinder for a pinch-hitter, Boston manager Joe McCarthy sent twenty-five-game winner Mel Parnell in as relief. Parnell gave up a home run to Tommy Henrich and a single to Yogi Berra. Tex Hughson, in the last year of his Major League career, came in next and gave up three more runs. The Red Sox, down 5 to 0 in the top of the ninth, rallied for three runs, but could not close the gap. The Yanks won the 1949 pennant.[55]

For fans not yet born in 1978 and inexperienced in the rivalry, something similar happened in 2003. Tied at three games each in the League Championship playoffs, the Yankees came back to tie the score in the final game against Pedro Martinez, one of the best pitchers in the American League. The Yankee rally had about it an air of inevitability. Even with Martinez pitching, rather than one of the lesser arms from a frazzled and inadequate bullpen, the Sox could not hold the lead, just as in 1978 and 1949. The end came suddenly, but to no one's surprise. In the last of the twelfth inning, Aaron Boone, a Yankee infielder who had been benched for repeated failures at bat and afield, hit a home run. Boone won the game, the League Championship Series, and sent Boston home to defeat. The Red Sox will break your heart.

The events of 1949, 1979 and 2003 are authentic examples of the Curse of the Bambino, and, when a curse can be established its ramifications are wide indeed. Although the Curse of the Bambino has struck only four times, first in selling the rest of the Boston team to the Yankees and then on the three occasions aforementioned, *all* the numerous woes of the Red Sox since 1920 have been understood as falling under the penumbra of the curse. But this mistakes the everyday for the extraordinary. Most disasters do not derive from the curse, but from ordinary *hamartia*, literally missing the target (in archery) but more generally denoting the inevitable imperfections in people and things.[56] Agamemnon struggled with numerous contretemps, but Aeschylus understood that the Curse of the House of Atreus, originating in a father's butchery of his children to feed the gods, applied only to Agamemnon's sacrifice of his daughter Iphigeneia so the Trojan War could began.[57] All else was happenstance, often catastrophic in effect but standing apart from the curse. So it is with the Red Sox. Losing to the Indians (1948) or the Cardinals (1946, 1967) or the Reds (1975) and the Mets (1986) were just things that happen, merely missing the mark. But losing to the Yankees, in the most crucial situations, should be seen as the workings of the curse. In dealing with the tragic view of life, one is always well advised to go with Aristotle and Aeschylus.

Playoffs still tend to reinforce the tragic view of life, even though that once extraordinary event that focused the entire attention of baseball, have become routine. The playoffs often generate interest, as they did in 2003, but lack the surprise and delight and tension of a late rally to force extra innings, which is what, on a season scale, the playoffs used to do. Playoffs have become another in the long line of victims of Gresham's law that bad money drives good out of circulation. Sir Thomas Gresham originally conceived his law in the wake of responses to the calamitous wave of royal and private bankruptcies in the 1550s, but it applies to the structure of baseball as well. Baseball, after all, is mostly about losing.

III

Winners and Losers

8

America's Team

In 1938, Walt Disney expanded his cartoon artistry to a full-length feature musical film, *Snow White and the Seven Dwarfs*. The film had everything, from an evil queen to a Prince Charming, to say nothing of the heroine, Snow White, and her faithful followers, the Seven Dwarfs. For Snow White the film provided a happy ending. But the Seven Dwarfs received less. Snow White did not abandon them, but the Seven Dwarfs obtained no guarantee that they, too, would live happily ever after. In America, where life imitates art, *Snow White and the Seven Dwarfs* was not just an old fairy tale cleaned up to become suitable for children. It also described the American League, where the mighty New York Yankees, America's team, almost always won, and the seven lesser teams trundled along behind as best they could. The American League was a one-team show. In the years between the sale of Babe Ruth (1920) and *Snow White*, the Yanks won ten pennants, while the rest of the league won nine, and the gap would grow over the next quarter century. The Yankees' star turn lasted for forty-five years; in the process, the Yankees, fortunate in name and location, became America's team.

I

The core of the Yankees' success rested on two things. For three baseball generations, America's team had several of the best players in baseball, and so they won consistently. More significant by far, the Yankees had the most celebrated players, whom the fans loved, admired and saw as bigger than life, or at least as bigger than baseball. Consequently, the Yanks attracted national attention. Though affection for the Yankees did not necessarily displace attachment to local teams, it did expand general interest in the game. Stories about the Yankees began to appear regularly in smaller newspapers around the country during the 1920s, and in the Depression decade radio brought the Yankee games to audiences beyond New York. Movies such as *Pride of the Yankees* about Lou Gehrig and musicals that became movies after the end of their useful life on Broadway, as did *Damn Yankees*, helped spread the impression that the Yankees belonged to everyone, not just the fans in New York. Television completed the nationalization of interest in the New York Yankees by showing them more often than any other team. Cable and satellite broadcast added convenience for the national fan base of the Yankees.

The media responded to an already existing interest in the Yankees more than they created it. Babe Ruth was the initial reason for it all. It began with home runs. In 1918, although winning thirteen games as a pitcher, including two more in the World Series, Babe Ruth played fifty-nine games in the outfield and hit eleven home runs, which led the league.[1] The next year Boston manager Ed Barrow played the Babe mainly in the outfield, where the not-yet-but-soon-to-become Sultan of Swat hit .322 and a staggering total of twenty-nine home runs. No one had ever hit that many in a single season, though Gavvy Cravath of the usually downtrodden, but for once triumphant Philadelphia Phillies, had twenty-four in 1915, and Wildfire Schulte had hit twenty-one for the Chicago Cubs in 1911. Until Babe Ruth, the National had been the league of sluggers. In one year the mighty Babe changed all that. His home runs caught the national imagination. The *Boston Post* carried an article on "Busting Babe and His Diadem," asserting that the "Clouting Hercules is one of the Celebrities of the Country." The article also carried seven seriatim photographs of the Ruthian swing, which had as its headline: "Now Everyone Can Make a Home Run As Babe Shows How to Do It."[2]

The article was about half right, which was pretty good for the sporting press. The Babe might show you how he did it, but no one else could hit like Ruth. Babe Ruth was, however, already an entertainment celebrity. Some Hall of Fame hitters, like Jimmie Foxx, Hack Wilson, Mel Ott and Lou Gehrig, tried mighty hard to hit like Ruth, but their efforts only reinforced a sense that Babe was unique.

After being traded to the Yankees on January 3, 1920, Babe Ruth brought his incomparable skills and boisterous personality into intimate contact with one of the great publicity machines in the Western world, the New York media. It was a perfect fit. Until Charles Lindbergh crossed the Atlantic in 1927, Babe Ruth was the most famous person in America, with the possible exception Rudolph Valentino, who materially aided his own notoriety by dying, slowly and in New York, a costly way for a movie star to increase his fame. Stanley Walker, city editor of the *New York Herald Tribune*, saw the whole gaudy passing of "The Sheik," and noted that Valentino "was the symbol of romance; his death meant that love itself was dead."[3] Valentino died on August 23, 1926, at about ten minutes after noon, in plenty of time for evening paper deadlines and morning paper commentary. Walker watched from his perch of virtue as the tabloids "indulged in a magnificent orgy of stallion-like headlines, sobbing chronicles of the life and death of the actor, and as many photographs of the hero, alive and dead, as the traffic would bear."[4] All of this took place during the pennant race, which the Yankees would win by only three games over the Cleveland Indians, and for a week or so blotted out even Yankees baseball. But the whole maudlin story lasted less than a month. While Valentino remained dead, Ruth continued to hit home runs (forty-seven for 1926), and the Yankees won the pennant. For sustained popularity, over decades not years, the Bambino eclipsed the Sheik.

Babe Ruth was not the last Yankee who transcended baseball and became a cultural phenomenon. In 1934, Ed Barrow, the Yankees General Manager, made a complex deal with the nearly bankrupt Charley Graham, owner of the San Francisco Seals. The subject of the deal was Joe DiMaggio, an eighteen-year-old local kid who, in 1933, had jumped straight from the sandlots to the Pacific Coast League. He did just fine. In 1933, he hit .340, with twenty-eight homers while driving in 169 runs. He also "achieved nationwide attention by his remarkable record of hitting safely in 61 consecutive games."[5] The Seals finished in sixth place, but the local lad had generated enough fan interest to keep Graham afloat. The next year DiMaggio hurt his knee, and Graham had to suspend his happy hopes of a high price for his star player's contract. Then Ed Barrow suggested a deal. Barrow offered $25,000 for DiMaggio, plus five players, and Graham could keep the kid for another season. Graham could be certain of another good year at the gate, and the Yankees could be sure that DiMaggio's knee had healed.[6] In 1935, Joe DiMaggio hit .398 and was a paragon of grace in center field, amply proving both his skill and his health.

JOSEPH MCCARTHY, YANKEES MANAGER. A photograph from the early thirties, the era of the called home run. In the early thirties the Yankees were not the best team in baseball, winning the pennant only once (1932) between 1929 and 1936. McCarthy was Ruppert's choice to fix that. He did.

Although DiMaggio hardly needed another year in the Coast League — like Mel Ott he could have jumped directly from the sandlots to the Bigs — the 1935 season in San Francisco was one of the best breaks he ever had in baseball. DiMaggio got to spend a season with Frank "Lefty" O'Doul, a home-town San Francisco hero, and one who understood the hero's life. Lefty had hit .398 with the Phillies in 1929 and had won a World Series ring with the New York Giants in 1933. O'Doul had not only been a good player, he was also a courtly gentleman whose manners were from the old school. He was gracious to all he met, graceful and apposite in all he said and did. He dressed elegantly, he knew, liked, and remembered everyone from top to bottom on the formal social ladder, and he loved kids. This could only come from two things, the focus and discipline necessary to be "on" all the time, and a gen-erosity of spirit as well as of purse. As a hero, Lefty O'Doul knew that the worst sin was to let the side down. Heroism is not only the result of a moment, but also the work of a lifetime.

As manager of the Seals in 1935, O'Doul gave Joe DiMaggio some use-ful batting tips, but his greatest gift to Joe was time. Lefty took Joe with him

JOE DIMAGGIO. A standard baseball pose, with the hitter shown finishing his swing. Action photographs were more difficult to get, so the completed swing filled news-paper pages and baseball publicity literature.

when he toured San Francisco, going to lunch with important people, greeting everyone, and introducing Joe around. DiMaggio got to see the hero's life lived, both the many benefits and the many more responsibilities. The gregarious, open and optimistic good fellowship, well lubricated with booze and beer, that Lefty O'Doul practiced did not suit the reticent Joe DiMaggio. Reserved, silent, shy, and cautious, DiMaggio could not exude the bonhommie of the outgoing O'Doul. But DiMaggio did have an elegance and grace off the field as well as on it. If he could not emulate the style he could understand the essence of Lefty O'Doul's heroic stature. Though not bookish, DiMaggio was exceptionally smart. He could and would learn, and not just baseball, possessing a skill that has eluded huge numbers of players, including some who were quite good.

So Joe DiMaggio built what he already was into a public persona that steadily became larger than baseball. His natural grace, beauty and elegance became his form of the hero's life. Silence became aristocratic reserve, and shyness and caution became appropriate modesty. Focus and discipline were seen as a steely resolve to do his duty, whether it or he hurt or not. Joe DiMaggio became the model of grace under pressure, the American ideal of a gentleman. By contrast, people wanted to play like Babe Ruth, not be like him. Few wished their kids to grow up living as the Babe had lived. But Joe DiMaggio became the ideal for life, not just baseball, the man to be emulated by adolescent and adult alike. His persona became one of character, not just skill. In the late thirties and early forties, Joe DiMaggio steadily emerged as a national hero come in a time of great need and danger to inspire and give comfort. He tied the fans, the Yankees, and the game to the best in the American ideal. Like Hamlet, he was

> The glass of fashion and the mould of form,
> Th' observed of all observers.[7]

In 1936, Joe DiMaggio came to the Yankees and made an immediate difference. In the seven years prior to 1936, the Yanks won only once, in 1932; in the eight years before Joltin' Joe entered the service in 1944 the Yanks won seven times, including six World Series. Like Babe Ruth, Joe DiMaggio led his team to triumph beyond dreaming, and no one could doubt that without him the Yanks would have been just another good team, and not the dominant sports franchise in America. Credit for that domination of the American League and the World Series went to Joe DiMaggio, both from the fans and the sports writers. Although nothing lasts forever in the American cult of celebrity, the Babe defied oblivion and remained a hero all his life. Joe DiMaggio continues to do the same thing, for "age cannot wither, nor custom stale"[8] his heroic stature. The Yankee Clipper today is bigger than ever.

Even the Yankee Clipper could not play forever, and in baseball one is "on the door-sill of sorrowful old age" by one's mid-thirties. The love given him by the fans did not diminish, but his skills inevitably did. When DiMaggio retired in 1951, the Yankees were in danger of becoming simply the best team in baseball, rather than the mythic core of the game. Yankees management was up to the task of remaining the symbolic heart of baseball. They found a new hero; indeed, they found two. Yogi Berra came up to stay in 1947, and Mickey Mantle joined the Yanks in 1951. With Yogi and the Mick, the Yanks won at an even more furious pace than they had with DiMaggio. The Yankees won fifteen pennants in eighteen years, from 1947 through 1964, and won the World Series ten times. That will likely be the gold standard for franchise success, unless, of course, the current and future Yankees surpass it. Surely, no other team will.

Both Mantle and Berra played superb baseball and both transcended mere athletic excellence. Mantle became part of a popular song about Mickey, Willie and the Duke, the premier hitters of the three New York teams in the fifties. Yogi surpassed this by becoming the namesake for a cartoon hero, Yogi Bear, and, more important yet, became a folk hero and one of modern America's philosophers. Whether or not Yogi actually uttered any of the phrases and comments attributed to him may be regarded as irrelevant. They all fit his public personality, which is cheerful, friendly, and wise. They have all become part of Yogi's legend, which, by definition, is always greater than reality.

In February 2004, the Yankees, who have lacked a hero possibly since Reggie Jackson and certainly since Yogi and the Mick, tried to fill that void. They signed Alex Rodriguez, the best player in the American League.[9] Will A-Rod meet the imprecise but exacting standards of the New York media and attain the rank of a legend and hero? There is no guarantee. It certainly will not happen if Rodriguez is right in his comments after the first Yankee–Red Sox spring training game: "I think its going to settle down. I think the major craziness is behind us."[10] An emotional connection, often defined by those unaffected as similar to craziness, is a significant ingredient in heroic stature, perhaps not in the hero himself, but certainly in the public reaction to him. Myth arises from love.

The last word, for the time being, on the Yankees' acquisition of A-Rod must be given to a Boston Red Sox fan. The Yankees snatched Rodriguez from the grasp of the Red Sox and will pay A-Rod $112 million over the next seven years. The numbers have changed, but the Yankee habit of buying the player needed goes back to the mighty Babe. A Red Sox fan, architect Joe Lafo, understood both the curse of the Bambino and the size of the Yankees' purse, and commented, "It's just the Yankees being the Yankees."[11]

II

January 1920 saw a lot of history. On January 3, Boston Red Sox owner Harry Frazee sold Babe Ruth to the New York Yankees, who signed him to a contract two days later.[12] And, at the stroke of midnight on the night of January 16, the Eighteenth Amendment went into effect and Prohibition became the law of the land.[13] At the time, both the growing celebrity of Babe Ruth and the coming of Prohibition received extensive coverage in the public press. Prohibition was not altogether a story of crime, of the difficulties inherent in moral crusades launched by the earnest to reform the behavior of the lapsed or indifferent. It also played a major role in the Ruthian legend; by making booze illegal Prohibition gave Ruth, who drank much and often, an aura of edginess as well as fun.

Prohibition was one of the two last victories (women's suffrage was the other) of the Progressive Movement, a reform era that had dominated American society and politics for the first two decades of the twentieth century. In the days when the Boston Red Sox were one of the dominant teams in baseball, Prohibition and the vote reigned as the two major political and social issues affecting the condition of women, and of the two, Prohibition was probably the more important to contemporary feminists. Both were proclaimed as necessary to the moral improvement of American life, a powerful appeal in an America which, from the Puritan city on a hill to making the world safe for democracy, saw itself as playing a special role in God's divine plan.

Part of American exceptionalism was to be the moral ascent from the iniquities of the saloon up to the purity of Uncle Sam's Water Wagon. Some hotels dissented from the evangelical view of booze, and on January 16, 1920, decorated their bars in black. People stocked up, buying liquor at substantial discount for extended future consumption. But more common were thanksgiving services, often in church, thanking God for grace in bringing the hideous evil of drink to an end. That was certainly the view of the Reverend Billy Sunday, who held a mock funeral for John Barleycorn on January 15 at Norfolk, Virginia. Billy had been a Major League player in the 1880s, but decades as an itinerant evangelist had dulled the worldly wisdom he had gained in Chicago so long ago. "Good-bye," Billy called to the presumably recumbent John Barleycorn. "You were God's worst enemy. You were hell's best friend." In the new dry America, Billy claimed,

> the reign of tears is over. The slums will soon be a memory. We will turn our prisons into factories and our jails into storehouses and corncribs. Men will walk upright now, women will smile and children will laugh. Hell will be forever for rent.[14]

One of those Christians who believed, despite the unaided majesty of God's creation otherwise, He could not bring His Kingdom on Earth without the help of mere men, Billy Sunday saw Prohibition as a long step on the rocky road toward the New Jerusalem. His peroration was quoted everywhere, became widely celebrated, and justly so. Rarely in the history of human prophecy has a man been so wrong about so much in a single speech.

In light of subsequent events, it is hard to believe that in January 1920 most Americans thought that Prohibition would prohibit. Except for the general Northern refusal to enforce national fugitive slave laws, Americans had no experience with widespread and unwavering disobedience to a duly consecrated statute, particularly a constitutional one. The experience of the war on drugs had not yet come. In that more innocent time, the will of the majority had sanctity about it. The law was the law, and respect for the law was taken more or less for granted. Why else would the Yale club expend the funds to lay in a fourteen-year supply of whisky, a precise calculation of need that one would expect of Yale men? Why else would innumerable private citizens stock up as the phrase then had it? Why would the Anti-Saloon League, which had put Prohibition over in the first place, anticipate no difficulty in enforcement, if not because there would be general obedience? And the initial opposition was muted. In running for governor of New York during the fall of 1918, Al Smith did not mention Prohibition. He concentrated on high public utility rates, which he successfully blamed on the Republicans.[15] The brewers and distillers said nothing at all. Prohibition slipped quietly in, amid the general assumption that this new law would change the country.

So important was respect for the law as a national virtue that the one thing those opposing and those defending Prohibition agreed on was the damage being done to the sanctity of the law. Even President Harding, a personal wet though a political dry, issued a few comments supporting Prohibition and dealing with the reverent subject of law. More in sorrow than in anger, the president said: "I do not see how any citizen who cherishes the protection of the law in organized society may feel himself secure when he himself is the example of contempt for law."[16] Could more be done for observance of law than a presidential comment?

After Prohibition had been the law for a couple of years, the wets, who wanted it modified, began to complain of the inconveniences of the "great social and economic experiment, noble in motive and far-reaching in purpose," to use Herbert Hoover's immortal phrase.[17] They pointed out the unenforceability of the Volstead Act, and the consequent increase in crime and police harassment, as well as the decline in respect for law. But though the facts were clearly with them, they made no headway. For all of the 1920s the dry majority in Congress actually grew. Prohibition was as American as apple pie.

So was baseball, and the sale of Babe Ruth to the Yankees was front page news everywhere. The sum mentioned, $125,000, was enormous, the largest sum ever paid for a player, and the loan to the Boston owner, Harry Frazee, $300,000, was even larger. In the late 1880s, Albert Spalding had sold John Clarkson and Mike Kelly to Boston for $10,000 each, sales that produced comment and amazement at the time.[18] Even allowing for wartime inflation, the price paid for Ruth was an order of magnitude higher, both mathematically and psychologically.

As they had a generation earlier, the papers reported a good deal of comment of the morality of spending that much money on a baseball player. Baseball might be the national pastime, but it was only a pastime, and leisure then lacked the moral value of work. The other complaint concerned the money. In 1919–20, America struggled to adjust to postwar life, which proved to be surprisingly difficult and unpleasant. In November 1918, President Woodrow Wilson had penned a few chaste and measured sentences to the American people of the occasion of victory in the Great War. "My Fellow Countrymen: The Armistice was signed this morning. Everything for which America fought has been accomplished. It will now be our fortunate duty to assist by example, by sober, friendly counsel, and by material aid in the establishment of just democracy throughout the world."[19] President Wilson held an absolutely unshakeable opinion that God would ensure that the future would be duty, example, counsel and aid. But one is often deceived about the *vox dei* and the *vox populi*, and throughout 1919 and 1920 Americans found it increasingly hard to believe that the social and economic dislocations and the disruptions of demobilization described the world for which they had fought.

The high lost of living was the worst problem and the one closest to home. The price of everything had shot up during the war, and after the war prices continued to rise. Food prices were the worst. Milk had risen to fifteen cents a quart, up from nine cents before the war. Eggs were a staggering sixty-two cents a dozen, rising from thirty-four cents before the war. Steak, of course, was higher, double its prewar price of thirty-two cents a pound, and that was itself a substantial increase from the two bits a pound a tough cut had cost in 1900. In New York, where food (along with coal and shelter) was one of the major working- and middle-class expenses, prices in general had risen nearly 80 percent over the course of two years. Wages and salaries remained by and large at prewar levels, and those working felt the pinch.

The cost of living wasn't everything; there was also the nearness of death. The influenza epidemic, called Spanish flu although it was a toxic variant of bird flu from China, began in the late summer of 1918. At Fort Riley, Kansas, soldiers became sick for no apparent reason and did not respond to treatment. On August 27, two sailors in Boston reported for sick bay, and four days later the navy had 106 cases. By mid–September, after the end of the World Series in that war-shortened season, the flu had spread to all of the major cities of the East Coast. Things got much worse that winter and spring. Perhaps thirty million Americans caught the flu and a half a million died. The authorities did what they could, closing schools, banning public meetings, and passing out face masks. America escaped the worst of the pandemic, though few at home drew much comfort from that. Worldwide, the flu killed close to fifty million people in a single year, more than the Great War had killed in five.

Flu and the high cost of living simply made the postwar depression, which lasted through 1921, that much worse. Jobs had become scarce, and income increasingly required stretching to cover "normal" living expenses. On the farm, prices paid for food and fiber began to drop, a trend that would continue throughout the twenties and thirties. Labor unrest, including a strike by the Boston police (September 9–12, 1919), which led to an orgy of looting, culminated in a coal miners' strike on November 1 that threatened the winter fuel supply. A Red Scare was conducted with verve and enthusiasm by Woodrow Wilson's attorney general, A. Mitchell Palmer, who, like Senator McCarthy later, believed in monsters under the bed and wanted to be president. It preyed on the already vulnerable, immigrants and social radicals, and it afflicted those still comfortable with the anxious suspicion that the world they had known and American values they cherished were under violent attack. In the midst of all this came the sale of Babe Ruth for an excessive sum, an immoral sum, a sum few Americans could earn in a lifetime. It was worse than immoral; it was unseemly.[20]

III

The new Yankees owners, Colonel Jacob Ruppert, a beer baron, and Captain Tillinghast L'Hommedieu Huston, were convinced that this deal, enormous as it was, would pay equally enormous dividends. The Babe was unlike any other player in baseball, and he would transform an already good team into a winner, both in the pennant race and at the gate. The Bambino was not the first important player they had obtained from the always impecunious Harry Frazee. On June 29, 1919, the Yanks paid $40,000, a hefty sum, and two pitchers for Carl Mays, who won 208 games in the Bigs, including two in the 1918 World Series, the recent Series victory for the Red Sox. Even with Mays's help, the Yanks came in third in 1919, and would do the same in 1920, although Mays won twenty-six games and the mighty Babe had fifty-four homers. Babe Ruth, even with Carl Mays, was not yet enough. Although no guarantee existed that the young Babe would become the immortal Babe, the Yankee owners, who had sunk almost half a million into baseball at a time when that was real money, saw greater rewards in the future if they just kept on. After all, had the Yankees not outdrawn the Giants for the first time? Next year would be even better.

And thank God for Boston. The Red Sox had some good players left and, if Carl Mays and the mighty Babe were not enough, Ruppert and Huston would visit the Boston larder again. On December 15, 1920, the Yanks obtained Waite Charles Hoyt, a twenty-one-year-old pitcher who had gone six and six in his second year with Boston. New York manager Miller Huggins saw something in young Hoyt, who came over with catcher Wally Schang and reserve infielder Mike McNally in exchange for four players. No mention of money. Of course, the $300,000 loan was still outstanding. Hoyt and Schang helped a lot, with Hoyt winning nineteen games and Schang hitting .316 in 1921. Carl Mays won twenty-seven games in his second full season in New York, and the Babe hit 59 home runs, driving in 171 runs. The quartet of former Red Sox led the Yankees to the 1921 pennant, their first. But Boston still had some pitching left, and the Yankee owners were determined to get it. After all, 1922 was another year, the Yanks had lost the 1921 Series to the Giants, and there is never enough pitching. On December 20, 1921, Boston traded infielder Everett Scott, twenty-three-game winner Sad Sam Jones, and sixteen-game winner Bullet Joe Bush to New York for four players. Again, there was no mention of money. In 1922, Bullet Joe won twenty-six games, but Sad Sam Jones sunk to thirteen, and the Yanks again lost the World Series to the Giants. It was time for more Boston pitching, and, on January 30, 1923, Boston sent Hall of Fame pitcher Herb Pennock, the Knight of Kennett Square, to the Yanks for three players, along with $50,000. The Knight of Kennett Square won nineteen games with the Yanks in 1923, who won their first World Series, but one more Boston trade really put the seal on the season. Boston sold infielder Jumping Joe Dugan to New York for the waiver price. The Yankees opened the 1923 World Series with four starting pitchers and four position players who had come from Boston since the Armistice. In baseball, good management counts, in the front office as well as on the field, and the Yankee management, from top on down, was genuinely superb.

IV

The New York Yankees won their first pennant in 1921, eighteen years after their entry into the American League in 1903. In the years before 1913, when they were not known as the Yankees but the Highlanders, the American League entry from New York was not, legends to the contrary, one of the doormats of baseball. They came in second in 1904, 1906 and 1910, and finished in third place in 1919 and 1920. They ended in the cellar only twice (1908 and 1912), and were a seventh-place team in 1913 and 1914. Their average for the years before 1921 was fifth place, and they had winning seasons for eight of the eighteen years.

The problem with the Highlanders/Yankees did not consist of their mediocrity as also-rans, but rested in the sustained excellence and popularity of their New York rivals, the Giants, managed by the already legendary John McGraw. McGraw had rescued a foundering team when he became manager in 1902, and produced an almost immediate winner.[21] The Giants won the pennant in 1904 and again in 1905, when they defeated the Philadelphia Athletics in the World Series. In the decade and a half between the 1905 Series triumph and the arrival of Babe Ruth in New York, the Giants continued to win. They became synonymous with the "dead ball" game, of low-run games dominated by pitching, stealing bases, hitting behind the runners and playing for one run. The Giants also enjoyed the approval of the newspaper reporters, as well as stockbrokers, politicians, theatrical folk and the sporting crowd. The Giants had social cachet, and the Yankees were merely poor relations.

The modern era for the Yankees started when Ruppert and Huston bought the franchise in January 1915, and steadily gained momentum over the next half decade. They began to obtain some good players, notably Wally Pipp, a first baseman, and pitcher Bob Shawkey, and in their first season the Yanks improved to a fifth-place finish. The next year, 1916, the Yanks added third baseman Frank "Home Run" Baker, and finished in fourth place with a winning record (eighty to seventy-four). In 1918, with Huston away at war in France, Ruppert brought in Miller Huggins to manage the Yankees. Huggins was a quiet man with a law degree, and he was not likely to be a drinking companion or source of information for the gregarious New York sports writers. But he did know something about baseball, and in 1918 and 1919 he brought the Yanks in with winning records and first division finishes. Even better, from the ownership perspective, in 1919, the now competitive Yanks drew over 600,000 fans to the Polo Grounds, a record for the team, though it was still a smaller gate than the host the New York Giants drew. Nonetheless, things were clearly looking up for New York's other team. And then came Babe Ruth.

In 1920, the Babe's first year with New York, the Yanks opened on the road at Shibe Park in Philadelphia. April 14, 1920, was a cold day, but more than 15,000 fans came to see the Babe, and paid premium prices, $1 for a grandstand seat. The Athletics were really terrible, having come in last every year since 1914, and would do so again in 1920 and 1921, the longest record of consecutive ineptitude up to that time.[22] Never mind. There was plenty of excitement, with most of it surrounding the Babe. He did not hit a home run, but he did make an error allowing the hapless As to score two runs in the eighth inning and win the game, 3 to 1.[23]

The rest of the season went better for the Yankees than the opener. New York finished in third place again, but with a vastly improved record of ninety-five and fifty-nine, were only three games behind Cleveland, which won its first pennant. The Bambino hit the incredible total of fifty-four home runs, and, for the second year in a row, he set a Major League record for homers in a season. The Yankees also drew over a million fans into the Polo Grounds, outdrawing the Giants for the first time. It was the promise of a new day in New York baseball. But even the unprecedented success of 1920 was not the real beginning of the modern Yankees.

The real opening game for the Babe and the new New York Yankees came on April 13, 1921, as the Yanks opened the season at home. The Philadelphia Athletics were the visitors, but no one cared; even the dozen or so Athletics fans came to see the Babe. The Athletics were the same wretched crew they had been the year before, but the Yankees were considerably better, and in an unexpected way. Edward Grant Barrow, the former Red Sox field manager, had come to New York as general manager, where he would run the franchise for the next quarter century, proving to be one of the great executives in the history of baseball.[24]

Plenty of pundits, and a lot of fans as well, thought the Yankees had a real chance to win their first pennant in 1921. About 37,000 fans, near capacity, packed the Polo Grounds on a warm and pleasant spring day to see the Babe and the Yanks start the year off. As he so often did when on center stage, the Babe responded magnificently. He went five for five, including two doubles and two runs batted in. Carl Mays held the woeful Athletics at bay, and the Yanks scored nine runs in the last two innings to win, 11 to 1.[25] The game only took an hour and a half, two hours less than it would today, and the fans left happy and got home in time for dinner.

The Yankees fulfilled that opening day promise and won their first pennant in 1921, finishing four and a half games ahead of Cleveland with a record of ninety-eight victories and fifty-five defeats. The team again drew over a million fans, and the Bambino, for the third consecutive year, set a new record for home runs in a season. He hit fifty-nine. The Yankees had arrived. They were now the dominant team in New York and the source of endless municipal pride.

The Yanks may have finally become Gotham's favorite team, but they were not the only good team in New York in 1921. The Giants also won the pennant, their ninth since 1883 and their seventh for John McGraw. Coming on with a rush in September, the Giants overcame a seven-game Pittsburgh lead and finished four games ahead of the fading Pirates. It was going to be the first Subway Series, though only for the fans as both teams played in the Polo Grounds.

The World Series of 1921 was the last in a three-year experiment with a nine-game series. Looking over the match-up, the pundits generally agreed that the Yankees had the best player, but, overall, the Giants had the better team. The pundits were right. The Series would be dominated by pitching and defense, with a lot of low-scoring games. Babe Ruth did hit a home run, but was hurt for much of the Series. His replacement, Chick Fewster, filled in adequately and hit a home run of his own, but it was not the same. The Series did not turn out to be a showcase for the Bambino, as so many fans had hoped. It did not turn out to be a showcase for the Yankees either, as the Giants won four of the last five games to win the Series, 5 games to 3.

Both New York teams won again in 1922, but the Babe had an off-year. He only played in 110 games, and his average fell from .378 to .315, and he hit only 35 home runs. His illness was popularly attributed to wild dissipation and loose living on a scale excessive even for the Babe, which only made him more popular. In the Series Ruth hit a less than robust .118, with only a single run batted in and no home runs. This was worse than it had been in 1921, and if the Babe was worse, the Yanks were worse. The Giants won the Series, 4 games to 0, with a tie caused by darkness being the best the Yankees could do.

The Yankees fully arrived in 1923, and it began with Yankee Stadium itself. Given the extraordinary celebrity of Babe Ruth, a new park for the Yankees was inevitable, but the Giants, driven by pique and jealousy, accelerated the process. In 1922, the Giants' owner, Charlie Stoneham, told Ruppert and Huston that after the current season, the Yankees would have to find another place to play. Ruppert and Huston bought ten acres in the south Bronx, then a peaceful neighborhood of homes, churches and synagogues. You could see the site for the new ballpark from the Polo Grounds. The land cost $625,000, a truly fabulous sum in those days. Construction began in May 1922, and, as the season progressed fans at the Polo Grounds could see the new park go up. Reportage about Yankee victories was punctuated with progress bulletins from the construction front. Early on, everyone understood that this would

YANKEE STADIUM IN 1923. The overwhelming impression is one of size. Colonel Ruppert had built one of the largest structures in New York, nearly twice the size of the Polo Grounds. The new Yankee Stadium was, by far, the largest baseball park in the country, and implied a new era of baseball in which the size of the crowds and the size of payrolls would be double, or more, from what they had been before the Great War.

be no ordinary park. It would be the biggest baseball stadium in the country, maybe the world, maybe the biggest since the Hippodrome in Constantinople or the Coliseum in Rome. Maybe bigger. On the morning of Opening Day, April 18, 1923, the *New York Times* commented:

> But in the busy borough of the Bronx, close to the shore of Manhattan Island, the real monument to baseball will be unveiled this afternoon — the new Yankee Stadium, erected at the cost of $2,500,000, seating some 70,000 people and comprising in its broad reaches of concrete and steel the last word in baseball arenas.[26]

Ruppert and Huston had impressed the newspaper writers, a cynical crew more accustomed to knock than to boost. The Yankee owners had also lived up to the famous advice given by Daniel Burnham about city planning and building. "Make no little plans; they have no magic to stir men's blood, and probably themselves will not be realized."[27]

The Opening Day game was treated by the press as an event, with the story on the front page above the fold. Reporters concentrated on the crowd. Hours before the gates opened, people began to arrive at the stadium. By the time the gates did open, a crowd estimated at 2,000 people milled around in the streets surrounding the new park. As people streamed into the stadium, the club lost accurate count, and the general estimate stood at 74,000, probably an exaggeration, but not by much. Regardless of the exact figure, it was by far the largest crowd to see a game in the history of baseball. Even so, Yankee Stadium was too small that day. Inside, and lucky to be there, "The greatest crowd that ever saw a baseball game sat and stood in this biggest of all baseball stadia."[28]

Outside and unable to get in were an additional 20,000 or so who were part of the event but not spectators of the game. Nor did they see the civic festivities that preceded the game. Accompanied by the Seventh Regiment Band, led by John Philip Sousa himself, a parade of notables, including the Happy Warrior, New York Governor Al Smith, and Baseball Commissioner Kenesaw Mountain Landis, marched to center field and raised the flag and the Yankees' American League pennant for 1922. Governor Smith threw the first ball to Yankee catcher, Wally Schang, and umpire Tom Connolly called, "Play ball."

This year the Yankees played the Boston Red Sox, most of whose good players were now wearing a New York uniform. The high point of the game came early. "In the third inning, with two team mates on the base lines, Babe Ruth smashed a savage home run into the right field bleachers, and that was the real baptism of the new Yankee Stadium."[29] The Yankees got four runs in the third inning, and Bob Shawkey, the senior member of the Yankees pitching staff, made the rally stand up. The Yanks won, 4 to 1. New York also won the next day. The second game always lacks the ceremony and drama of the

GOVERNOR AL SMITH, COLONEL RUPPERT AND OTHER DIGNITARIES IN YANKEE STADIUM ON OPENING DAY, 1923. Colonel Ruppert persuaded Governor Alfred E. Smith, the Happy Warrior, to attend the opening of the stadium, thus lending quasi-official dignity to the occasion. Al Smith had a genius for attending the proper events, like this one. Although all were dressed in black, this was far from a funeral, but instead a celebration of the future of baseball and of New York.

first, but about 10,000 fans showed up anyway. The *New York Times* noted "they were completely swallowed up in the depths of the big stand."[30] But 10,000 was a large crowd for an ordinary weekday game, and they saw the Yanks again defeat Boston, 8 to 2. It looked as if Ruppert and Huston, as well as the Yankees, were going to have a good year in the new stadium.

Everyone in New York hoped that the Giants and the Yankees would win again in 1923, and they both did. The Giants had won the two previous World Series, but the pre–Series betting favored the Yankees. Not until the eve of the first game, on October 10, did the odds reach even money. Pundit opinion reflected the attitude of the bettors the *New York Times* asked: "Will Ruth redeem his failure of 1922 and step forward as the outstanding star of the Yankees?"[31] The other theme of pre–Series analysis also concerned money. In a front page article the *Times* assured its readers that this Series "also promises to be the most lucrative, the biggest 'money series' that the national sport has ever seen. The total attendance and the gate receipts threaten to break all previous records."[32] In the midst of fan excitement, the *Times*, at least, kept a firm grip on the core of American culture.

The first game of the 1923 World Series, played at Yankee Stadium, drew about 58,000 fans and brought in gate receipts of $181,912, both large numbers in their time. The Giants won, 5 to 4, as Casey Stengel hit an inside-the-park home run in the top of the ninth inning. It was the eighth consecutive Series win for the Giants over the Yankees. The next game, at the Polo Grounds, saw the end of that streak, as the Yanks won, 4 to 2. Babe Ruth was the dominant player in the game, hitting two home runs, one in the fourth inning and another in the fifth. The *New York Times* provided a sober commentary that hit exactly the right note. "Perhaps it would not be too much to say that Ruth saved the series for the Yankees."[33] The Giants fought back, and won the third game, again at Yankee Stadium. Casey Stengel hit his second game-winning home run, this time in the top of the seventh, as the Giants won, 1 to 0. The gate was as satisfactory as the game was exciting. Over 62,000 fans filled the stadium, and the gate receipts topped $200,000. This was the high point for the Giants. They led the Series, two games to one, and some of the smart money began to favor them. After all, the Giants had won the two previous years.

But this was 1923. The Yanks won the next game, 8 to 4. Over 45,000 fans filled the Polo Grounds, and their number included Charlie Chaplin, who rooted for the Giants. The gate reached $181,622, the largest of the Series for the Polo Grounds. The fifth game, played at the stadium on a Sunday, drew more than 62,000 fans, and again netted more than $200,000 in gate receipts. The Yankees won this one as well, 8 to 1, and moved within one game of taking the Series. That was certainly worth notice, but the *Times* was as interested in the crowd and the money as the game. The *Times* kept up with what was changing, and that was scale. This would be a million-dollar Series.

> The marvel of it all, however, was not the crowd inside but the crowd outside.
> At times it seemed as if all New York with a little of New Jersey thrown in was trying to squeeze into the ball park. Apparently every citizen who could walk had come to see the Giants play the Yankees in the Sunday game....
> The anguish of this series for the club owners is not that the parks are too big but that they are too small.[34]

The final game, in the Polo Grounds, did not draw the same size crowd. The park was smaller and it was a weekday game. Still, 34,000 fans saw the Yankees score five runs in the eighth inning to win, 6 to 4. For the most part, those at the game were rooting for the Yankees.[35]

The Giants could have won the Series in 1923. Although they lacked Babe Ruth, the Giants were not a bad team. But in the world beyond the diamond it would have made no difference. The Series of 1923 marked the end of the old order, when the Giants had been the local favorites. The Yankees had the most exciting player in baseball and the new and stupendous stadium, and they had forever replaced the Giants as the local team. But there was more than the changing of the guard. The scale of sports, along with the scale of celebrity, had also changed in the years since the war to make the world safe for democracy, to use Woodrow Wilson's noble but fatuous pronouncement. Movies, radio, even prohibition, added to the national dimension of what went on in places like New York, Chicago, or Los Angeles. The Yankees had gone beyond being New York's team. In October, 1923, the Yankees first became, and were to remain, America's team.

9

America's Other Team

In the movie *Patton*, George C. Scott, portraying General George Patton, declared theatrically that Americans love a winner and will not tolerate a loser. *Patton* was about half right, which is pretty good for a movie made during wartime about a general in wartime. Americans do love a winner, aspire to be winners, and assume that, in limited ways at least, they will be winners themselves. It is part of the American belief in the myth of progress. Things will continue to improve, and the golden age is in the future. America is a land of civic faith and personal hope, not fashionable doubt and cynicism. Politicians, though never professors, like to proclaim that it is "morning in America," even for the underdog, and politicians, not professors, have caught the prevailing cultural attitude. Perhaps that is why they are paid more and are more highly regarded generally.

Damon Runyon, a New York journalist and short story writer, once remarked that "the race is not always to the swift nor the battle to the strong, but that is the way to bet." That advice would make perfect sense but for one thing; it is awfully hard to tell with any certainty who the swift and the strong are. Many are cast into the role of long-odds underdogs because they are bedraggled and unkempt, but bestowing slight regard on the superficialities of appearance alone can be dangerous and costly. Henry V at Agincourt, Seabiscuit in the late thirties, or the Miracle Braves in 1914 illustrate the dangers of failing to discern the identity of the really swift and genuinely strong. The story of the underdog triumphant has been told many times; a notable recent version being the *Rocky* movies, in which Rocky wins again and again against yet another, and increasingly malodorous, favorite.

Most underdogs, however, even the most charming and feisty, simply lose, often by quite substantial margins, and give wistful pangs to those deeply attached to challenging the world. There are reasons aplenty why the underdog is so far under, and upon sober reflection, these reasons usually make sense. The underdog lacks the physical skills, the grasp of the game and the experience to prevail. Baseball fans were not shy about admitting those inconvenient facts, and would often shout out the shortcomings of their favorites.

145

But they rooted for their team in bad years as well as good. As it turns out, General Patton to the contrary notwithstanding, while Americans do not happily tolerate losers, they sometimes come to love them.

Part of the reason for this cultural compartmentalization lies in the daily drama of the game and the extended drama of the season. No matter how long the odds, the most sodden and woebegone underdog had his occasional day. In 1946, the Giants finished last but split the season series with the World Champion Cardinals (they lost the season series to the rest of the league). I saw one of those victories, and for one game resignation and defeat were punctuated by a moment of hope. The struggle, the game itself, and the journey through the season also count for the fans of even the worst collection of also-rans. The result does not count alone; indeed, in terms of myth, memory and moment, defeat can be as significant as victory. In America, mythology is not immune to the charms of the lost cause.

I

When the Brooklyn Dodgers failed to win, their devoted fans would say, "Wait till next year." Next year finally came, in 1955, but it came only once. In 1958, three years after their greatest triumph, the Dodgers had moved to a place H. L. Mencken called, with characteristic understatement, "Los Angeles the Damned." But while the Dodgers were in Brooklyn, they were clearly America's other team. The Brooklyn Dodgers inspired fierce devotion in their fans, had a large national audience of those sympathetic, and embodied the connection to community that is part of the baseball myth of virtue. Now, the Brooklyn Dodgers and the New York Giants exist only in the mind of God and the memory of mankind. America's other team needs still to be playing on the field.

The demise of the franchise also rules out the St. Louis Browns, who fit a distinct niche in the ecology of losing, those who lose habitually without style or panache, and make only ineffective efforts to improve. The Browns exemplified the nineteenth-century moral and social category of the undeserving poor. Upon joining the American League in 1902 the Browns began as losers, remained losers and would always remain losers until translated into glory, which happened when they moved to Baltimore after the 1953 season, having again finished last. The Browns had won a single pennant, in 1944, and then lost the Series to the Cardinals. Losing had become a habit. But no one though much about it, since the Browns had few fans and they had the good taste to avoid the ball park. Resignation and acceptance rarely inspire affection, and few lamented their remove to Baltimore in 1953.

The Boston Red Sox represented a second type of losing, far removed from the predictable debility of the Browns. The Red Sox, to use John Milton's phrase from *Paradise Lost*, were "authors to themselves," deliberately, like Satan and Adam before them, having created their own fall.[1] In a fallen world this happens often, yet the experience remains morally and socially instructive in site of frequency.

Unlike Adam or Satan, the exact date of the Red Sox demise can be ascertained: January 3, 1920. On that date Boston sold Babe Ruth to New York, and the sale of the Babe was so monstrous and consequential that the Curse of the Bambino dates from that event. The Boston fall from glory resembled a descent into "the pit that is bottomlesse" only in the twenties, when the Sox finished in the cellar in 1922 and 1923, and from 1925 through 1930. Thereafter the Red Sox did better, rising by the end of the thirties to the first division, signing Ted Williams, and winning pennants in 1946, 1967, 1975, 1986, and 2004. The Red Sox were often good and always a part of the New England civic culture. They play in Fenway Park, with its irregular angles, green monsters and historic moments. Mike Barnicle, as Boston man of letters, has caught the "mystic chords" of Red Sox rooting. "Baseball isn't a life-and-death matter, but the Red Sox are."[2]

The Curse of the Bambino did not prevent the Red Sox from giving sustenance to hope, but it did keep the Sox from the full measure of victory against their cultural rival, the hated and envied New York Yankees. This perennial hand-to-hand struggle against America's team has stamped the Red Sox as a favorite among those who loathe the Yankees, giving the Sox a national fan base notable both for geographical extent and intense devotion. The Red Sox certainly have a potent claim to the status of America's other team, one rooted in theology as well as history. The Red Sox are a national object of love.

But the Red Sox are not the only "other team." The Chicago Cubs fit the paradigm as well. They are a connection to the beginning of the National League (1876), which antedated organized ball (1883) itself, and they are the only franchise which has never moved, dropped out for a while, or changed leagues. Like Boston, the Cubs have had a long history of success and a substantial dollop of failure. The Cubs play in "friendly confines" of Wrigley Field, built for the Chicago Whales of the Federal League (1914–15). Wrigley Field and Fenway Park are the two remaining old parks, the rest having been torn down in a continuing display of cultural vandalism. Both Wrigley and Fenway were built to a human scale with the fans close to the players and a sense of the game's past functions as a constant subliminal companion to the game on the field. The Cubs also have a national fan base, nurtured by legendary announcer Harry Caray and transmitted by cable and satellite to the known world, even as far as Los Angeles. The Cubs play in the National League, giving balance to comment about the Yankees.

Even with all rational and visible factors considered, the Cubs' rise to national mythic status remains mysterious. The Cubs have only played the

Yankees twice (1932 and 1938), and did not win a single game. In 1945, when the Cubs lost their last series, they were a regional team in a genuinely divided hometown. Over the course of more losing than winning seasons, and winning seasons that stopped short of the World Series, the Cubs became a national team and then a national icon. There is no precise moment when this happened, just as there is no precise reason. By the 1990s, perhaps a bit earlier, the Cubs had arrived. The whims and ways of fashion are unfathomable.

II

Looking back on it all, the serious observer can see that the 1929 World Series marked the beginnings of the modern Cubs. That Series, now utterly forgotten, seems to have stamped the Cubs with their apparently permanent character. A pennant leads to losing the Series; a division championship (1984, 1989, or 2003) leads to defeat in the playoffs. Mostly, of course, years of defeat led to more years of defeat. The story that the Cubs must expiate the sin of refusing to admit a goat to the 1945 World Series is silly on its face. There were plenty of fans in 1945 sufficiently indistinguishable from a goat, even on close inspection, that a real goat would have gone unnoticed. The goat story may be dismissed as merely curse envy, an attempt to imitate the Red Sox. No curse story is needed; in matters of style mystery itself explains all.

The World Series of 1929, which the Cubs lost to the Philadelphia Athletics, was marked by spectacular and improbable Philadelphia comeback wins. The Cubs did not have a bad team, far from it. Chicago manager Joe McCarthy, who would later lead the mighty Yankees to eight pennants, had put together a strong squad for the 1929 campaign. The Cubs had a terrific outfield with Hack Wilson, Kiki Cuyler and Riggs Stephenson, whose lifetime batting average of .336 is the highest of any player *not* in the Hall of Fame and is higher than the averages of most of the players who are. All were exceptional players, and Wilson combined ability with an unquenchable thirst. In 1929 he hit .345 with 39 homers, and drove in 159 runs. That was in daylight. He really came alive after dark. Hack was a two-fisted drinker, and if he had had a couple of extra fists he would have used them too. But, drunk as he got, Hack Wilson always made it to the game and played well. He later claimed: "I've never played drunk; hung over, yes, but never drunk."[3] Probably more or less true, but it is equally true that he played hung over every day. After having been traded to Brooklyn in 1932, Wilson was standing in center field sweating alcoholic rivulets in the sun when Dodgers manager Max Carey went out to get the always ineffective Walter Boom-Boom Beck. Boom-Boom, enraged at being lifted, threw the ball against the sheet metal wall in center field. The ball made a deep hollow boom and bounced back toward Wilson. The nearly comatose Hack reacted instantly. He ran the ball down and made a perfect throw to second base. Hack always knew how to play the game.

In the infield the Cubs were almost as good. Jolly Cholly Grimm played first base, Rogers Hornsby, who hit .380 and did not lead the league (Lefty O'Doul hit .398) was at second, Woody English was a competent shortstop, and journeyman Norm McMillan played third. The pitching was exceptional. Pat Malone won twenty-two games, Charley Root won nineteen, Guy Bush won eighteen, and Sheriff Blake won fourteen. The Cubs won ninety-eight games and finished ten and a half ahead of the Pirates. After regaining first place the third week of July, the Cubs remained in first for the rest of the season, gradually widening their lead over Pittsburgh. They were a good team with a good manager. Should do fine in the Series.

The American League champion, the Philadelphia Athletics, won the pennant by 18 games over the New York Yankees, who still led the American League with 142 home runs. Even Tom Zachary, who won 12 games and lost none at all, could not lift the mighty Yankees to the pennant. The Athletics had everything, terrific hitting and even better pitching. By the third week in May they were in first place, and remained there until the end. It had taken Connie Mack fifteen years to rebuild after the World Series loss in 1914, but at last he had fine team.

The first three games of the World Series were ordinary. The Cubs lost both games at home, but then won in Philadelphia when Guy Bush, giving up nine hits and pitching out of trouble, held the Athletics to a single run and came out on top, 3 to 1. The Athletics later said that they had stolen the Chicago signs, and knew what Bush would throw. But the Mississippi Mudcat had his best stuff and won anyway. The Cubs were behind two games to one. That had happened before.

This time everything but the eventual outcome was different. In Game 4 the Cubs jumped out to a big lead, and by the home half of the seventh inning were leading, 8 to 0. Charley Root was pitching well, and the Athletics had only nine outs left. But those are hard outs to get. Al Simmons led off the Philadelphia seventh inning with a home run. Then Jimmie Foxx singled to right field and Hack Wilson lost Bing Miller's Texas leaguer in the sun. Jimmie Dykes hit a sharp grounder back to Root who deflected the ball enough so that Foxx scored and Dykes and Miller were both safe. Joe Boley, the Athletics shortstop, singled to center scoring Bing Miller. George Burns, pinch-hitting for pitcher Eddie Rommel, popped out, but leadoff hitter, second baseman Max Bishop singled to right scoring Jimmie Dykes. At this point, with four runs in, Joe McCarthy took Root out and brought in left-hander Art Nehf. Mule Haas hit a high fly to center field which Hack Wilson lost in the sun for an inside park home run scoring Bishop and Boley ahead of him. The score was now 8 to 7. Nehf walked Mickey Cochrane and Sheriff Blake replaced him for Chicago. Al Simmons got a hit on a grounder that bounced over McMillan at third. Jimmie Foxx singled, driving in Cochrane with the tying run. Blake was finished and Pat Malone came in. Malone promptly hit Bing Miller with his first pitch and then gave up a double to Jimmie Dykes, scoring Simmons and Foxx. Boley and Burns struck out, but the Athletics had scored ten runs in the seventh inning and won the game, 10 to 8.[4]

The *Spalding Official Base Ball Guide* reported that this was "an inning unlike any that had ever been witnessed in a world series."[5] It sure was. Ten was a lot of runs. The Athletics got more runs in one inning than the Boston Red Sox scored in winning a six-game Series from the Cubs in 1918. Boston had nine. The Cubs had had ten in a losing effort. The mighty Murderers Row of the 1927 Yankees scored only twenty runs in their Series victory over the Pirates.

These things happen in baseball and you can come back and get them tomorrow. At least, that's the way you must think if you're in baseball. And that's what the Chicago players did think, for they came back the next day with unimpaired determination. Things began well. Chicago pitcher Pat Malone had his good stuff. The Cubs scored two runs in the top of the fourth and knocked Howard Ehmke, the Philadelphia pitcher, out of the box. Those two runs stood up until the last of the ninth. With one out Max Bishop singled, and on the first pitch from Malone, Mule Haas hit a two-run homer to tie the game. Malone got Mickey Cochrane, but Al Simmons doubled. Jimmie Foxx drew an intentional walk. Malone went to work on Bing Miller. He got two strikes on the Philadelphia right fielder, but Malone made the next pitch too fat and Miller doubled to right, driving Simmons with the winning run in the 1929 World Series.[6]

For the second game in a row the Philadelphia Athletics had come back from substantial deficit to defeat the Cubs. The first hill to climb, in the fourth game, was one of eight runs, and required the biggest inning in Series history. The second deficit was a question of time, the last of the ninth inning. Philadelphia, which only had to score three runs, was down to its last strike, which is as close as you can cut it. But the Athletics were up to the challenge, and Bing Miller got the winning hit. The Cubs had a genuine chance to win both games and lead the Series, but disaster, of a kind familiar in baseball but on a wholly different scale, overtook the Cubs.

President Herbert Hoover and his wife were at the game, and after the Athletics won in such dramatic fashion, the crowd stood and waited for the president and his party to leave. This was an appropriate gesture of respect for the office. It was also an indication of respect and affection for the man. The fifth game was on October 14, 1929. The Wall Street crash was still a fortnight in the future. No one knew and few suspected what was coming. Most were convinced, as was the national chief engineer himself, that the prosperity of the twenties would roll on and on, if not forever then almost. Conditions were fundamentally sound, as optimists at the time were fond of saying. It was often a self-interested comment, but it was also a cry from the American heart. America is not a land that usually favors the tragic view of life.

No one could be expected to understand that the spectacular loss in the 1929 World Series was the first discernible indication of the "Cubs Factor" as Mike Royko called it. But things kept happening. Individually they might be entirely random, but collectively, well... In the 1932 World Series Babe Ruth hit his called homer off Charlie Root. That had never been seen before and nothing like it has happened since. The Cubs lost in 1935 to the Detroit Tigers, the only team they had ever defeated in a Series. In 1938 the Yanks again took four straight games from the Cubs. The last wartime Series, in 1945, went to the Tigers, who again beat the Cubs.

During those years when the Cubs didn't win the National League pennant they were a factor in the race. And other teams were also losing in the World Series, especially in the National League, which won only seven Series (five by the Cardinals, one each by the Giants and Reds) in the quarter century from 1927 to 1954. The Cubs seemed to be like the rest of the better National League Clubs. And perhaps they were.

After losing the Series in 1945 to Detroit, the Cubs sank rapidly into the lower depths of the National League. In 1947, the Cubs finished in sixth place, and for the next nineteen years they were never out of the second division, a Major League record for ineptitude. In 1962, the Cubs finished ninth, behind the expansion entry from Houston. That year was certainly the worst. The team lost 103 games and finished 42½ games out of first place. Chicago attendance fell to a bit over 600,000, the lowest since the war, and the Cubs only drew about 8,000 fans a game.[7] Wrigley Field was empty, the Cubs were terrible, no one had any hope, and the ridicule heaped upon all Cubs players except Ernie Banks lacked the core of love that informed Brooklyn plaint. Those were the years in the desert, a multigenerational (by baseball standards) failure. No one then thought of the Cubs as having a special aura of any sort. They just stunk.

The worst years were the early 1960s. The Cubs not only finished ninth, next to last, in 1962, they finished seventh, also next to the cellar in 1960 and 1961. In 1963 the Cubs rallied to win more games than they lost, a record of eighty-two and eighty, but they still finished seventh, and in 1964 the Cubs resumed an accustomed ineptitude and sank to eighth, which they repeated in 1965 before finishing tenth, firmly in the cellar, in 1966. This was really terrible baseball, reminiscent of the Browns and the Phillies, though probably not as bad as the Red Sox in the twenties or the Athletics after 1915. Still, Cubs fans booed the team and gave way to cynicism, gallows humor and existential despair. In the arid years the Cubs inspired more contempt than love. But historically, time in the desert, though long and difficult, has led to good results.

It is not altogether clear why the Cubs performed quite as badly as they did. They had some good players. Ernie Banks, the best shortstop in the National League, played for the Cubs through all the worst years. Lou Brock played in the Chicago outfield in 1962 and 1963, and Billy Williams was a Cubs outfielder from 1959 through 1974. All three went to the Hall of Fame. Ron Santo played third base for Chicago during the worst years, and he was a perennial member of the All-Star squads. Dick Ellsworth won twenty-two games for the Cubs in 1963, the first left-hander to win twenty games since Hippo Vaughn in 1919. The Cubs had some superb players, but they seemed to specialize in doing less with the available talent than any team in the league, and comment at the time indicated that the fans noticed. They certainly noticed the June 15, 1964, trade of Lou Brock to the Cardinals for Ernie Broglio, one of the poorer deals in baseball history. Taking it all and all, the fans could only conclude that the Cubs were badly managed, both in the front office and on the field.

Then, quite suddenly and entirely surprisingly, the Cubs got much better. In 1967, Leo Durocher brought the Cubs home in third place (eighty-seven and seventy-one), although he had more or less the same team he had managed to tenth place the year before. Some changes had been made, notably the acquisition of Hall of Fame pitcher Ferguson Jenkins from the equally mismanaged Phillies. In his first full season with the Cubs Jenkins won twenty games, and that helped. Showing this was no fluke, the Cubs came in third again in 1968 (eighty-four and seventy-eight), and Ferguson Jenkins again won twenty games. This was the real thing. Cubs fans began to cherish wild and outrageous hopes. Perhaps next year...

The Cubs opened the 1969 season on April 8 at home against the Philadelphia Phillies. Opening Day is always a time for celebration, and the Cubs sent the fans home happy with a 7 to 6 win in eleven innings. Having started the season in first place, the Cubs stayed there. Posting a winning record for every month from April through August, the Cubs held a five-game lead over their unlikely challengers, the New York Mets, on September 2. The season had one month to go.

April is the cruelest month, T. S. Eliot assures us in "The Waste Land," but in reality, it is September. Pennants are lost and won in September, and in 1969 it was the Cubs' time to sing a sad September song. On September 3, the Cubs lost to Cincinnati, 2 to 0, and followed this by three home losses to Pittsburgh, before heading to New York to lose two more to the charging Mets. The Chicago lead had dropped to half a game. The next day, September 10, the Cubs lost to the Phillies and fell out of first place as Chicago lost eleven of twelve. At the same time, the Amazing Mets won ten straight games. The Cubs dropped four and a half games behind the Mets on September 15, and finished eight behind, in second place, on October 2. In September, the Cubs had won eight and lost seventeen, a flashback to the way it had been in 1966 or 1962. The season had not been a total loss; the Cubs won ninety-two games, the most since 1945, had drawn 1,674,993 fans into Wrigley Field, the most ever.[8]

But the season left a sour aftertaste among the Cubs' faithful, and for the more thoughtful, including columnist Mike Royko, it hinted at a problem beyond this team and this year. The Cubs were not always going to finish at the bottom of the league, but the desired prize would always elude them. Good teams would finish second instead of first; better teams would lose in postseason play. Royko called it the Cubs Factor. Any team with more than three ex–Cubs could not win the World Series, and most could not even get that far. There was something about the Cubs that included the players as well as the team. The exact nature of the Cubs Factor remains elusive; its reality has become increasingly obvious. None of this surprises anyone. Baseball contains more than its share of cultural mythic truth.

III

The Cubs' embodiment of the tragic nature of life shows most clearly in the league playoffs. In these years the Cubs have shaken free from the lethargy of losing and finally won something. They have advanced to postseason play, with every game on national television and every player potentially a hero. This first occurred in 1984, the year chosen by George Orwell for the triumph of fascism, and thirty-nine years since the Cubs had last been in the center ring. Chicago won the East Division with a record of ninety-six and sixty-five, finishing six and a half games ahead of preseason favorites New York Mets. The Cubs surprised nearly everyone in 1984, having finished in fifth place the year before, twenty games under .500 and nineteen behind the division champion Phillies. All in all, that had been a typical Cubs year.

For the 1984 campaign the Cubs management revamped their team. They got a new first baseman, Leon "Bull" Durham, and two new outfielders, Gary Matthews and Bob Dernier, both coming over from Philadelphia. The biggest improvement came in pitching. Rick Sutcliffe came from Cleveland on June 13 for four players, and won sixteen games with only a single loss for the Cubs. Acquiring Scott Sanderson from Montreal helped as well, as did the midseason (March 30) trade of Dennis Eckersley from the Boston Red Sox for Bill Buckner. Retaining only Steve Trout and Dick Ruthven, the Cubs remade their starting rotation. Pitching is, as Yogi Berra has remarked, 90 percent of the game.

Having won the division title, the Cubs faced another newcomer to postseason and also a surprise winner, the San Diego Padres. The Padres had finished third in 1983, but with a new outfield, Graig Nettles at third base and Goose Gossage in relief of an undistinguished pitching staff, Dick

Williams bought them home twelve games ahead of Atlanta. It was hard to pick a favorite between the two unexpected winners, but the sentimental choice, outside of southern California, was the Cubs, whose long-suffering fans deserved to cheer at last.

The 1984 League Championship Series began on October 2, a beautiful, clear Chicago afternoon. In spite of the audience needs of television, the game was played during daytime. There were already dark and muttered threats from callow television executives that should the Cubs keep winning, Wrigley Field must get lights or the networks could not cover the game. But on this day television covered the game as it ought to be played, in daylight and on grass.

The Cubs sent Rick Sutcliffe against Eric Show, as both managers started their best. Sutcliffe was at his best, but Show had his troubles, and San Diego relief pitcher Greg Harris was even worse. The Cubs scored twice in the first inning and three more in the third. In the fifth inning Harris gave up six runs, along with two more in the sixth. The Cubs hit five home runs, one by Sutcliffe himself, to support Sutcliffe who pitched a six-hit shutout. Chicago won, 13 to 0, in their first postseason game since October 10, 1945, when the Cubs had lost. It was also the most decisive victory in playoff history.

Chicago followed this by winning the next game as well, though it was a much tighter contest. This time there were no home runs, but the Cubs again jumped out to the early lead. Chicago scored a run in the first inning and two more in the third off Mark Thurmond. Steve Trout gave up a run in the fourth innings and another in the sixth, but he only allowed five hits before giving way to Lee Smith with one out in the ninth inning. The Padres' relief pitching was much better than it had been the day before, with Andy Hawkins, coming in the game in the fourth inning, followed by Dave Dravecky and Craig Lefferts, none of whom allowed a run. The Cubs held on, and won the game, 4 to 2. It was the final game in Chicago, and the Cubs took a two-game lead into San Diego. One more victory and the Cubs would be in the Series for the first time since 1945.

But for the Cubs, so close to the pennant, so dominant at home, winning at San Diego would be a difficult task. With their backs to the wall, the Padres sent Ed Whitson to the mound. He had a record of fourteen and eight in 1984, his best in eight years in the Show, along with a quite respectable 3.24 ERA. Chicago countered with Dennis Eckersley, who had also won fourteen games. The smart money tended slightly to favor the Padres, mostly on the basis of home field advantage. The Cubs scored a run in the second inning, and Eckersley made that hold up until the fifth, when Garry Templeton, the Padres shortstop, doubled in two runs to give San Diego its first lead in the series. Kevin McReynolds hit a three-run homer off Eckersley in the sixth inning, and Whitson kept the Cubs from scoring. San Diego won, 7 to 1, and kept hope alive.

The next game, on October 6, saw both teams use the back of their starting rotations. Chicago started Scott Sanderson, who had won eight and lost five, but had a good ERA at 3.14. The Padres went with Tim Lollar, who won eleven and lost thirteen, and had an ERA of 3.91. Both pitchers were unexpectedly strong. San Diego got two runs in the bottom of the third inning, but the Cubs came back with three in the top of the fourth to take the lead. San Diego tied the game with a run in the bottom of the fifth, and both teams turned the game over to the bullpen. The Padres got two runs off Tim Stoddard in the bottom of the seventh, but the Cubs tied the score off Goose Gossage with two in the top of the eighth. The Cubs put their ace relief pitcher, Lee Smith, who had saved thirty-three games in 1984. Surely Smith could hold the Padres down. In the bottom of the ninth, with one out and one man on, Steve Garvey hit a home run to win the game, 7 to 5, and tie the series at two games apiece. The Padres had come back from the brink of elimination to become the team with the momentum.

For the final game of the league championship series, both teams went back to their opening game pitchers, Rick Sutcliffe for Chicago and Eric Show for San Diego. Show was again ineffective, giving up a first inning two-run homer to Bull Durham, the Cubs' first baseman, and a second inning solo home run to catcher Jody Davis. Show didn't last through the second inning and the Cubs had a three-run lead. Sutcliffe rolled along, pitching five scoreless innings before running into trouble. The Padres scored twice in the sixth, to close the gap to one run. In the seventh, Bull Durham's error allowed the tying run to score, and three consecutive singles drove in three more runs. The Padres led, 6 to 3, and their bullpen had held the Cubs scoreless since the second inning. Goose Gossage pitched the last two innings and set the Cubs down. San Diego won the game, 6 to 3, and the series three games to two. The Cubs, like the 1960 Yankees, had a better team earned ran average, had gotten more hits, had hit more home runs, had scored more runs and had lost more games. For the Yankees in 1960, this had been a statistical oddity; for the Cubs this might be understood as the inexorable workings of fate.

The full impact of the Cubs' defeat in 1984 did not emerge in 1989, though Chicago lost in the playoffs to the San Francisco Giants, four games to one, but only two decades later. In the 2003 league championship series (second round) against the Florida Marlins, the Cubs, having defeated Atlanta in the preliminary round, had another chance to win the National League pennant. On October 14, the Cubs, leading the series, three games to two, were playing at Wrigley Field, needing just one more victory, as in 1984, to go to the World Series. The Cubs, behind their ace, Mark Prior, had a 3 to 0 lead in the eighth inning of Game 6, with five outs to go. Frequently, five is a lot of outs, and it was in this game as well. The Marlins rallied, and a pop fly foul ball drifted down the left field line. Moises Alou, the Cubs' left fielder, came over to the stands, hoping to lean into the first row and snag the ball.

He reached in, but other hands above his also reached for the ball. Luckless fan Steve Bartman tried to catch the foul ball and deflected it back into the stands. Alou might have had a play, but once a fan had touched it, the ball was out of play. Bartman's effort to grab a foul ball drew instant denunciation from Alou and the fans, and security police had to extricate him from the outraged mob. The Cubs, of course, promptly fell apart, losing Game 6, 8 to 3 and Game 7, 9 to 6.

Cubs fans were not surprised at the Chicago collapse, though they were certainly not happy about it. They blamed Bartman rather than the team, since defeat involved more than the game itself. Bartman, an ardent Cubs fan, issued a statement.

> Had I thought for one second that the ball was playable or had I seen Alou approaching, I would have done whatever I could to get out of the way and give Alou a chance to make the catch.
> I am so truly sorry from the bottom of this Cubs fan's broken heart.[9]

No one doubted the truth of the statement, but no one cared either. Bartman was about to discover the anguish of his fifteen minutes of fame. He became the story of the Cubs' latest disaster, and a popular culture villain. Associated Press writer Nancy Armour described the process precisely: "In a society where placing the blame is a constant game, Bartman was a very convenient target."[10] The frustration of a century, or at least sixty years, was heaped upon him. Entrepreneurs of the bottom feeding variety produced Bartman trading cards and T-shirts. He became the butt of jokes on late-night television, to say nothing of the Chicago bars. A Bartman costume became popular for Halloween. Fame may not have ruined his life, though it yet may, but the days and months since October 14 have certainty had a large component of nightmare. Unwittingly, and clearly with no desire or effort to make this happen, Steve Bartman had committed *ate*, enormous folly, which can only be followed by *nemesis* for the hero and *katharsis*, fear and pity, for the entire culture. Like Orestes before him, though he may be discharged by the gods, he will remain a tragic exemplum for a tragic team.

Bartman himself has shunned publicity, shrunk from notoriety, and made no attempt to profit from his perfectly reasonable and legitimate effort to catch a foul ball. And, perhaps, things will slowly return to normal. Bartman will gradually fade into deserved and desired obscurity, becoming an increasingly arcane sporting allusion, and the Cubs will return to losing in the old way, decisively rather than barely. It seems likely, however, that the Cubs must lose dramatically again for Bartman to escape popular culture. There must be a new Bartman to replace the old, a new scapegoat to explain the loving combined with losing that describes the tragic way of the Cubs.

IV

Andy Warhol once remarked that in the future everyone would be famous for fifteen minutes. This is less a comment on the fleeting nature of fame — where are they now — than it is on the insatiable need of American electronic media for new celebrities and for something new to be fashionable, but not for long. America suffers from cultural neophilia, a love for the new, which means novelty alone suffices for celebrity. This includes eating worms and bugs on reality television shows, or running into poles or falling off houses as home video shows demonstrate, or standing on stage with a paper bag over your head before being yanked off with a big hook. All were (or are) successful staples of television, which indicates that the professional entertainers are too few, too familiar and too similar to fill the culture's need for novelty. Even with the constant help of sports, commentary, "reality shows," games, commercials, news, replays and reruns, soaps and movies, television finds it a continuing challenge just to fill the air.

While fame, fashion or glam do not get around to absolutely everything and everyone (yet), they do cut a substantial swath through American institutions, places and personalities. Winners in every conceivable venue of life, including poker, qualify for at least a modest recognition, but there are not enough winners, so the frantic search for the new and perhaps interesting includes also-rans who seem quirky, edgy, available, unlucky, beautiful or historical. Combining all these qualities, pre- as well as post–Bartman, the Chicago Cubs have succeeded in becoming fashionable as well as lovable, not just at home but throughout the nation. Sometimes dubbed as "lovable losers," particularly by White Sox fans (and these exist; I've met some) who don't understand it at all, the Cubs have been transformed by popular culture from bums who lose into good guys for whom losing doesn't matter. Joining the Red Sox as the antithesis of the Yankees, the Cubs have entered that narrow niche of myth where there is no need to be a hero. Like the Mets of the early 1960s, the Cubs are loved for themselves, not the result of their activities.

The visible continuing element in the Cubs' popularity and glam is Wrigley Field. The Cubs acquired Wrigley Field after the Federal League had collapsed following the 1915 season. Standing at Addison, Waveland and Clark, Wrigley Field firmly established the Cubs as Chicago's north-side team, and north was the more fashionable side of town. For a couple of decades Wrigley Field was a workaday ball park, as was Comiskey to the south, Forbes Field in Pittsburgh, Ebbets Field in Brooklyn or Crosley Field in Cincinnati. Between the wars beautiful ball parks were commonplace, and few thought of them as endangered national treasures.

Wrigley Field did not acquire its distinctive ivy until the late thirties, when Bill Veeck planted it along the outfield wall. The ivy was an immensely

successful effort at improving the park, but the lack of lights, also an improvement, was an accident. Phil Wrigley had acquired light standards in 1941, but
the war intervened and he donated them to the war effort. As night baseball
came to dominate the schedule by the sixties, Wrigley Field became the lone
holdout against the increasingly strident demands of television. That only
added to its charm. The Cubs also held out against the monstrosity of artificial
turf, made necessary by domed stadia and convenient in places that housed
both baseball and football. The Cubs continued to play on grass and in daylight, giving fans an increasingly rare connection with the history of the game
and the experience of how baseball once had been. "This is not your father's
car," automobile ads bellowed to hippies turned yuppies in the 1980s, but
baseball in Wrigley was your father's and grandfather's game.

Wrigley Field's greatest asset was its increasing rarity as one of the few
old-time baseball parks that had been built to a human scale. Both teams that
moved, like the Braves or the Dodgers, and teams that stayed, like the Cardinals, the Pirates or the Reds built large new stadia, in each case places of
aesthetic sterility. But the Cubs played on in Wrigley, and the Red Sox did
the same in Fenway, and they are now the only teams to play in the old parks.
Louts and boosters continue to demand that Boston and Chicago require
gaudy new stadia — those like O'Malley are among us always— but the Cubs
and the Red Sox manage to make do with the best places to play in all of baseball.

The Cubs did put lights in Wrigley Field in the eighties, after television
moguls said they would not carry World Series day games from Wrigley,
should there ever be any. That did not destroy the park's ambience. The night
games quickly acquired a charm of their own, becoming a chic Chicago social
event that always filled the park.

Filling the park at Wrigley meant more than selling seats inside; it meant
filling the rooftop and upper-story window seats across the streets from
bleachers. Homeowners built elaborate stands, some with three stories and
complete with roof grilling area, overlooking Wrigley. A full house meant
filling these seats as well, which the Cubs always did for night and weekend
games. Advertisers took advantage of the Wrigley exposure. For years, the sign
along a house beyond right field held the simple message TORCO, which is
a company rather than a person or product. Beyond left field was a sign for
Budweiser, the beer that sponsored the electronic Cubs. Greater Wrigley Field
offered an experience unavailable anywhere else, and an opportunity for fashionable entertainment that Hollywood or Vegas could not match. Wrigley
Field stands as a remnant of baseball more than half a century before, played
in smaller parks set on a city block in a residential neighborhoods, surrounded
by houses not parking lots, served by public transportation and played in
daylight. Wrigley is both a functioning antique and the myth of *The Natural*
made manifest.

Having preserved Wrigley Field, whether from wisdom or inertia, the Cubs added a second element to their popularity. Fabled announcer Harry Caray, after a career announcing for the Cardinals, joined the Cubs' broadcast booth. Caray began announcing in the forties, and he belonged to the second generation of the "maestros of the microphone." As was then the custom, he developed an individual combination of baseball knowledge and personal enthusiasm, which was designed to enhance games that all knew about but few could ever see. In those days, broadcasters described home games on site, but were in a studio for away games re-creating the action coming in over a ticker tape. Either way, broadcasting required verve and imagination as well as a grasp of the game. Ronald Reagan and Red Barber developed these skills, and so did Harry Caray.

As the Cubs announcer, Caray created the tag lines so essential to electronic success. He described himself as a "Cubs Fan and a Bud Man," bringing together baseball and beer into a happy combination that symbolized middle America. His exclamation "Holy Cow" appeared on a T-shirt, one of the ultimate indicators of success in modern America. His happy comment "Cubs win! Cubs win!" was imitated by other announcers celebrating other teams. He established the custom of singing Van Tilzer's ditty, "Take Me Out to the Ball Game" during the seventh inning stretch, and that has become emblematic of Cubs baseball. The announcers added something to the game, and an afternoon spent with Caray and his "color" man, for many years former pitcher Steve Stone, was time well invested. The Cubs might not have won as often as the fans or the announcers wished, but Caray and Stone always gave an upbeat and cheerful account of the game. They gave the distinct impression that baseball was more exciting and more fun at Wrigley than it was anywhere else.

It was also baseball that fans everywhere in the country could share. The Cubs were favorably situated electronically to acquire a national audience since the station which televises the Cubs was (and is) a mainstay on satellite and cable packages. Wrigley Field and the Cubs became as well known as local teams, and fans in distant parts could see the Cubs. Caray and Stone developed a national following, as Red Barber and Mel Allen had done in New York fifty years earlier, and Cubs hats and shirts displayed a translocal loyalty that could be seen everywhere. The Cubs continued to lose, and everyone saw them do it, but with the Cubs, as with the Red Sox, love conquered disappointment. And the fan base grew steadily larger.

Cultural resonance is the Holy Grail of American showbiz, and entertainment executives strive ceaselessly to attain it. Economic success is a byproduct of cultural approval rather than its cause, so the secret of cultural connection lies in the soul rather than the purse. Since the mix of cultural elements necessary for success requires judgment rather than measurement and resists being quantified, attaining and retaining cultural approval is an artistic pursuit. Putting together the elements of the Cubs' cultural approval, whatever these might have been, and whether by design or accident, was a work of art by the Chicago management. Maintaining the Cubs as a national favorite will be an even harder artistic task, demanding even more subtle judgment. Times change and preferences change with them. Once the Cubs were just another terrible team, and this could well happen again. But for now, the Cubs have transcended the characteristic American emphasis on result, and have entered the realm of myth as America's other team.

IV

Time and Memory

10

The Bambino

Harry Hooper, a Hall of Fame outfielder who was Babe Ruth's teammate on the Boston Red Sox for six years (1914–19), watched the whole saga, and tried to sum it up.

> You know, I saw it all happen, from beginning to end. But sometimes I still can't believe what I saw: this nineteen year old kid, crude, poorly educated, only lightly brushed by the social veneer we call civilization, gradually trans- formed into the idol of American youth and the symbol of baseball the world over — a man loved by more people and with intensity of feeling that perhaps has never been equaled before or since. I saw a man transformed from a human being into something pretty close to a god.[1]

Hooper was a sophisticated man, but he could only begin to describe the phenomenon of Babe Ruth. Hooper was also a mighty good player, one of the best of his era, but he had never seen anything like the Babe. And neither had anyone else, not then or now. Babe Ruth simply transcended conventional description and became an Aristotelian category of one.

I

The year 1919 was difficult in America. The Spanish flu infected millions of Americans; there were strikes, anarchist bombings, and labor unrest; the cost of living was twice what it had been in 1913; the country suffered from a Red Scare; and the horrors of Prohibition approached. Into this mix of social trauma, economic downturn, and personal anxiety, the boys began to come home. They didn't seem to be the same kids who had left, won the War To End All Wars and made the world safe for democracy. The sense of unease was caught in a popular song of 1919, which asked: "How Ya Gonna Keep 'Em Down on the Farm? / After They've Seen Pa-ree." The song was a hit, selling a lot of sheet music and becoming a staple of night club requests. In New York, the home of Tin Pan Alley, the song was funny and topical; in the small towns of rural America it provoked anxiety and anger. All too often, the returning veteran did return to the city rather than home. Disease, high prices, no jobs, and mothers, sisters and wives greeting young men who seemed suspiciously worldly and acquainted with sin — was this the world for which men had bled and died?

Theater confirmed the musical straw in the wind. In 1923, as the Yankees opened the Stadium, *Abie's Irish Rose* was well into its run at the Republic Theatre, and when the Yankees gladdened the heart of most of New York by winning the Series, *Abie's Irish Rose* still had an audience. A heart-warming comedy on the surface, the play was also about marrying outside the tribe. Before the Great War, that had been a rather rare occurrence, always provoking disapproval among family and tribal elders and not infrequently leading to (often temporary, until the arrival of grandchildren) the young couple being disowned. After the war, disapproval continued, but the practice increased, particularly among the well educated, whose greater chances provided wider choices. In America, the young are ever a problem.

Babe Ruth became part of the postwar world during the 1919 season, when he was still playing in the relative obscurity of Boston. Early in the season the Boston manager, Ed Barrow, moved the Babe from the mound to right field, where he hit .322. More important, Ruth had twenty-nine home runs, then the Major League season record. Babe Ruth was something new in the game, a home run hitter on scale not seen before or (by most), even imagined. The public took to it immediately, on a scale that allowed the Boston owner to sell the Babe to New York before the 1920 season for a sum of money never before heard of in baseball or even imagined by most.

A substantial part of the Ruthian phenomenon lay outside the Babe himself, in changes in American public attitudes over the war years. Babe Ruth had been born in prewar America, which combined the social reforms of the Progressive era with a public culture of patriotism, religion, optimism and community. Before the Great War this duality of political reform within a cultural context of traditional values had been taken for granted, and Americans felt they lived in a land of "balance and harmony ... the old values of neighborliness and love of country, cooperation and hard work, decorum and discretion, peace and serenity."[2]

The war, somehow, seemed to have swept all that away. The tranquility and prosperity of prewar America gave way to the disquieting sense that the country had fundamentally changed. In an effort to recover the increasingly idealized past Americans voted overwhelmingly for Warren Harding in 1920, but he was as helpless as his constituents to stop the world. The Jazz Age had dawned; a time of automobiles, movies, radio, flappers, speakeasies, bootleggers; of hard, high, fast living, of rising hemlines, of a taste for the new, the exotic, the dangerous. "So we beat on, boats against the current, borne back ceaselessly into the past."[3] The ending of Fitzgerald's *The Great Gatsby* is a celebrated definition of displacement. But time's current also drifts forward while we grope toward receding familiarity. America had moved to join the Babe, his values, his attitudes, his lifestyle of booze and women, his home runs, while prewar baseball (like prewar America) appeared slowly but inexorably just to evaporate.

By 1920, America had become essentially urban, industrial and big, but the existential transition had barely begun. The new urban and immigrant America did not replace the old rural society and economy; the two coexisted uneasily. But the excitement, the novelty, the sheer glamour, epitomized by movies, music, the Babe, and the city bought increased cultural resonance to the Jazz Age, and the world cherished by William Jennings Bryan, although very much alive and persistent, seemed to be fading from view. In prewar America, the Babe had been, much like Ty Cobb, something of a wild man and an outlaw; in the Roaring Twenties and beyond he become an ideal held up to American kids. Babe Ruth became for boys something like Rudolph Valentino became for young girls—the idea of life and love. Unbidden, unexpected, by most Americans unwanted, a new cultural era grew gradually more distinct and enticing after 1919. The change in cultural attitudes did not make the Bambino into a great ball player; it made him into an icon.

II

In the America that entered the Great War, Protestant rural counties and small towns governed the country as they always had, and the middle border dominated the majority Republican Party, as it had since Lincoln. The cultural and political attitudes of Booth Tarkington's small town America came to the public square from the family of course, but also from social institutions that stood with the family. Dominating them all was the church, with its revivals, its temperance leagues, its schools and sermons and publications and its role in every person's identity. The church was not alone in the great work of moral instruction. The common schools, many of one room, all utilizing the McGuffey readers, tried their best to teach morality and patriotism, as well as literacy, to the young. Periodically, small towns would be visited by the Chautauqua troop, combining entertainment with culture, instruction and moral precept, at once both a school and a revival.

All taught the same virtues of patriotism and good citizenship, which seemed the appropriate American public attitudes and conduct. If Athens was the school of Hellas, as Pericles proclaimed in his funeral oration, then the family, churches, common schools, the lodge, and the Chautauqua combined to form the school of small town America.[4] It was deemed by those who remembered it, and in 1920 almost everyone did, to have been a good school in a good America.

The schools of America taught moral and religious lessons without any hint of ambiguity. No doubt as to the correctness of doctrine or discipline crept into church teachings, and modernism, whether pastoral (Roman Catholicism) or scientific (Protestant) was found only in the major cities. Equal certitude prevailed in civic lessons and in American history, usually taught in the ecclesiastical fashion by using parables and stories that taught moral lessons. America was the greatest country in the history of the world, Americans were uniquely good, God loved America and had a special divine mission for this most faithful people. Skepticism, "critical thinking," and dissent provoked immediate corporal punishment along with threats of later divine retribution. Rowdiness, a disinclination to learn and playing hooky were tolerable, but a rejection of theological Americanism meant a rejection of the community of one's fathers.

What was taught in church, school or lodge reflected what was taught at home. Society and family reinforced with other with simple lessons of piety, patriotism and morality. General social agreement meant that church and local government cooperated and overlapped. The message was the same wherever one turned. As Sinclair Lewis noticed, the small towns enforced an orthodoxy composed of a firm belief in God and Church, along with

> true patriotism, integrity, honesty, industry, temperance, courage, politeness and all the other moral and intellectual virtues ... which are at the foundation of character.[5]

This seemed good for both individual and community.[6] It was absolutely essential for the common schools, the community institution that was supported by public funds and public faith.

The public school system itself was decentralized to the local level, where the local school board ran it parsimoniously and guarded its independence and their authority fiercely. But if the schools all had different political masters, they also had about the same curriculum. What was nationalized about the American common school was not the system but the studies. This was largely the result of book publishing companies, most particularly Van Antwerp, Bragg and its successor after 1890, the American Book Company. This outfit owned the McGuffey readers, and by the time of the Great War they had sold over 100 million of them. Virtually no one in prewar America, and this included the young George Herman Ruth, was totally unfamiliar with the McGuffey readers, spellers, and speakers. In the days before Normal Schools, the NEA, federal legislation, accreditation and political correctness, they formed the unifying core of American public education.[7] The McGuffey readers contained the socially approved view of things, extolling freedom and giving a Christian religious gloss to their stories and lessons. A civic and moral life without God was inconceivable.[8]

Since the McGuffey readers emphasized the spectrum of values and attitudes Americans thought were important, these could be imparted by rote learning, by precept, by parable, and by paddle, all administered without psychobabble and with parental and cultural approval and support. Contained within the McGuffey curriculum was

> rugged individualism, the dignity of labor, the basic virtues of thrift, honesty, and charity, and ... the punishment of doers of evil in a hundred examples.[9]

No gaps existed between secular virtues and their social and religious matrix. Religion, wrote William Ellery Channing in an early reader, "is a social concern, for it operates powerfully on society, contributing, in various ways, to its stability and prosperity."[10] The religion on tap during the nineteenth century was often Protestantism of the enthusiastic variety, and consequently was centered on the Bible, which McGuffey called the "best of classics," whose authority "came from heaven in vision and prophecy under the sanction of Him who is Creator of all things, and the Giver of every good and perfect gift."[11] Other passages on the Bible described it as "a transcript of infinite power and perfection" and is therefore

> the only universal classic ... of every age and country, of time and eternity, more humble and simple than the primer of a child, more grand and magnificent than the epic and the orator, the ode and the drama, when genius, with his cheviot of fire and his horses of fire, ascends in whirlwind, into the heaven of his own inventions. It is the best classic the world has ever seen.[12]

Such emphasis on the Bible as the center of both religious and communal experience was intensely Protestant, indeed Puritan, but the law and the mores of the time did not disdain denominationally based moral instruction.

Religious faith, of course, engendered fierce and fervent belief, along with vast doubt among the adherents of any one denomination that the others had much of grasp on eternal truth or God's will. Nonetheless, there was a general social consensus that religion was good for society as well as the soul, and it was undeniable that religion, primarily Protestant, had turned Abolition from politics into a crusade and into reality.

In education, religion would show each child the right way. A McGuffey aphorism stated that: "Appetites in man are capable of being made subsidiary to the sacred affecters and to religion."[13] The appropriate social virtues were certainly clear. In the *Eclectic First Reader* children were taught the story of foundling Mary taken in by old Mr. Post, who kindness and charity were repaid with service and gratitude.[14] Bread cast upon the waters had indeed returned after many days. Honesty was equally a prime virtue. The little boy in lesson XXXI of the *Eclectic Third Reader* who took a larger piece of cake than his mother would permit, and, hiding the evidence in his lap, deceived her and was punished by a guilty conscience.

> If you would have the approbation of your conscience, and the approval of friends, never do that which you shall desire to have concealed ... Be above deceit, and then you will having nothing to fear.[15]

Young lads were also admonished to practice temperance, while girls, presumably, were too pure and too sensible to give way to the snares and wiles of John Barleycorn. Temperance lessons began early. In the *Eclectic Third Reader* the young students were instructed to "beware of the first drink," lest they become "a perfect sot" and wind up in the pen.[16] Lads were instead enjoined to drink "water ... pure and cold," which was the "fountain, the source of health, peace, and happiness."[17]

Temperance reinforced other desirable social virtues, one of which was labor. In the *Eclectic Fourth Reader* the morality tale of "Hugh Idle and Mr. Toil" was adapted from Hawthorne's tale "Little Daffydowndilly." In this moral parable, young Hugh Idle had been sent to a strict and disagreeable schoolmaster who made him work and learn. "This will never do for me" young Hugh thought, and he ran away. Coming into the company an old stranger on the road, Hugh went with him in an effort to escape Mr. Toil. But to his shock and horror, everywhere he went he found Mr. Toil's spiritual brothers and relatives, some farmers, others working as carpenters, officers in the army, even fiddlers, and in every house, whether grand or humble, work was to be found and honored. Finally, young Hugh gave up in fatigue and frustration. "If there is nothing but Toil all the world over, I may just as well go back to the school-house."[18]

He did return, certainly wiser and perhaps sadder, for he now applied himself to his schoolwork and earned the approval of old Mr. Toil. And, if this affecting tale were insufficient, the *Fifth Reader* contained an essay by William Wirt, who was an author, lawyer, attorney general, and presidential candidate (1832). Wirt declared that "there is no excellence without great labor," a sentiment rephrased later by Thomas A. Edison when he remarked that genius was 1 percent inspiration and 99 percent perspiration.[19]

Allied to labor was perseverance. The *Fourth Eclectic Reader* contained the short poem "Try, Try Again," a piece so simple and direct that it passed into the langue as a general moral proverb and was invoked by Neville Chamberlain as he set out for Munich in 1938. Earlier, for a couple of generations in America, it had been a little golden memory verse that began as follows:

> 'Tis a lesson you should heed
> Try, try again
> If at first you don't succeed
> Try, try again.[20]

The complementary lesson was also taught in the *Fourth Eclectic Reader*, by the anonymous poem "Lazy Ned." Ned, who loved sledding, was too lazy to climb back up the hill, and for his general laziness, "died a dunce at last."[21] At a time when most jobs, whether agricultural, industrial or domestic were muscle jobs, laziness was a primal social sin, and the McGuffey schools were solidly against it. Prewar America was also a time with private charity alone providing a safety net, and it was literally true that one worked or starved. The Aesop fable of the grasshopper and the ant described reality as well as approved social values, as did William Hogarth's etchings concerning the idle apprentice.

The appropriate social values were contained within a short poem by Robert Southey, "Father William," which first appeared in the antebellum editions of the *Second Eclectic Reader*. In the well-known and often parodied poem (by Lewis Carroll, for one), young Theophilus declared Father William to be old and gray, but also in good health, and asked how this could be. The old man replied:

> I abused not my health and my vigor at first
> That I might never need them at last.

Theophilus remarked that Father William did not seem to repent the lost pleasure of youth, but the old man replied that he always knew youth would not last and he did not abuse the worldly pleasures that had been then available. Finally Theophilus noted that Father William was cheerful in his old age and did not fear death. The old man said:

> In the days of my youth I remembered my God!
> And he hath not forgotten my age.[22]

Here a biblical passage, the virtues of temperance, prudence, respect for one's elders and oneself, and love of God were all combined into a single moral lesson, which, like all McGuffey morality, was designed to last a lifetime.

The McGuffey spirit also proclaimed the goodness and greatness of America. Manifest destiny here acquired a moral as well as imperial dimension. Patriotism was an essential social virtue for an American, often taught as existing in combination with personal morality. Never was this clearer than in the civic piety of Mason Locke Weems, an Episcopal clergyman whose *Life of Washington* (1800) ran through seventy editions and was part of the *McGuffey Eclectic Third* (before 1857, the Second) *Reader* until 1879.[23] Parson Weems's biography of Washington was mostly fiction, though presented as fact, and specialized in moral instruction of the sentimental variety. In Weems's version, Washington's father told him that

> "Truth, George ... is the most lovely quality of youth. I would ride fifty miles, my son, to see the boy whose heart is ... honest..."
> How lovely does such a child appear in the eyes of everbody.[24]

The still-young and not-yet father of our country took this to heart, as it was meant for him to do, and, when he had killed the cherry tree with his "little hatchet" he confessed in the following terms: "I can't tell a lie, father; you know I can't tell a lie. I cut it with my hatchet." His father rewarded the young woodsman by saying "Such proof of heroic truth in my son is of more value than a thousand trees, though they were all of the purest gold."[25] This story passed from fiction into the empyrean realms of national myth where symbolic truth overtakes more mundane reliance upon facts. Its moral became part of how Americans of the years before 1917 (though no longer) saw themselves, their history, and their country.

Epideictic fiction was not the only examples of patriotism praised in McGuffey. In 1799 General "Light Horse Harry" Lee delivered the Congressional Eulogy on Washington, the peroration of which found its way into the Sixth reader.

> First in war, first in peace, and first in the hearts of his countrymen, he was second to none in humble and endearing scenes of private life. Pious, just, humane, temperate, sincere, uniform, dignified, and commanding, his example was edifying to all around him, as were the effects of that example lasting.[26]

Patriotism may have been, as Johnson commented, the last refuge of scoundrels, but that idea had not taken hold in prewar America. Consequently, the speech of Patrick Henry to the Virginia Convention on March 23, 1775, was reprinted in every edition of McGuffey's readers. Although the speech was not written down at the time, and the text is reconstructed, the official version was established by McGuffey. The conclusion was memorized by a hundred years of American children (among them myself), and entered the general culture

> Is life so dear, or peace so sweet, as to be purchased at the price of chains and slavery? Forbid it, Almighty God! I know not what course others may take; but As for me, give me liberty, or give me death.[27]

This was the way Americans wished to see themselves: as heroic and great-spirited, as devoted above all to liberty. Patrick Henry expressed the earlier American version of "the right stuff," and helped give McGuffey schools a clear public purpose and meaning.

The social goal of education in prewar America, obtained by immersing the child in McGuffey for a decade, was a 100 percent American. This had an obvious tinge of nativeism, but urban schools, which struggled with the children of immigrants, also confidently taught that a real American, which these children should become, loved his country, was polite and virtuous, obedient to his parents, read his Bible, attended church, practiced temperance or at least moderation, worked hard and was cheerful and pleasant with his neighbors. Of course, he also held foreigners in contempt, viewed unfamiliar religions with suspicion, thought of much domestic violence as godly admonition, and was not entirely trustworthy in all matters of business. But if Americans fell short of the mark in actual virtue, they did not fall short in supporting virtue.

Americanism (morally defined), religion (generally Protestant), and patriotism (America the good), generally enabled the young student to fit in to Gilded Age society. And the schools better not fall short, either. Nor did they, though often adjuncts to Protestant churches of the Calvinist variety, in all cases the schools were uninfected with ambiguity or multiculturalism. They endlessly preached approved moral doctrine, which was both true and eternal. Graduates of these academies might not practice all they had learned, and might hold it in contempt, but few made a point of proclaiming such heresy. It was not good social policy to condemn the local schools to neighbors whose daughters taught there and whose wealthier relations were on the school board.

It takes an effort of imagination to reenter the attitudes of the common schools of the McGuffey era. There are, of course, books of personal improvement today. These generally involve mental health, nutrition, muscles or money. You can learn how to make a million bucks in real estate or franchising. You can learn the fabulous secrets of a nutrition program which, if followed religiously, will enable you to live to be 100, or at least it will seem that long. You can smooth out every emotional kink and quirk, and become sublimely happy, well-adjusted, focused, organized, in control of your life, utterly unafraid and unaddicted, and even more happily married than Jason and Medea. You can sculpt a body so perfect that the opposite gender, whatever that might be, will follow you down the street in a condition of hopeless drool. But none of this touches the moral and social values that the American common schools of the Gilded Age so endlessly taught. A McGuffey education would "rouse the moral sentiments ... elevate and establish the moral sentiments ... elevate and establish character ... Character is more valuable than knowledge."[28] Victorian self-improvement was moral and social and anagogic. Modern self-help is profoundly secular; education in the McGuffey era was profoundly moral and religious.

The common schools may have been uncomfortable and the actual learning somewhat thin, but the social values of goodness, patriotism and religion had a tendency to stick, at least in memory. They were endlessly repeated in church, in revival meetings, in the Grange or Rotary, in temperance lectures and in traveling theatrical troupes. One could not escape them; even in the big city. As they grew older, people remembered that they had met their spouses in school, had been inspired there to read the law, had acquired the virtues of thrift and diligence necessary to succeed in the hardware business. Memory of discomfort faded. A sense of romance grew. With nostalgia, the past grows warmer, fonder, more inviting. Lemonade on the front porch is remembered. The bugs are not. The schools weren't so bad, not so bad at all. Since it was good for me, people thought, it would be just fine for the kids. After all, the schools taught the proper American social virtues. And, by God, Americans knew what was right and what was good for the community.

III

There can be little doubt that this form of education and perhaps the particular books were inflicted upon the young and recalcitrant George Herman Ruth at St. Mary's Industrial School in Baltimore. Certainly, the Xaverian Brothers who labored in that stony vineyard of immense challenge and small chance of success believed in the development of character, which had long been the foundation of Roman Catholic education.[29] If the boy is the father of the man, Brothers Matthias, Paul and Gilbert succeeded brilliantly in George's case, for he became a kindly, open, and generous adult. As for the "book-larnin'," young George missed most of that. Perhaps just as well. The Brothers were unable to separate George from his love of wine, women, song and night-life, which he learned in his father's saloon. George was never attracted to the abstemious existence of Puritan rectitude, which the women's movement and small town America thought necessary for earthly virtue and divine election. Perhaps just as well.

The Babe described his youth of misadventure in tones of decorous reminiscence, appropriate for conduct long outlived and publicly repudiated. He alluded to a spacious life of urban living, which alarmed those charged with his care at home and the Brothers at St. Mary's, as well as those who later employed him in baseball. He described his vivid life in terms of travail endured, of dedication and hard work in a difficult profession and of a growing sense of responsibility toward kids. It was a tale of temptation surmounted that McGuffey himself would have applauded.

These formed the basic themes of his book, *The Babe Ruth Story*, written with the assistance of Bob Considine in 1948, the year the Babe died of cancer. *The Babe Ruth Story* was a dying declaration to which the law gives a special weight. It placed Ruth's stupendous and by then already mythic athletic skills in a social useful context. The Babe not only did something enormous and unprecedented, he also did something good in the McGuffey mold. The values taught in youth are never utterly repudiated in old age.

The central story in the Babe's book concerns Johnny Sylvester, a sick boy who "was a terrific fan of mine. The kid had saved my box scores and stories about me and pasted them in a scrapbook."[30] Ruth took the father's call, and, in response to a request for a letter or an autographed ball, said he would pay a visit. The family was in Essex Fells, New Jersey, which is beyond Montclair and the Oranges. This was a substantial haul for the cars and roads of the mid-twenties, but the Babe used the day before the 1926 World Series to make the trip. He brought the youngster a bat, ball, and glove, and told him that he had to get up to play ball. Johnny asked the Babe

> if I could hit a home run for him in the World Series which was about to open with the Cardinals.
>
> I said sure, rubbed his head for luck and started back for New York.[31]

The Babe's generosity of time and spirit combined with his overwhelming physical vitality worked a sort of miracle cure.

> I had no way of knowing it, but the kid improved not only from the hour of my visit but each home run seemed to give him a new strength. They were "his."[32]

Babe Ruth and Johnny Sylvester stayed in touch for the rest of Ruth's life. After Babe Ruth had nearly died in 1946, baseball held a Babe Ruth Day on April 27, 1947, to be celebrated at every Major League game that Sunday. The day before, Johnny Sylvester came to visit the Babe. Johnny had gotten well, gone to Princeton, served as a submarine officer in the Pacific during the war, and then ran a machine-making firm on Long Island. Johnny's comments fit the moment.

> Hello Babe, ... I'm grown up now, thanks to you. And I figured it was only right for me to visit you, after your visit to me — a long time ago — did me so much good.[33]

Johnny Sylvester's relationship with Babe Ruth was exceptional in hagiography, in medical terms, and in duration, but it was only one among the many encounters Babe Ruth had with kids. Early in his career, with the Boston Red Sox, Ruth went back to St. Mary's to talk to the students, and he always gave autographs. After most games, the Babe greeted a sea of kids who stuck around the player's gate after the game. He visited hospitals and orphanages and answered his mail.

> I spent a fair portion of every day, during the summer, signing my way though a mob of kids before and after a ball game. I guess I've had as much direct contact with kids as any American who ever lived.[34]

The message that Babe Ruth conveyed to the youngsters, almost all male in those days of defined gender roles, was always one of good humor and optimism. Long before the official invention of positive thinking by Norman Vincent Peale, the Babe thought positively. Work hard, respect your craft and things will work out. It was right out of Mr. Toil in McGuffey. Optimism, respect for religion, and a general kindliness were things that Babe Ruth lived as well as preached; clean, sober, and abstemious living he just preached. The Bambino might live expansively, but he did not approve of such things in the youth whom he visited. He urged respect for teachers and elders, and for religion as well. Babe Ruth's style suited the Roaring Twenties, with his life a continuous toot and his message reflecting tradition. This was probably not the first time that has happened.

The second theme running through Babe Ruth's book expressed his consuming love for baseball. It was all he had ever done, and he never wanted to leave the game. Managing the Yankees was his fondest wish, but neither Jack Ruppert, the owner, nor Edward Grant Barrow, the general manager, were at all inclined to give him that job. Ruth put himself forward for the first time in 1930, after the death of Miller Huggins, who had managed the Yanks since 1918. Colonel Ruppert was ready for the Babe.

> I told him everything I could think of, but when I had finished he just shook his head, kind of sadly.
> "You can't manage yourself, 'Root,'" he said. "How do you expect to manage others?"[35]

The Babe had an answer for that, along the line that the best gamekeepers are reformed poachers. But there was no managerial offer in 1930, nor again in 1931, when the Babe asked again. This time Ruppert had ready a long list of Ruthian foibles and misadventures, and there were a great many of these. The Colonel read them out,

> and at the end he shrugged.
> "Under the circumstances, 'Root,' how can I turn my team over to you?"[36]

The New York general manager, Ed Barrow, summed the whole issue up succinctly.

> But the facts are that at no time during the years he was with the club, from 1920 until 1934, was Ruth ever considered a candidate for manager of the Yankees.[37]

But if managing the team he made into America's team was never a possibility, Babe Ruth did have two legitimate chances to manage. They both came in the twilight of his playing career. The Yanks offered Ruth the managership of the Newark farm club in the International League. Barrow argued that managing Newark would give Ruth some experience and help him live down his reputation for excessive joie de vivre. The Babe turned it down. In 1933, Frank Navin, who owned Detroit, wanted Babe Ruth to manage the Tigers. Getting permission from Barrow to talk to the Babe, Navin called him and asked him to come to Detroit to talk things over. Babe told Navin about a tightly scheduled barnstorming trip that he agreed to, and suggested seeing him when he got home. Navin called Barrow, who called Ruth and advised him to see Navin immediately. It would be a mistake to put the meeting off. But the Babe did, and when he got back he found that Navin had bough catcher Mickey Cochrane from Philadelphia and made him the manager.[38] It would be the Babe's only chance to manage a Major League club.

The alternative to managing or coaching at the end of a playing career is to leave baseball. Some have prepared for life after baseball, but Babe Ruth had not. While he played, he was so good that it was possible to imagine that his skills would never erode to ineffectiveness. The Babe only intermittently went in for the relentless physical conditioning required for an extended career. His style ran more to booze, babes, junk food, and late hours, and his staggering skills could offset the good times only for a while. Nor had the Babe made much effort to repair the deficiencies of his formal education and find something else he could do. Personal charm and a generous spirit had always made the Babe a popular figure, both in and out of the game. That should be good enough; the Babe was, after all, the Babe, and the biggest draw in baseball.

It was not good enough. The fans remember, but baseball is a business and the owners move on. This puzzled the Babe.

> From the mail I got — and always answered — and the receptions I had every place I went ... I felt that the public was as bewildered over my absence from baseball as I was. A second-stringer can go back to the farm or get some other kind of job and fit into the routine of life. But I had had too much publicity, had been too well-known, had been too much a part of baseball for that to happen.[39]

So the Babe left the game, and left himself at loose ends without a purpose, and haunted by a constant sadness.

In his last testament, Babe Ruth alluded to the sense of being lost. In 1942, Walter Johnson and the Babe put on a benefit for Army-Navy Relief. They appeared in Yankee Stadium, and about 60,000 fans came out to see Walter pitch to the Babe. Walter Johnson threw twenty-one pitches, and Babe Ruth hit the last one into the third deck in right field, a vintage Ruthian clout. The fans exploded into cheers, and

> were still yelling for us as we disappeared into the Yankee dugout and started down to the dressing room. We walked along, gabbing and signing autographs, but there was a kind of sadness in both of us. Walter had been the greatest pitcher in the league; I had been the greatest slugger. But he was no longer a part of the game and the same was true of me.[40]

It was the Bambino's last appearance in a Yankee uniform, and his next official appearance would be for Babe Ruth Day on April 27, 1947. He had nearly died the year before, and would die a year later; this celebration was baseball's tribute to him, long after he had left the game. Babe Ruth Day was a moving moment, and illuminated both the Babe's place in baseball and his absence from it. As always, Babe Ruth's feelings were clear to see. "I wanted to stay in baseball more than I ever wanted anything in my life."[41] It was a cry from the heart, and also an indication that, until near the end and looking back, Babe Ruth had no difficultly viewing his life as a whole.

IV

Baseball record books, most notably *The Baseball Encyclopedia*, have collected and checked the statistics and records of baseball in one united whole covering the game from 1871 up through the date of publication. The records are exhaustive, and baseball researchers constantly refine and update them. I daresay no other comprehensive set of records in the Western world is as accurate, and few are as important. In human affairs, however, precision is often the enemy of reality. Where there is one set of baseball records there ought to be three, which would reflect more precisely the changing nature of the game. The first set should cover the years from 1976 to 1894, when the rules were flexible and pitchers threw underhanded from the box. The second set would chronicle the years from 1894 to 1919, the era of the dead ball, spitballs and other ingenious doctored deliveries, and strategies built around manufacturing runs. The third set would describe the power game from 1920 on into the future, the era of the rabbit ball, relief pitching and massively muscled sluggers. In the first two periods, pitchers set records, with Radbourn's 60 wins in a single season, and a dozen pitchers winning 300 games. The hitters also set records, Hugh Duffy hitting .438 in 1894. These achievements seem permanent in a single record book that covers the game from Anson to the end of time. It was a different game then. In the modern era, the slugging and the relief pitching records also appear permanent, like night baseball and modern gloves. It is a new game now. The first two eras were the creation of rule makers, who tinkered with the game to achieve balance among all the elements of the game, from pitching and fielding to hitting, base running and baseball tactics. The third era was the creation of Babe Ruth, whose talents simply transcended the current form of the game, and created something new, modern baseball.

11

Baseball on Television

So much was exciting and novel about the 1947 World Series that it is easy to overlook the most important aspect of that most important event. It is not Cookie Lavagetto's ninth inning double to break up Bill Bevens's no-hitter, nor Al Gionfriddo's stupendous catch of Joe DiMaggio's long drive. Certainly, the expected Yankees victory in the Series is now just a footnote, only another in a long list of Yankees World Series triumphs. The key factor in that Series occurred off the field. The World Series of 1947 was the first to be televised and generate television revenue. The total from television was $65,000. In subsequent years the sum would rise, but televised World Series, which are a fixture in network programming, began long ago with Bevens, Cookie, and Al.[1]

I

Television, like the weather, has proved to be more difficult to understand than to predict. The most accurate forecast about the new medium, and the one most often made by sponsors and media moguls alike, predicted an ever growing and perhaps never to be diminished popularity for the new medium. No one ever went broke by being bullish on television. By the time of the Korean War, the rooftops of New York had become a scrub land of antennas bringing those housed below the endless commercials of Mad Man Muntz (or was it Martz), who sold something or other at peak pitch. As commercials blared and multiplied, making television the essential medium for peddling anything, sponsors understood that the quality of television must improve. They were right. Early television, of the 1947–49 variety, had five- or seven-inch screens which required a piece of green plastic in front of the screen to make the black and white image appear in suitable shades of snowy gray. Even with that help, one had to sit several minutes in front of the screen fiddling with the knobs to make the test pattern abandon its incurable predilection for appearing in wavy rather than straight lines.

177

The picture may have been terrible, and, even worse, the roller derby had become a program staple, but everyone, from the manufacturers to the moguls, promised constant improvement. Both groups succeeded. The screens got bigger, the antennae improved, the picture became less snowy and more detailed, and even the programs improved. Olsen and Johnson gave way to Lucille Ball, Jack Webb, Sid Caesar and Milton Berle. Network television (1951) nationalized the medium, and provided an even more powerful financial incentive to standardize programs that would appeal nationally, attract viewers, and sell stuff. There was sustained debate, at the time and subsequently, over whether the programming, generally estimated to be at about the intellectual level of age twelve, or perhaps ten or eleven, might not have been set too low. Substantial growth in both audience and revenues, however, confirmed that the programming level had general appeal and was about right.

General appeal is never universal appeal, and three commentators have made important remarks on the state of American television. The first of these was widely disseminated and widely discussed. Newton Minow, head of the FCC, described television in a 1961 speech as a "vast wasteland." He meant a wasteland of intelligence, public service, educational value, of moral and social uplift, of beauty and charm, and he did not exclude commercials. Those making money in television howled in rage. Critics, who had been saying these things and worse for years, howled in glee. The debate produced more heat than light; these things always do. But it did indicate that the American intellectual establishment, both public and academic, thought television ought to do more for the public interest, variously defined.

Minow's comment gained notoriety because it dealt not merely with the quality of the programs but also carried an unsettling implication about viewer reaction. Television sold ideas, attitudes and values as well as products because viewers reacted emotionally as well as intellectually. They liked this character, disliked that show, wanted to use this product, and wanted to avoid that one. The trick to making money in television lay in the realm of social and psychological attitudes. The advertiser had to find the program, or better yet create the commercial, that carried positive moments of emotional impact, thus ensuring that the viewer would reschedule the program and remember the commercial.

Minow's observations produced a variety of responses among those trying to make money from television. Few took the need for public service too seriously, but almost everyone believed that better commercials could be made. Many thought in terms of increasing the positive emotional impact of specific moments in their shows and commercials. Raw, gut-wrenching emotion might work. John Wayne, dying of cancer himself, made a commercial for the American Cancer Society. Standing on a bare stage, Wayne said that the society needed the viewers' help. He then added that things could be worse. The viewer could need the society's help. Some, opting for a lighter touch, tried humor. A celebrated commercial for a pain reliever showed a bloated and uncomfortable man sitting on a bed complaining that he had eaten too much. An unsympathetic wife completed the picture of domestic pathos. Others tried the power of association. Celebrity endorsement of a product carried a direct message. Use the product and be associated with fashion and glam. A more subtle variety involved having an ordinary citizen wearing a hat or shirt emblazoned with a product logo standing next to a NASCAR winner being interviewed after the race. Still others tried love. A Coca-Cola commercial, often regarded as one of the most successful ever made, showed a hundred young people standing on a Tuscan hillside singing about brotherhood and Coca-Cola. Most tried wish fulfillment. Buy this car, cosmetic, diet regimen, exercise machine, or beer, and you will become instantly more sleek, sexy, desirable, admired and successful. You will enter the mainstream of the cutting edge of the new and chic. Some, taking advantage of cable television and digital cartoons, have merged commercial into show. Entire info-channels are next. Indeed, they are here now. Whatever Newton Minow meant to convey, he succeeded in convincing those in television to try harder to make their shows and commercials even more seductive, even more subtle and sophisticated, so that the most mundane bar of soap became enticing and exotic.

A second important comment on the nature of television came from Van Gordon Sauter, in the mid-eighties the president of CBS News. In a moment of candor, he described television news as a series of moments that carried an emotional impact, which might increase viewer intensity or certainty, but worked less well in increasing viewer intellectual sophistication. Television news was just like television programs; indeed, it was quite like television commercials. Pretentious and outraged critics drove Sauter from his job for claiming that the news, regarded by critics as a sacred public service, was not different from programs and commercials, regarded by critics as false and grotesque. The moral indignation of public-spirited critics was entirely misplaced. Everyone literate in English had known of the congruity of news, sales, and entertainment at least since Ben Jonson's comedy, *The Staple of News*, produced in 1625.[2] Sauter left his position, saying that he was ahead of his time, meaning, in this case, that he was farther behind his times than were his critics.

A third important comment, this one on the beginnings of television, came from Doris Kearns Goodwin, a television pundit and one of America's leading historians. In her memoir of childhood in Rockville Centre on Long Island, she noted:

> Television entered our lives robed as the bearer of communal bonds, providing a new set of common experiences, block parties, and festive gatherings shared by children and adults alike.[3]

This did not seem implausible at the time, although today only an acute social memory can recall it. People then assumed, reasonably enough, that families would gather around the television set as they had around the radio and around the breakfast table with the morning paper. And for a while they did. Those of a certain age (among them myself) can remember gathering around a neighbor's television set to watch baseball.

The communal aspect of television, as with radio and the newspaper, depended upon singleness of source. Most families got one morning paper so everyone shared it. On commuter trains and subways, everyone had his/her own paper, folded in half and then half again, so people separated. Radio presented the same phenomenon. When there was a family radio people gathered around it. I remember a Sunday dinner, listening to the New York Philharmonic, when an announcer broke in with what he called important news. It was about the attack on Pearl Harbor. After the war, with multiple radios, each listener chose different programming. Television went through this same individuation process, first family by family, then viewer by viewer, and did so very quickly. The social solvent of increasing wealth, which made television possible in the first place, also allowed a second set for the kids, who, unaccountably, did not wish to watch the shows favored by their parents. A television set for each child helped tamp down squalid sibling conflict which had been amplified by fewer jobs and more free time for the young. The process of reducing communal viewing to individuals or pairs took only a couple of decades. By the late sixties or early seventies, television had brought peace through separation to many American families.

Social separation traced to television did not involve every level of American communal life. Small communities, such as families and neighborhoods, broke down into groups of disparate individuals more fully after television than before it. At this level, individual taste trumped collective solidarity. With large numbers of people the opposite occurred. Network broadcasting rather quickly created a national common experience through shows, ball games, commercials, and newscasts that all America could see and many millions did see. The larger community was brought together as national homogeneity emerged through the same medium that encouraged local diversity. Television fulfilled its communal promise, although it did not do so in ways originally expected.

II

These observations on television as a social force carry, to differing degrees, negative connotations about the medium, but none of these criticisms could be thought damaging to televised baseball. Not only was baseball beautiful, wholesome, and a constant reminder that character should accompany skill, it also fit perfectly into the basic function of television, which is to sell things. In the American model of corporate ownership the sales mix leans away from politicians and policies toward cars, cosmetics, and beer, while the public model in Europe concentrates more on politicians and policies. But these differences, while crucial within the First Amendment, are actually just details within the structure of the medium. However organized, television sells things, and baseball fits nicely into that paradigm.

As a program like any other, baseball punctuates the game with commercials, spreading them out so that the advertising moments arrive with appropriate impact. Structurally, baseball functions better as a television program than does tennis, hockey or football, where the game must stop arbitrarily for commercial time-outs. Baseball is certainly better than soccer, which puts viewers to sleep so quickly that they miss the artificial commercial respites. The nineteenth-century tempo of baseball, often described as too measured for the manic modern taste, is actually perfect for television. Baseball contains numerous normal pauses in the game, beginning with the end of each half inning and extending to pitching changes and conferences on the mound. Both game and commercials flow naturally. Pauses in the action of baseball allow for a full schedule of commercial moments, which those who run television think ought to be at least a half of every hour of real time.

Success in fitting in with television's sales function also derives from baseball's essential imitation of life. The drama of baseball acts as a metaphor for the appropriate social values of courage, fairness, skill, application, diligence, and running out every pop fly and ground ball. Baseball also moves at the regular pace of life lived in the normal way, absent emergencies or pharmaceuticals. In life and in baseball, time exists to let the mind wander and regain focus, to chat with the fan in the next seat, to have a beer and a Polish, to keep score, to reflect on the game and still see and comprehend all of the action. People live this way, when they can, in spite of the ubiquity of office and industrial efficiency programs and the popularity of managerial snooping on employee computers, both practices striving endlessly to attune the human to the mechanical or electronic. Baseball moves at the tempo of life lived as a person, not an adjunct to a machine or process, and it is persons who buy things. Baseball moves at the pace of sales.

Were this not so, the major teams, Cubs, Red Sox, Yankees, Mets, Dodgers, Braves or Mariners, would not have national and international television networks. Even the smaller market teams, such as the Pirates, the Twins, or the Royals achieve limited television exposure. Teams make money off television, but so do the stations and so do the sponsors. Baseball lives in the comfort zone of electronic commerce, and, in the case of baseball, that generally refers to lifelong consumption, not just the ephemeral fads of the young.

Tempo alone suffices to explain the symbiosis between baseball and television, but moments of high excitement within the game also matter. Baseball has enough extraordinary action to interest even the casual viewer/fan/consumer. In baseball, unlike most standard shows, the game is better than the commercials. Even the most cunningly concocted commercial lacks the intensity of a play at the plate. Moreover, in nearly every inning the viewer/fan/consumer sees a great play afield, a stolen base, a clutch hit, and good and bad pitching. I recall an inning pitched by Dale Mohorcic against the Yankees, a single inning in a game that had no great connection to the pennant race. Mohorcic struck the side out on ten pitches, all of them strikes. One hitter got a two-strike foul ball, so he saw a fourth pitch and struck out on that one. A random inning of superb, dominant, focused pitching became a memorable moment in an otherwise ordinary game. Baseball highlights are not confined to the World Series. Those comprise the realm of myth, but do not exhaust that of excellence. Brilliant play occurs daily. Whether television in general is a wasteland or not forms a continuing debate among the cognoscenti of the medium, but baseball on television displays a variegated tapestry of life well lived, for both player and viewer, in both moment and memory.

III

Baseball has not had a significant impact on the direction and development of television, in spite of providing large blocks of interesting programming. By contrast, youth culture has been the great influence on programming, on commercials, on the language used over the air. Television, however, has had a stunning influence on baseball, which may be summed up in a single word: money. Because television sells stuff so well, it is, given the nature of things, quite rich, while baseball is basically poor, routinely requiring hundreds of millions in municipal and state support to provide land for stadia, for construction and maintenance of the parks, for roads and parking, for rapid transit access, and for tax breaks. The public frequently balks at these outlays, and politicians and people always complain about them, but, in the end, funds usually become available, in part because being a Major League city on television has immense psychic and civic appeal.

The transfer, over several decades, of some of television's billions to baseball in exchange for programming (games) has changed organized ball in terms of its internal numbers, raising them by an order of magnitude from hundreds of thousands to millions. This notably has included salaries, and baseball players have begun to make what television, music, or movie stars do; indeed, since players work all the time, their income has exceeded that of the lesser or lazier rock stars. In fiscal terms, television has made baseball part of show biz, and brought even to average Major League players the celebrity, the temptations, and the routine risks faced in Hollywood as part of living large and dangerously in the public eye.

While television money has changed the scale of baseball income, it did not change either the nature or the parameters of internal baseball conflict. The formal relationship of the league to the owners and the owners to the players has remained constant since Abraham G. Mills hammered out the National Agreement in 1883. Owners still fight each other, and owners still fight players, mostly over money. Baseball's conflicts, like its uniforms, have remained constant since the days of John Montgomery Ward, the Players' League (1890), and the baseball syndicate scheme (1900–1901).[4]

Television has also left undisturbed the fiscal gap between the large market (national in fan interest) and the small market (local in fan interest) teams. Since clubs share equally in the national television money, all have become somewhat more solvent, but the gap in local or satellite or cable television contracts continues. Local television contracts exacerbate fiscal inequality by giving huge sums to specific teams, such as the Cubs, the Braves, the Mets or the Yankees. In economic theory, at least, the favored clubs with fat electronic contracts could drive players' salaries up to the point where small market teams could not compete on the field. This has not yet happened all across baseball, but there are small market teams, like Kansas City, Pittsburgh, Detroit or Minnesota, that seem uncomfortably close to being "Four-A" clubs, developmental franchises seasoning players for stardom elsewhere. This stands as the constant nightmare for baseball. Executives and pundits have floated plans to equalize revenues, a bit or a lot, but very little has happened.

As it now stands, the recent inequality of electronic revenue has not altered the traditional inequality of baseball competition. The Yankees remain the dominant team in baseball, as they have been since the days of Babe Ruth, and are less dominant now than they were in the early days of television when the revenues were small. The Cubs are much, much worse than they were before the 1950s when television began to affect baseball, but they are one of the fortunate large electronic market teams. The Curse of the Bambino may once have doomed the Red Sox on the field (against the Yankees), but it has not prevented the Sox from gaining a national electronic fan base and the funds that follow it. The Mets, with a huge payroll and local television contract, usually settle near the bottom of their division, getting less for their money than even the Cubs. Indeed, competitive inequality has always been part of the game. In the National League, the Pirates, Giants, and Cubs won all the pennants between 1901 and 1914, and the same teams, plus the Cardinals, won them all between 1921 and 1939. In the American League, the Athletics, Tigers, Red Sox and White Sox won all the pennants from 1901 through 1919, and the Yanks, Senators, Athletics, and Tigers won them all between 1921 and 1944. From 1947 through 1964, the Yankees lost the pennant twice to Cleveland and once to the White Sox, while winning the other fifteen flags themselves. Baseball is actually more competitive on the field now than it was a generation ago and before.

Television has ameliorated some of the disadvantages of bad baseball management, just as it has added to long-standing fiscal inequalities. Combined with free agency, the most important internal development in baseball since Jackie Robinson, television money has enabled well-run smaller market teams to build fleeting success around young players and a couple or three major and expensive stars. Pittsburgh, Kansas City, Toronto, and Minnesota have all done this. Success is temporary; the income needed to preserve the team is usually more than the team can generate. The Mets and the Rangers, though, demonstrate how huge salaries for huge stars can produce very little on the field. Television can't do everything. A good general manager and skillful handling of players in the clubhouse and on the field still matter. The Atlanta Braves stand as a recent example of that.

The changes wrought by television on baseball have been spectacular, but the essential structure of both organized ball and the game itself has remained about the same. Television money, combined with free agency, which functions as an auction market for that money, has catapulted the players beyond the economic circumstances in which the fans live, but that is true for all forms of American entertainment. The fans still see the same game their grandparents did, though breaks in the action caused by home runs and relief pitching have lengthened the game by perhaps an hour. But thanks to television, the fans did notice one change. The best seat in the stadium has become an easy chair at home in front of the tube.

IV

Television fits the rhythms of baseball not only because the inning break precisely suited the medium's insatiable need to sell something but also because television emulated baseball's combination of long-running acts and constantly changing faces. Most players stay for two, three or four years, if that long, and then they are through. Many others come up for a cup of coffee, staying in the Show for only part of a single season. Bobby Cox, manager of the Atlanta Braves, calls them Four-A players, pretty good in the high minors but unable to establish themselves in the Major Leagues. Television operates on the same system. Every season dozens of actors appear in bit parts and supporting roles, gain a part on a series destined for the trash, make a commercial or two, and then are replaced by a new crop of faces, equally attractive, hopeful, determined, diligent, and doomed.

This does not describe the entertainment/athletic fate of everyone. There are the stars; indeed, the nature of entertainment demands that there always be stars. What makes a star in television is unclear (at least to me), but in baseball it is ability frequently augmented with charm and usually enhanced by character. The stars remain the Show for fifteen or twenty years, or even more, and give continuity to fan interest and to the game itself. Television combines with time to make the stars visible, and ultimately familiar and comfortable. Stars become the subject of inevitable comparison to their predecessors, who were equally "the wonder of their generation." In memory, those gone before become better, as the idealized past always surpasses the inevitably degraded present Baseball is continually self-referential, as is any activity that has value.

The mix of stars and supporting cast has made baseball just another television program of the reality genre, better than the rest of course, but still in the standard paradigm. This was (and is) how television moguls saw (and see) the game. It is niche programming, relatively inexpensive, drawing a limited audience, but selling a lot of beer and cars. Televised baseball has expanded with the number of television channels, sets, cables and satellites. It is now possible for any fan to see any game in either league; in television, niches form within niches and broadcasting inevitably devolves into narrowcasting. In the drama of baseball, like the drama of television, the game or program ends while the season continues, and the season ends but the game/medium continues. Instant replay and reruns catch it all. It has become difficult to imagine baseball and television without each other.

V

The best seat in the house is not necessarily the best seat in the heart. A common observation from those who discuss television holds that viewing an event on the tube remains a lesser version of physical presence at the game. It is always better to be part of the studio audience. While one may see the action, the whole ambience, the sounds, smells, taste and feel of the game in the park are all occluded by television. This is certainly true, although the game, like the show, remains the same. Jim Bunning's perfect game against the Mets on June 21, 1964, at Shea Stadium was not less perfect for those who saw it on television (and that includes me) than it was for those at the park. Nonetheless, those at home rightly wish to be at the park; attendance makes a game special while television reduces it to routine. But attendance does not, in itself, make a moment into a myth. Bobby Thomson's home run to win the 1951 playoff was seen by a few thousand at the Polo Grounds; it was seen on television by millions more. For all, it was "the shot heard round the world," as the suddenness and drama of the event obliterated whatever sense of distance or remove that television engendered.

As a medium, television adds immediacy to other forms of distance communication, and in baseball television has followed the trail blazed by newspapers and then radio by bringing the game and the players to those who could not be there. The fan, from whatever distance, could join in the myth and the moment that are designated by the wider culture, or the memory that always belongs to one alone. All are treasured as markers of life lived and then revisited, of a journey once taken and now comprehended. For each and for all, in that circular way that memory, moment, and myth reinforce each other in an ever-growing sense of cultural and personal past, baseball becomes as a talisman of the self.

> We shall not cease from exploration
> And the end of all our exploring
> Will be to arrive at where we started
> And know the place for the first time.[5]

Notes

Chapter 1

1. On the Depression, a convenient place to begin is David Kennedy, *Freedom from Fear: The American People in Depression and War, 1929–1945* (New York: Oxford University Press, 1980), which is part of the Oxford History of the United Sates series. It will surprise no one to hear that historians and participants have written a great deal about the New Deal. Readers who prefer something more substantial than Kennedy's excellent book may turn to Kenneth S. Davis, *FDR*, 4 vols. (New York: Random House, 1945–1993), or the earlier classic by Frank Freidel, *Franklin D. Roosevelt*, 4 vols. (Boston: Little, Brown, 1942–1976), or James MacGregor Burns, *Roosevelt: The Lion and the Fox* (New York: Harcourt, Brace, 1956) and *Roosevelt: The Soldier of Freedom* (New York: Harcourt Brace Jovanovich, 1970). The *Public Papers and Addresses of Franklin D. Roosevelt*, 13 vols. (New York: Random House, 1938–1950) provide an essential source for his presidency.

For studies on the Depression as its own phenomenon, see Michael Bernstein, *The Great Depression: Delayed Recovery and Economic Change in America, 1929–1939* (New York: Cambridge University Press, 1987), and Lester Chandler, *America's Greatest Depression* (New York: Harper & Row, 1970). On the beginning of the Depression, see the delightful little book by John Kenneth Galbraith, *The Great Crash* (Boston: Houghton Mifflin, 1955). On the era leading up to the Depression, see Frederick Lewis Allen, *Only Yesterday* (New York: Harper & Brothers, 1931).

On Prohibition, the place to begin is the politics of the dry crusade. See, for example, Charles L. Mee, Jr., *The Ohio Gang: The World of Warren G. Harding* (New York: M. Evans, 1981). See an early evaluation on the dry era,

Charles Merz, *The Dry Decade* (New York, 1932), along with Herbert Asbury, *The Great Illusion: An Informal History of Prohibition* (Garden City, N.Y.: Doubleday, 1950), a popular history that is hostile to Prohibition. On establishing Prohibition, from an author highly placed in the Anti-Saloon League, see Ernest Cherrington, *The Evolution of Prohibition in the United States of America* (Westerville, Ohio: American Issue Press, 1920). On the electoral tactics and successes, see The *New York Times*, March 29, 1926; on the Anti-Saloon League, which put Prohibition across, one can do no better than their own words, *Proceedings Fifteen National Convention of the Anti-Saloon League of American Twenty Year Jubilee Convention* (Westerville, Ohio: American Issue Press, 1913). But do not forget the crucial role played by the women's movement in the success of the dry crusade. See Eleanor Flexner, *Century of Struggle: The Woman's Rights Movement in the United States* (Cambridge, Mass.: Harvard University Press, 1975). On the women's movement, as feminism was then called, and Prohibition see particularly Frances E. Willard, *Woman and Temperance or, The Work and Workers of the Woman's Christian Temperance Union* (Hartford, Conn., 1883, reprinted New York, 1972). Willard was the president of Union. See also Ruth Bordin, *Woman and Temperance: The Quest for Power and Liberty 1873–1900* (Philadelphia: Temple University 1981). On Methodist Bishop Cannon, who played a major role in Prohibition, see Virginius Dabney, *Dry Messiah, The Life of Bishop Cannon* (New York: A. A. Knopf, 1949). See also on Prohibition generally Norman A. Clark, *Deliver Us from Evil An Interpretation of American Prohibition* (New York: W. W. Norton, 1976); on Harding, a personal wet but the first dry president, see Randolph C. Downes, *The Rise of Warren Harding 1865–1920* (Columbus,

Ohio: n.p., 1970); see also Robert K. Murray, *The Harding Era: Warren G. Harding and His Administration* (Minneapolis: University of Minnesota Press, 1969); see also Francis Russell, *The Shadow of Blooming Grove: Warren G. Harding in His Time* (New York: McGraw-Hill,1968); see also Geoffrey Perrett, *America in the Twenties: A History* (New York: Simon & Schuster, 1982).

Finally, the quote on Prohibition is from a letter by Herbert Hoover to Senator William Borah, February 28, 1928.

2. Kennedy, *Freedom from Fear*, p. 100. On Holmes, a convenient place to begin is Max Lerner, ed., *The Mind and Faith of Justice Holmes His Speeches, Essays, Letters, and Judicial Opinions* (New Brunswick, N.J.: Rutgers University Press, 1989; New York, 1943).

3. Kennedy, *Freedom from Fear*, p. 98.

4. On the personal havoc wrought by the Depression, see Studs Terkel, *Hard Times: An Oral History of the Great Depression* (New York: W. W. Norton, 2000).

5. *New York Times*, October 1, 1932.

6. Babe Ruth as told to Bob Considine, *The Babe Ruth Story* (New York: E. P. Dutton, 1948), p. 190. It is impossible to imagine what those words might have been, considering Ruth's early years in a Baltimore waterfront tavern, but it is also perfectly clear that he did not regard them as appropriate for the kids who would be reading his book.

7. *New York Times*, October 2, 1932.

8. *Sunday News*, June 22, 1952, from the "Ask Anybody" column.

9. Ruth, *The Babe Ruth Story*, p. 194.

10. *Sunday News*, June 22, 1952. Regardless of what Charlie Root said, or the recently unearthed home movie might show or not show, Americans seem to favor Tertullian over Augustine in matters of belief and incredulity concerning this central myth of baseball. In *On the Body of Christ* (*De Carne Christi*), c. 210, Tertullian wrote that the death of the Son of God "can be believed only because it is absurd" (*Et mortus est Dei Filius; prorsus credibile, quia ineptum est*). The saying has been modified by continuous misquotation to become: "I believe because it is absurd" (*Credo, quia absurdum*). Augustine, by contrast, wrote in the *City of God* (*Civitas Dei*), c. 427, in Bk. XXII, chap. v: "If the thing believed is incredible, it is also incredible that the incredible should have been so believed" (*Si autem credita est, etiam hoc utile incredibile est, sic creditam esse quod incredibile est*).

11. This attitude has found its spiritual home in Albert G. Spalding, *America's National Game: Historic Facts Concerning the Beginning,* *Evolution, Development, and Popularity of Baseball with Personal Reminiscences of its Vicissitudes, its Victories and its Votaries* (New York: American Sports Publishing, 1911). An opposite view is found in Steven Riess, *City Games: The Evolution of American Urban Society and the Rise of Sports* (Urbana: University of Illinois Press, 1989); and Melvin Adelman, *A Sporting Time: New York City and the Rise of Modern Athletics 1820–1870* (Urbana: University of Illinois Press, 1986). Riess and Adelman have on their side historical fact, which is comparatively unimportant. The mythic appeal is entirely on the side of Albert Spalding.

Myth as story about the past antedates baseball. For a good summary of classical myth, see Mark P. O. Morford and Robert J. Lenardon, *Classical Mythology* (New York: Oxford University Press, 1971); see also as particularly useful Michael Grant, *Myths of the Greeks and the Romans* (New York: New American Library, 1964) and H. J. Rose, *A Handbook of Greek Mythology*, 6th ed. (London, 1958) and H. J. Rose, *Religion in Greece and Rome* (New York: Harper & Row, 1959). The basic book is, of course, Sir James George Frazer, *The Golden Bough: A Study in Magic and Religion* (London, Oxford: Oxford University Press 1944), an abridgement of the second and third editions. Frazer combined classical scholarship with an interest in cultural anthropology and a belief that all myth everywhere was similar in content, purpose and technique.

On baseball as an example of the varieties and nature of myth, see Deanne Westbrook, *Ground Rules: Baseball and Myth* (Urbana: University of Illinois Press, 1996). In this excellent book, Westbrook brings the example of baseball to bear on the nature of myth; *The Called Home Run* reverses the process, bringing myth to bear upon baseball.

12. WFAN in New York and the ESPN system nationwide perform these functions *con brio*, but they are not alone. Every radio and television station devotes time (and money) to Hot Stove League activities, particularly when they reek of scandal.

13. The basic study of the nature of orality and literacy, and the cultural difference made by writing, a technology that change how one thinks, is Walter Ong, S.J., *Orality and Literacy: The Technologizing of the Word* (New York: Mothmen, 1982); see also Walter Ong, S.J., "Voice as Summons to Belief," in *Literature and Belief*, ed. M. H. Abrams (New York, 1965), pp. 80–105.

14. Errors creep into even the most carefully edited texts, including the annual *Official Base Ball Guide* and the *Baseball Encyclopedia*, now

in its 10th edition, soon to be extended further. In the case of baseball, however, these errors and omissions are self-correcting, as members of the Society for American Baseball Research (SABR), armed with old newspapers and team archives constantly improve the written record. Perfection is the goal, providing a written summary of baseball history and statistics as perfect as the game they describe.

15. In the *Theogony*, Hesiod explained forces and conditions that all experienced: sea, sun, earth, life, death and the like, in metaphorical and anthropomorphic form, thus connecting the experienced, but also unknowable both in origin and nature, to the experienced and understood, both in meaning and function. Thus forces and conditions become gods and stories about gods, the truth of which involved not the gods (natural forces and conditions) but human understanding. Hence artistic creativity is born from Mnemosyne (Memory) understood as a goddess, since humanity recognizes and experiences artistic creativity but does not understand it and cannot summon it up by an act of will. The story connected the individual to things greater, and made the world more comfortable. There remained one exception to this. We all recall Aeschylus' line from the lost *Niobe*: "Death is the only god who / Is not moved by gifts." Quoted in Aristophanes, *The Frogs*. The definition of *myth* is mine, it is the opposite of Euhemerus, as can easily been seen, and it tends instead to be metaphorical.

For Hesiod, see Stanley Lombardo (trans.) and Robert Lamberton (intro.), *Hesiod Works and Days: Theogony* (Indianapolis: Hackett, 1993).

16. Aristotle, *The Poetics*, VII.2–3. All citations from Aristotle come from the Loeb Classical Library Edition, *Aristotle*, vol. 23 (London and Cambridge: Harvard University Press, 1973).

17. The two major Western examples of cosmic myth presented as epic are the *Commedia* of Dante and *Paradise Lost* by John Milton. Both combine the belief in doctrine with faith and with the known human condition to illustrate the essential truths of myth.

18. Ovid, *Metamorphoses*, Bk. VI. See *Ovid: The Metamorphoses*, trans. Horace Gregory (New York: New American Library, 1958), pp. 163–65.

19. The Aristotelian soul had three parts. At the lowest level was the nutritive soul, which humanity shared with plants and animals. Next came the sensitive soul, which people shared with animals, involving sensations, motions and emotions. At the top came the rational soul, which humanity alone possessed, and which involved reason.

20. The Latin phrase for "once upon a time," *olim*, was used as the opening of medieval law cases decided and recorded in the early thirteenth century by the French Parliament of Paris. The "Olim rolls" reflect the view that a law case is a human story, including myth, that deals with fundamental values and realities.

21. The phrase means "once, always, everywhere and to all."

22. Heracleitus, frag. 10. See also fragments 47 and 51 in Milton C. Nahm, *Selections from Early Greek Philosophy* (New York: Appleton-Century-Crofts, 1964), pp. 68 and 71.

23. See, as an example, *Riggs et al. v. Palmer et al.*, 115 N.Y. 506 (1889). In this case a greedy heir, whose grandfather had left him the bulk of a considerable estate, feared that the old man would either change his mind or live on for an inconveniently long time. Palmer solved the problem by murdering his grandfather, thus ensuring the inheritance and advancing its arrival. The New York Court of Errors and Appeals held that, regardless of the sanctity of a last will and testament, the general principle that no one could profit from his criminal act must prevail.

24. In myth, as in law, the local and the domestic are consequential. The myth of Semele is, in part, about the perils to hearth and home of unthinking promises and nagging.

25. Ovid, *Metamorphoses*, Bk. III, Gregory, pp. 92–94.

26. Heraclitus, fragment 121, in *Selections*, Nahm, p. 75.

27. Shakespeare, "Sonnet 30," ll.1–4.

28. Stephen Ambrose, *D-Day June 6, 1944: The Climactic Battle of World War II* (New York: Simon & Schuster, 1994), and Stephen Ambrose, *Citizen Soldier: The U.S. Army from the Normandy Beaches to the Bulge to the Surrender of Germany June 7, 1944 to May 7, 1945* (New York: Simon & Schuster, 1997). Others beside Ambrose have written on D-Day, but his books have become popular classics.

29. John K. Ryan, ed., *The Confessions of St. Augustine* (Garden City, N.Y.: Doubleday 1960), see particularly Bk. XI, ch. 28, par. 37. The first eight books illustrate Augustine's spiritual journey from sin through false doctrine to the truth faith, while Book XI deals with the working of time on the mind and on faith. The faith of the believer and the searcher (catechumen) gains in depth and nuance of understanding through constant reconsideration in memory. The same process, of course, applies to an understanding of myth.

30. Louis D. Rubin, Jr., ed., *The Quotable Baseball Fanatic* (New York: Lyons Press, 2000), p. 194.

31. Stephen Jay Gould, *Bully for Brontosaurus: Reflections in Natural History* (New York: W. W. Norton, 1991), chapter 31, which deals with the DiMaggio hitting streak.

32. Gould, *Bully for Brontosaurus*, p. 464.

33. See, for example, in the vast medieval and Renaissance literature on the wheel of fortune, Niccolo Machiavelli, "Capitolo on Fortune" (1515).

34. Michael Seidel, *Streak: Joe DiMaggio and the Summer of '41* (New York: McGraw-Hill, 1988). See also *Official Baseball Record Book: 1942*, pp. 149–51.

35. Shakespeare, *Othello*, V. ii. 338.

36. *The Confessions of St. Augustine*, Bk. XI, ch. 28, par. 37.

37. Rubin, *The Quotable Baseball Fanatic*, p. 9.

38. George Herbert, "A Prayer," 11.8, 14.

39. T. S. Eliot, "Little Gidding," 11.239–42. This is the last of the *Four Quartets* (1943).

Chapter 2

1. See James D Hardy, Jr., *The New York Giants Base Ball Club: The Growth of a Team and a Sport 1870–1900*, p. 77, and note 11, p. 213. See also DeWolfe Hopper and W. W. Stout, *The Reminiscences of DeWolfe Hopper: Once a Clown Always a Clown* (Garden City, N.Y., 1925), pp. 72–98.

2. Tony Lazzeri, the New York Yankees second baseman, struck out with three men on base and two out in the seventh inning of the last game of the 1926 World Series. The Cards, deep underdogs, led the deciding game, 3 to 2, when Earle Combs singled and Babe Ruth received an intentional pass, as did Lou Gehrig. Rogers Hornsby, the Cardinals manager, called in Grover Cleveland Alexander to face Lazzeri and put out the fire. "Ol' Pete" was certainly hung over a bit, but he was a great pitcher and immune to pressure. Alexander came in and the fog lifted, as it always did when he pitched. The first pitch to Lazzeri was a ball, the next a strike, and Lazzeri hit the third down the left field line into the seats, in foul territory. Then Alexander struck him out, ending the threat and wining the Series. See Babe Ruth, as told to Bob Considine, *The Babe Ruth Story*, pp. 151–152. In his earlier book, the Babe also described the strikeout: In the 1926 World Series when Alexander struck out Tony Lazzeri in that crucial inning and won a championship,

a lot of fellows raved about Alex's great curves. Let me tell you a little secret. Alex threw Tony just one curve ball in all those pitches. And the ball Tony fanned on wasn't a curve at all. It wasn't even a fast one. It was a half-speed ball that cut the corner of the plate within a half inch of the spot Bob O'Farrell called for." See George Ruth, *Babe Ruth's Own Book of Baseball* (New York: A. L. Burt Co., 1928), p. 36.

3. *New York Times*, October 15, 1992.

4. *New York Times*, October 27, 28, 1991; *The Baseball Encyclopedia* (1993), p. 2822.

5. *Official Baseball Guide: 1945*, pp. 8–10; *New York Times*, October 1, 1945.

6. *Spalding's Official Base Ball Guide: 1939*, pp. 70, 88–89.

7. *New York Times*, September 28, 1938.

8. *New York Times*, September 29, 1938.

9. *New York Times*, September 29, 1938. Curiously, *Spalding's Guide* passed by the Hartnett Homer in the Gloaming with only a brief reference, rather than acknowledging it as the pennant-winning hit that it was.

10. *Spalding's Official Base Ball Guide: 1939*, p. 94.

11. *New York Times*, September 28, 1938.

12. *Ibid*.

13. *Ibid*.

14. *Id.*, September 29, 1938.

15. *Official Baseball Guide: 1951*, pp. 52–53.

16. *The Baseball Encyclopedia: 1993*, pp. 244–45.

17. *Id.*, pp. 189–90.

18. *Id.*, pp. 301, 309, 312, 315–17.

19. *Official Baseball Guide: 1951*, pp. 52–53, 56–57.

20. *Id.*, pp. 52–53; *New York Times*, October 2, 1951.

21. *The Baseball Encyclopedia: 1993*, p. 1385.

22. *Official Baseball Guide: 1955*, pp. 112–14, 118–21; *New York Times*, September 30, 1954.

23. A picture and diagram, including distance from home plate, for the Polo Grounds may be found in the *Baseball Guide* (1946), p. 79.

24. *The Baseball Encyclopedia*, 1993, p. 1320.

25. *Spalding's Official Base Ball Guide* (1934), pp. 114–15.

26. *Id.*, pp. 70–71.

27. *Id.*, p. 28; *New York Times*, October 8, 1933.

28. *New York Times*, October 15, 1988.

29. *New York Times*, October 14, 1988.

30. *Ibid*.

31. *Id.*, October 15, 1988.

32. *Ibid*.

33. *Id.*, October 16, 1988.

34. *New York Times*, October 24, 1993.

35. *Baseball Guide and Record Book: 1961*, pp.

131–39 for the play-by-play of the first three games. See also *New York Times*, October 6, 7, 9, 1960.

36. *Baseball Guide and Record Book: 1961*, pp. 139–43; *New York Times*, October 10, 1960.

37. *Baseball Guide and Record Book: 1961*, pp. 142–44; *New York Times*, October 11, 1960.

38. *Baseball Guide and Record Book: 1961*, pp. 144–47; *New York Times*, October 13, 1960.

39. *Baseball Guide and Record Book: 1961*, pp. 147–49; *New York Times*, October 14, 1960. This was an odd series. The Yankees had a team batting average of .338, highest in Series history. The Pirates hurlers gave up ninety-one hits, including twenty-seven for extra bases, along with eighteen bases on balls. The Pirates earned run average was an immense 7.11. And Pittsburgh won.

40. *New York Times*, October 14, 1960.

41. *Ibid.*

Chapter 3

1. The basic rule changes are outlined in convenient form in *The Baseball Encyclopedia, 1993*, Appendix C, p. 2853.

2. *Id.*, p. 2854.

3. Glenn Liebman, *Baseball Shorts* (Chicago: Contemporary Books, 1994), p. 25. This quote has also been attributed to Casey Stengel. From either man, it accurately describes the relationship of pitching to hitting.

4. No-hit games are listed in *The Baseball Encyclopedia, 1993*, pp. 2426.

5. *Official Baseball Guide: 1946*, pp. 151–53; *New York Times*, October 6, 1945.

6. *Official Baseball Guide: 1946*, p. 147.

7. *The New York Times*, May 15, 1920. This speech to the Home Market Club of Boston is reprinted in Frederick E. Schortemeier, ed., *Rededicating America: Life and Recent Speeches of Warren G. Harding* (Indianapolis: Bobbs-Merrill, 1920); and has been analyzed in Francis Russell, *The Shadow of Blooming Grove: Warren G. Harding in His Times*; Andrew Sinclair, *The Available Man: The Life Behind the Masks of Warren Gamaliel Harding* (New York: Macmillan 1965); Randolph C. Downes, *The Rise of Warren Gamaliel Harding*; Robert K. Murray, *The Harding Era: Warren G. Harding and His Administration*.

8. Data on baseball the records described here may be found in *The Baseball Encyclopedia, 1993*, p. 35 for Leonard and p. 36 for Radbourn. Leonard's full record can be found on p. 2028, and Radbourn's on p. 2179.

9. *Id.*, p. 2361.

10. On Carl Hubbell, see *Spalding Official Base Ball Guide* (1937), p. 49; see also *The Giants of New York*, the 1947 Yearbook. On Tim Keefe, see Hardy, *The New York Giants*, pp. 79–80; see also *New York Times*, June 24, 1888, for Keefe's first victory and August 12, 1888, for the last. For an overview of the winning streak, see Hy Turkin and S. C. Thompson, *The Official Encyclopedia of Baseball* (New York: A. S. Barnes, 1951, 1956, 1959, 1963, 1968), p. 502.

11. *Official Baseball Guide: 1969*, pp. 221–23.

12. *Id.*, p. 221 for game box score; *New York Times*, October 3, 1968.

13. See Homer, Iliad, bk. XVIII, ll. 483–607, containing the description of the shield of Achilles, an excellent and concise depiction of the Greek view of both the cosmos and the vital domestic virtues of piety and appreciation of beauty. For a second description, see Virgil, *The Aeneid*, particularly book I where such virtues, especially piety, appear, and compare with book IV where both are absent.

14. On the 1934 All-Star Game see *Spalding Official Base Ball Guide: 1935*, pp. 37–39, *New York Times*, July 11 1934.

15. Rubin, *The Quotable Baseball Fanatic*, p. 248.

16. Gould, *Bully for Brontosaurus*, p. 464.

17. Rubin, *The Quotable Baseball Fanatic*, p. 249.

18. Jocko Conlan and Robert Creamer, *Jocko* (Philadelphia: Lippincoff, 1967) p. 72.

19. This is the last line the classic motion picture *The Maltese Falcon* (1941).

20. *New York Times*, June 24, 1917.

21. *Official Baseball Guide: 1960*, pp. 112, 163–64.

22. *Official Baseball Guide: 1957*, pp. 115–31.

23. *Id.*, pp. 131–34; *New York Times*, October 9, 1957.

24. *The Baseball Encyclopedia, 1993*, p. 2017 for Larsen and p. 1954 for Hubbell.

Chapter 4

1. *Official Baseball Record Book: 1942*, pp. 126–28; *New York Times*, October 5, 1941.

2. *Official Baseball Record Book: 1942*, pp. 128–30; *New York Times* October 6, 1941.

3. Rubin, *Quotable Baseball Fanatic*, p. 220.

4. *Official Baseball Record Book: 1942*, p. 121.

5. Summary in *The Baseball Encyclopedia: 1993*, p. 2807; much fuller account in *New York Times*, October 26, 1986.

6. *Washington Post*, October 26, 1986.

7. Liebman, *Baseball Shorts*, p. 101.

8. *The Boston Post*, January 6, 1920; reproduced in Eric Caren, ed., *Baseball Extra: A Newspaper History of the Glorious Game from its Beginnings to the Present* (Edison, N.J.: Castle Books, 2000), p. 149.

9. Dante, *Inferno*, Canto 34.

10. Alexander Theroux, *Boston Globe Magazine*, July 2, 1989, p. 22.

11. *Ibid.*, pp. 38–39.

12. Homer *Iliad*, Books 19 and 24, in particular Book. 24.

13. *Official Baseball Guide: 1947*, pp. 180–81.

14. *Official Baseball Guide: 1956*, p. 138, photographs of Amoros's catch on p. 120.

15. *Official Baseball Guide: 1955*, p. 79. For Jansen's pitching career, see *The Baseball Encyclopedia 1993*, p. 1966.

16. Rubin, *Quotable Baseball Fanatic*, p. 262.

17. H. L. Mencken, *Prejudices,* 6 vols. (New York: A. A. Knopf, 1919–27), vol. 6, pp. 187–94.

18. *Official Baseball Guide: 1955*, photographs, p. 110, game description, pp. 118–21; *New York Times*, September 30, 1954.

19. Conlan and Creamer, *Jocko*, p. 130.

20. *Ibid.*, pp. 130–31.

21. *Official Baseball Guide: 1955*, p. 113.

22. Ovid, *Metamorphoses*, Book 13, p. 346, in the Gregory translation.

23. Cesare Ripa, *Iconologia* (1592), ed. Stephen Orgel (Ithaca, N.Y.: Cornell University Press, 1976), from the 1611 Padua edition. On image books and their cultural importance as sources of emblems, see Peter Daly, *Literature in the Light of the Emblem: Structural Parallels Between the Emblem and Literature in the Sixteenth and Seventeenth Centuries* (Toronto: University of Toronto Press, 1979). For a general discussion of emblems as cultural markers, with an emphasis on England, see Gale H. Carrithers, Jr. and James D. Hardy, Jr., *Age of Iron: English Renaissance Topologies of Lore and Power* (Baton Rouge: Louisiana State University Press, 1998), chapter 2.

Chapter 5

1. Liebman, *Baseball Shorts*, p. 86.

2. *Spalding's Official Base Ball Guide: 1928*, pp. 118–27; *The Baseball Encyclopedia: 1993*, p. 234.

3. Liebman, *Baseball Shorts*, p. 86.

4. *Spalding's Official Base Ball Guide: 1928*, pp. 69–72.

5. *Ibid.*, pp. 46–51; *New York Times*, October 6, 1927.

6. *Spalding's Official Base Ball Guide: 1928*, pp. 52–53; *New York Times*, October 7, 1927.

7. *Spalding's Official Base Ball Guide: 1928*, pp. 54–55; *New York Times*, October 8, 1927.

8. *Spalding's Official Base Ball Guide: 1928*, pp. 55–59; *New York Times*, October 9, 1927.

9. Liebman, *Baseball Shorts*, p. 220.

10. *The Baseball Encyclopedia* (1993), pp. 238–40.

11. *Spalding's Official Base Ball Guide: 1927*, pp. 57–59; see also George Herman Ruth, *Babe Ruth's Own Book*, p. 36; *New York Times*, October 11, 1926.

12. *New York Times*, October 5, 6, 8, 10, 1928, for coverage of the World Series that was predicated on an expected New York victory.

13. On the crash of October 29, 1929, see John Kenneth Galbraith *The Great Crash* (Boston: Houghton Mifflin, 1955).

14. *The Baseball Encyclopedia: 1993*, pp. 252–54, gives an epitome of the American League teams and season for 1932.

15. *The Baseball Encyclopedia: 1993*, pp. 251–52, for the 1932 National League season.

16. *New York Times*, September 29, 20, and October 2, 3, 1932.

Chapter 6

1. See Hardy, *The New York Giants*, p. 52.

2. John Donne, "A Lecture upon the Shadow," in C. A. Patrides, ed., *The Complete English Poems of John Donne* (London: Dent, 1985), pp. 123–24.

3. *New York Times*, April 11, 1947.

4. Rubin, *Quotable Baseball Fanatic*, p. 280.

5. *Ibid.*

6. *New York Times*, October 1, 1947; *Official Baseball Guide: 1948*. pp. 98–100.

7. *New York Times*, October 2, 1947; *Official Baseball Guide: 1948*, pp. 100–02.

8. *New York Times*, October 3, 1947; *Official Baseball Guide: 1948*, pp. 102–05.

9. *New York Times*, October 4, 1947; *Official Baseball Guide: 1948*, pp. 104–08.

10. *New York Times*, October 5, 1947; *Official Baseball Guide: 1948*, pp. 108–10.

11. *New York Times*, October 6, 1947; *Official Baseball Guide: 1948*, pp. 110–12.

12. *New York Times*, October 7, 1947; *Official baseball Guide: 1948*, pp. 113–14.

13. Rolfe Humphries, "Polo Grounds," (1940), *The Summer Landscape* (New York: Scribner's Sons, 1944), pp. 22–25.

Chapter 7

1. *Official Baseball Guide: 1947* contains the details of these stirring events on pp. 9–11. The excitement appears more clearly in the daily papers, even the austere *New York Times*, September 28, 29, 30, October 1, 1946.

2. *Official Baseball Guide: 1947*, pp. 191–94. See also *New York Times*, October 2, 1946.

3. *Official Baseball Guide: 1947*, pp. 191–94. See also *New York Times*, October 4, 1946.

4. Stephen Jay Gould, *Wonderful Life: The Burgess Shale and the Nature of History* (New York: W. W. Norton, 1989) esp. pp. 283–85 where Gould discusses contingency theory in terms of a finite historical event, the Civil War.

5. *Official Baseball Guide: 1949*, pp. 85–94.

6. *Ibid.*, pp. 95–96.

7. *Ibid.*, pp. 101–22.

8. Doris Kearns Goodwin, *Wait Till Next Year: A Memoir* (New York: Simon & Schuster, 1997), p. 125.

9. *Official Baseball Guide: 1952*, pp. 53–56; *New York Times*, September 30, October 1, 2, 3, 1951.

10. Rubin, *Quotable Baseball Fanatic*, p. 12.

11. *Official Baseball Guide: 1952*, p. 53; *New York Times*, May 2, 1883; Hardy, *The New York Giants*, chapter 2.

12. J. H. Hexter, *Doing History* (Bloomington: Indiana University Press, 1971), p. 41.

13. *Official Baseball Guide: 1952*, p. 53.

14. The streak is given, game by game, in the *Official Baseball Guide: 1952*, p. 54 and *New York Times*, October 1, 1951. I saw two of them, a 3 to 1 victory over Brooklyn on August 15 and a 6-to-5 victory over the Cardinals on August 24, before going off to college. The effect of the streak on the pennant race, game by game, can be seen in *New York Times* of October 1, 1951, and in Hexter, *Doing History*, p. 35.

15. Jocko Conlan and Robert Creamer, *Jocko* (Philadelphia: Lippincoff, 1967) p. 126.

16. *Ibid.*, pp. 126–27.

17. *Official Baseball Guide: 1952*, pp. 54–55; *New York Times*, September 29, 30, October 1, 1952.

18. *New York Times*, October 1, 1951.

19. *Ibid.*

20. Hexter, *Doing History*, p. 41.

21. In 1880 the Chicago Cubs had a winning percentage of .798 and finished fifteen games ahead of Providence. Even the record of St. Louis in the 1884 Union Association race, .832, for a twenty-one-game lead over Cincinnati fell short of the Giants' 84 percent spurt. In 1906, the Cubs won 116 and lost 36 for a paltry .763 mark, 20 games ahead of the New York

Giants. See *The Baseball Encyclopedia*: 1993, pp. 69–71, 84–87, 155–157.

22. *New York Times*, October 1, 1951.

23. *Ibid.*, October 2, 1951.

24. *Ibid.*; *Official Baseball Guide: 1952*, p. 55.

25. *New York Times*, October 3, 1951; *Official Baseball Guide: 1952*, pp. 55–56.

26. *New York Times*, October 3, 1951.

27. *Ibid.*

28. Conlan and Creamer, *Jocko*, p. 128.

29. Goodwin, *Wait Till Next Year*, pp. 152–53.

30. *Official Baseball Guide: 1952*, pp. 56–58; *New York Times*, October 4, 1951; Goodwin, *Wait Till Next Year*, p. 153. I am counted among those who heard the game. I was at Cornell, listening to the radio in Jerry Mendelsohn's room. Jerry and I were Giants' fans, surrounded by half a dozen or so rooting for Brooklyn. When Russ Hodges called Thomson's home run, the Dodgers' rooters silently rose and left the room. Jerry and I, grinning and laughing, remained to hear the postgame festivities. For Doris Kearns Goodwin, as for many another, it was the "worst day as a fan." For me, it was one of the best. In my youth, the Dodgers were consistently better than my beloved and bedraggled Giants. But for one fine day, one incredible day, the *Moirae* smiled.

31. *New York Times*, October 4, 1951.

32. *Ibid.*

33. *Ibid.*

34. *Ibid.*

35. An examination of the pennant races and winners in the *Official Baseball Guides* will indicate the long-term superiority of the Yankees and the Dodgers over the others.

36. *Official Baseball Guide: 1960*, pp. 56–58; *New York Times*, September 26, 27, 28, 1959.

37. *Official Baseball Guide: 1960*, p. 86.

38. *Official Baseball Guide: 1960*, pp. 58–59; *New York Times*, September 29, 1959.

39. *Official Baseball Guide: 1960*, pp. 58–59; *New York Times*, September 30, 1959.

40. *Official Baseball Guide: 1963*, pp. 76–77.

41. The worst team in Major League history was the Cleveland Spiders of 1899 with a record of 20 wins and 134 defeats, for a .130 record. They finished last in a twelve-team League. *The Baseball Encyclopedia: 1993*, pp. 135–36.

42. *Official Baseball Guide: 1963*, pp. 68–69.

43. *Ibid.*, p. 70; *New York Times*, October 2, 1962.

44. *Official Baseball Guide: 1963*, pp. 70–71; *New York Times*, October 3, 1962.

45. *Official Baseball Guide: 1963*, pp. 71–73; *New York Times*, October 4, 5, 1962.

46. *Official Baseball Guide: 1963*, pp. 149–73.

47. The details of these dismal doings can

be found in *The Baseball Encyclopedia* (1993), pp. 115–36.

48. The logical conclusion to all of this is to have each team in its own division, thus everyone wins ever year and the playoffs last for three months instead of three weeks.

49. *The Baseball Encyclopedia (1993)*, pp. 438, 441.

50. *The Baseball Encyclopedia (1993)*, p. 1902 for the full dimension of Guidry's astonishing record in 1978.

51. *New York Times*, October 3. 1978.

52. *New York Times*, October 1, 2, 3, 4, 1978 for comments on the season and the playoffs.

53. *The Baseball Encyclopedia (1993)*, p. 313.

54. *Official Baseball Guide (1950)*, pp. 86–87

55. *Ibid.*; *New York Times*, October 3, 1949.

56. Aristotle, *The Poetics*, XIII.5 (1453a).

57. Aeschylus, *Agamemnon*, described by the chorus and referred to only obliquely thereafter. Athenian audiences knew the myth before they saw the drama, and filling in the background to the events was a task the dramatist did not need to undertake.

Chapter 8

1. The records for Babe Ruth in 1918 can be found in *The Baseball Encyclopedia* (1993), pp. 1421, 2214, 2699. The World Series was front page news for the morning hometown *Boston Post*, September 6 and 10, for the Ruth victories, and September 12, 1918, for the final game, in Caren, ed., *Baseball Extra*, pp. 144, 145.

2. *Boston Post*, September 9, 1919, reprinted in Caren, ed., *Baseball Extra*, p. 146.

3. Stanley Walker, *Mrs. Astor's Horse* (New York: Frederick A. Stokes, 1935), p. 216.

4. Stanley Walker, *City Editor* (New York: Frederick A. Stokes, 1934), p. 28.

5. *Spalding Official Baseball Guide: 1934*, pp. 143 and 145 for DiMaggio's hitting statistics for 1933.

6. Richard Ben Cramer, *Joe DiMaggio: The Hero's Life* (New York: Simon & Schuster, 2000), pp. 68–74.

7. William Shakespeare, *Hamlet*, III.I.154–5.

8. William Shakespeare, *Antony and Cleopatra*, II.2.240.

9. *New York Times*, March 8, 2004.

10. *Baton Rouge Morning Advocate*, February 16, 2004.

11. *Ibid.*

12. *Boston Post*, January 6, 1920, in Caren, ed., *Baseball Extra*, p. 149; see also Babe Ruth, as told to Bob Considine, *The Babe Ruth Story*,

pp. 66–70.

13. This can be found in *New York Times*, January 19, 20, 21, 1920.

14. *New York Times*, January 16, 1920.

15. See Christopher M. Finan, *Alfred E. Smith: The Happy Warrior* (New York: Hill and Wang, 2002), chapter 5.

16. *New York Times*, June 26, 1923, quoted in Charles Merz, *The Dry Decade* (New York: Doubleday, 1932), p. 104.

17. Herbert Hoover to Senator William Borah, February 28, 1928.

18. Hardy, *The New York Giants*, p. 81.

19. Woodrow Wilson, "Message to the American People," November 11, 1918, in Frederick Lewis Allen, *Only Yesterday: An Informal History of the Nineteen-Twenties* (New York and London: Harper & Brothers, 1931), p. 15; see also Ray Stannard Baker, *Woodrow Wilson: Life and Letters*, 8 vols. (New York: Doubleday-Page, 1927–1939), VIII, p. 580.

20. On the social dislocations after the war, see David Kennedy, *Over Here: The First World War and American Society* (New York: Oxford University Press, 1980); see also Burl Noggle, *Into the Twenties: The United States from Armistice to Normalcy* (Urbana: University of Illinois Press, 1974); see Allen, *Only Yesterday*, chapter 1 for an account, focused on ordinary household expenditures, of the dramatic and painful rise in consumer prices and the social stress accompanying this during 1919 and 1920; for an examination of the tragic side of postwar America see William M. Tuttle, Jr., *Race Riot: Chicago in the Red Summer of 1919*.

21. Before McGraw, the Giants had been winners, had been fashionable, had been the toast of the sporting set, but this had been a sometime thing. The Giants had won in 1888, 1889, and 1894, but by the turn of the century those days were long past and the Giants were terrible, finishing in or near the cellar, with an unpopular owner, and were denounced daily by the sports writers. The few remaining fans were equally censorious. This is always discouraging. See Hardy, The New York Giants, chapters 7 and 8.

22. *The Baseball Encyclopedia: 1993*, pp. 190–214, for the sustained lack of success endured by the Philadelphia Athletics.

23. Lyle Spatz, *New York Yankee Openers: An Opening Day History of Baseball's Most Famous Team, 1903–1993* (Jefferson, N.C.: McFarland, 1997) p. 77–80.

24. See Edward Grant Barrow with James M. Kahn, *My Fifty Years in Baseball* (New York: Concord-McCann, 1951).

25. Spatz, *New York Yankee Openers*, pp. 80–81.

26. *New York Times*, April 18, 1924.
27. *Ibid.*
28. *Ibid.*
29. *Ibid.*; see also Spatz, *New York Yankee Openers*, pp. 90–94.
30. *New York Times*, April 20, 1923.
31. *Ibid.*, October 10, 1923.
32. *Ibid.*
33. *Ibid.*, October 12, 1923.
34. *Ibid.*, October 15, 1923.
35. *Ibid.*, October 16, 1923.

Chapter 9

1. John Milton, *Paradise Lost*.
2. Rubin, *Quotable Baseball Fanatic*, p. 12.
3. Liebman, *Baseball Shorts*, p. 60.
4. *Spalding Official Base Ball Guide: 1930*, pp. 52–53; *New York Times*, October 13, 1929.
5. *Spalding Official Base Ball Guide: 1930*, p. 53.
6. *Ibid.*, pp. 54–56; *New York Times*, October 15, 1929.
7. *The Official Baseball Guide: 1963*.
8. *The Official Baseball Guide: 1970*.
9. *Baton Rouge Morning Advocate*, October 16, 2003.
10. *Ibid.*, December 23, 2003. This is a superb piece of cultural commentary.

Chapter 10

1. Rubin, *Quotable Baseball Fanatic*, p. 286.
2. Charles L. Mee, Jr., *The Ohio Gang: The World of Warren G. Harding*, p. 102.
3. F. Scott Fitzgerald, *The Great Gatsby* (New York: Scribner's, 1925, 1950) p. 182.
4. See Robert B. Strassler, ed. and Victory Davis Hanson, intro, *The Landmark Thucydides: A Comprehensive Hide to the Peloponnesian War* (New York: Free Press, 1996), pp. 111–18, II.35–II.46.2. The "school of Hellas" is in II.41. On American education before the Great War, a good overview may be found in a neglected classic, Mark Sullivan, *Our Times: The United States 1900–1925*, 5 vols. (New York: Scribner's, 1925–35), II, chapters 1–12.
5. Henry Hobart Vail, *A History of the McGuffey Readers* (Cleveland: Burrows, 1911), p 2.
6. See Sinclair Lewis, *Main Street*. See also Sherwood Anderson, *Winesburg, Ohio*. Both were critical of the stultifying intellectual, religious, and cultural orthodoxy of small town

American in the era before radio and the movie, and both received extended critical acclaim in enemy territory, the urban literary and cultural circles. H. L. Mencken, the greatest of American literary critics, stated of Lewis's *Main Street*: "that god-damn slob has written a masterpiece."
7. Henry Vail was an early commentator on the McGuffey readers, and he noted their importance as a contemporary cultural phenomenon. Others have followed, writing after the McGuffey books no longer dominated American public education. See John H. Westerhoff III, *McGuffey and His Readers: Piety, Morality and Education in Nineteenth Century America* (Nashville: Abingdon, 1978); Harvey C. Minnich, *William Holmes McGuffey and His Readers* (New York and Cincinnati: n.p., 1936); Ruth Miller Elson, *Guardians of Tradition: American Schoolbooks of the Nineteenth Century* (Lincoln: University of Nebraska Press, 1964); Walter Sutton, *The Western Book Trade: Cincinnati or a Nineteenth-Century Publishing and Book Trade Center* (Columbus: Morgan Library of Ohio Imprints, 1961); see also Richard D. Mosier, *Making the American Mind: Social and Moral Ideas in the McGuffey Readers* (New York: Russell & Russell, 1947). Mosier wrote from the perspective of the far left, and was particularly hostile to the gospel of wealth and to the Protestant approval thereof, without, apparently, being a Marxist. There are also reprints of the contents of the McGuffey readers. The 1957 edition of the *McGuffey Eclectic Readers* were reprinted by Henry Ford in the 1930s, and *McGuffey's New Sixth Eclectic Reader* (1857–66) was reprinted by Garden Press in 1974. See also Harvey C. Minnich, ed., *Old Favorites from the McGuffey Readers* (New York and Cincinnati: American Book Company, 1936); Stanley W. Londberg, *The Annotated McGuffey: Selections from the McGuffey Eclectic Readers 1836–1920* (New York: Van Nostrand Reinhold, 1976).
8. Minnich, *Old Favorites from the McGuffey Readers*, p. v., wrote: "an introduction to McGuffey savors of the presumption of an introduction to the Bible."
9. *Ibid.*, p. vi.
10. Quoted from the 1837 edition of the Fourth Eclectic Reader by Mosier, *Making the American Mind*, p. 58; the entire lesson, numbered LI, may be found in Westerhoff, *McGuffey*, pp. 151–52.
11. Quoted by Minnich, *Old Favorites*, p. 352. IT was lesson CXVI from the *Fifth Reader*.
12. Quoted in Westerhoff, *McGuffey*, pp. 160–61. This came from lesson LXI in the

Fourth Reader, a passage written by South Carolinian Thomas Grimeke.

13. Quoted in Minnich, *Williams Holmes McGuffey,* p. 179.

14. Minnich, *Old Favorites,* pp. 5–6.

15. Westerhoff, *McGuffey,* pp. 142–43.

16. Minnich, *Old Favorites,* pp. 5–6.

17. *Ibid.,* p. 228, lesson XXIX from the *Eclectic Fifth Reader.*

18. Lindberg, *The Annotated McGuffey,* pp. 170–75. This first appeared as lessons LXXVI and LXXVII in the 1866 edition of the *Fourth Eclectic Reader,* and became a standard for subsequent editions. See also Minnich, *Old Favorites,* pp. 167–72.

19. Lindberg, *The Annotated McGuffey,* pp. 224–25; Minnich, *Old Favorites,* pp. 313–15. This piece appeared in every edition throughout the nineteenth century, in the *Fourth Eclectic Reader* until 1857 and the *Fifth* thereafter.

20. Minnich, *Old Favorites,* pp. 110–11.

21. Lindberg, *The Annotated McGuffey,* p. 178.

22. *Ibid.,* p. 29; Minnich, *Old Favorites,* p. 13.

23. Lindberg, *The Annotated McGuffey,* pp. 44–46.

24. *Ibid.,* p. 44.

25. *Ibid.,* p. 46.

26. Minnich, *Old Favorites,* p. 471.

27. Lindberg, *The Annotated McGuffey,* pp. 327–30.

28. Vail, *A History of the McGuffey Readers,* p. 65.

29. On the Bambino's days of youth and yore; see Babe Ruth, *The Babe Ruth Story,* chapter 1. This dying declaration was designed to present the Babe's often gaudy life in a manner suitable for the moral instruction of the young, as he himself had experienced it in the days of McGuffey. The Babe, and everyone else as well, wished to make his legend, which transcended both baseball and his personality, enter the realm of culturally approved myth.

30. Ruth, *The Babe Ruth Story,* p. 173.

31. *Ibid.*

32. *Ibid.,* p. 174.

33. *Ibid.,* p. 236.

34. *Ibid.,* p. 174.

35. *Ibid.,* p. 178.

36. *Ibid.,* p. 183.

37. Barrow with Kahn, *My Fifty Years in Baseball,* p. 154.

38. *Ibid.,* pp. 166–67; Ruth, *The Babe Ruth Story,* pp. 200–201.

39. Ruth, *The Babe Ruth Story,* pp. 218–19.

40. *Ibid.,* p. 218.

41. *Ibid.,* p. 212.

Chapter 11

1. *Official Baseball Guide: 1948,* p. 11.

2. Ben Jonson, *The Staple of News,* ed. Debra Rowland Kifer (Lincoln: University of Nebraska Press, 1975).

3. Doris Kearns Goodwin, *Wait Till Next Year,* p. 123.

4. See James D. Hardy, Jr., *The New York Giants,* pp. 29–32; see also Harold Seymour, *Baseball: The Early Years* (New York: Oxford University Press, 1960) pp. 75 and foreword; see also Peter Levine, *A. G. Spalding and the Rise of Baseball: The Promise of American Sport* (New York: Oxford University Press, 1988), pp. 21–29; see also David Quentin Voigt, *American Baseball: From Gentleman's Sport to the Commissioner System* (Norman: University of Oklahoma Press, 1966), vol. 1, pp. 3–99; see also Douglas Noverr and Lawrence Ziewaiez, *The Games They Played: Sports in American History, 1865–1980* (Chicago: Nelson-Hall, 1983), chapter 1. The text of the National Agreement may be found in Spalding, *America's National Game,* pp. 244–48 and in *Spalding's Official Base Ball Guide: 1884,* pp. 47–51.

5. T. S. Eliot, *Little Gidding,* 11.214–215 the last of *Four Quartets* (1943).

Bibliography

Introductory Note

Primary Sources

There are few public primary sources for baseball as a game, though, perhaps as recompense, the public sources are generally fairly accurate. They consist of newspaper accounts of the games, including the box scores. The papers, both daily and sporting, cover the seasons with daily statistics on who ranks where in the pennant races or in the struggle for the batting or home run titles. The papers also cover the entertaining and frequently strange antics of the owners. Newspapers are supplemented by the annual baseball guides and registers. The *Baseball Encyclopedia* has collected and refined these records for the Major Leagues, making them stunningly accurate, so it also may be considered a primary source.

Beyond this baseball has generated mountains of memorabilia, some of it now antique and all of it collectible. No physical remnant of baseball falls outside of this category, including baseball cards, uniforms, bats, balls, autographs, chunks of departed stadia, photographs, scorecards (whether filled out or not), baseball publications, newspaper clippings, gloves, paintings, letters—in general, objects and items in such variety and profusion that one cannot catalog them all. Since there is a huge market in baseball stuff, which shows no signs of losing value, there are an increasing number of fakes and forgeries that circulate, and in time these as well may become a special category of baseball collectibles. The remnants of baseball past are more familiar, as a field of study to archeologists than to historians, for they resemble shards of pottery and other artifacts dug up from civilizations long past. In a way they are, for seasons gone cannot be replayed, and, in a way they are not, for new seasons and players and balls and bats and cards come every year, and the supply of baseball memorabilia is constantly renewed. But the historian can use them, for collectively they show how the game looked, and indicate areas where the style of play has changed, probably forever.

Additionally, there are private primary sources for baseball, including club and league archives, along with the papers and reminiscences of those who played, administered and covered the game. These are enormously useful and can provide valuable insights into how the game was run and how the players felt about their teams, clubs and careers. As those who write about baseball interviews more and more players, managers, and executives, the volume of these sources brought to light increases, and so does their importance for the history of the game.

Finally, there is a fourth category of records: those that are, strictly speaking, not baseball records but sources about baseball. These include court reports and other legal documents dealing with clubs and players, along with congressional publications detailing the trials and travails before high public authorities that baseball and the players, from time to time, have endured.

Books by Baseball Participants

These were once rather rare and often pretty good (memoirs by Cap Anson and Johnny Evers) and now, after World War II, have become pretty common and much less good. Many were written with the help of a sports journalist or other ghost writer, and the memories of the player or umpire or executive are filtered through the judgment and attitudes of the writer. Ghost-written memoirs may be regarded as filling a separate category of baseball source material, certainly a primary source but of a particular sort.

General Sources

Given the focus of this book, which is baseball rather than the nature of myth and how baseball fits mythic categories, all other sources of information or inspiration, whether ancient, such as Aristotle or Heraclitus, or modern, such as the McGuffey readers or the poetry of T. S. Eliot, are listed in the general baseball. So the general sources are a kind of omnium-gatherum for all things not specifically pegged for another location.

List of Major Sources

Primary Sources

BASEBALL GUIDES

Major League Baseball (Whitman, then Dell), *The Baseball Register,* and the *Sporting News Dope Book* have been used to supplement the official *Guides.* Collectively, these sources present a rich contemporary statistical overview of the game, year by year.

Official Baseball Guide (and Record Book): 1942, 1945, 1946, 1947, 1948, 1949, 1950, 1951, 1952, 1955, 1956, 1957, 1960, 1961, 1963, 1969.
Spalding's Official Base Ball Guide: 1884, 1927, 1928, 1930, 1934, 1935, 1937, 1939.

NEWSPAPERS

The Baton Rouge Advocate
The Boston Globe
The New York Herald-Tribune
The New York Times
The Sporting News
Sunday News (New York)
Washington Post

ENCYCLOPEDIAS

The Baseball Encyclopedia, 9th edition (New York, 1993).
The Official Encyclopedia of Baseball, Hy Turkin and S. C. Thompson, ed. (New York: A. S. Barnes, 1951, and nine subsequent editions through 1977).

BOOKS BY BASEBALL PARTICIPANTS

Barrow, Edward Grant, and James M. Kahn. *My Fifty Years in Baseball* (New York: Coward-McCann, 1951).
Conlan, Jocko, and Robert Creamer. *Jocko* (Philadelphia: Lippincott, 1967).
DiMaggio, Joe. *Lucky to Be a Yankee* (New York: Grosset & Dunlap, 1946).
Durocher, Leo. *The Dodgers and Me: The Inside Story* (Chicago: Ziffs Davis, 1948).
Robinson, Jackie, and Wendell Smith. *My Own Story* (New York: Dell, 1948).
Ruth, Babe. *Babe Ruth's Own Book of Baseball* (New York: A. L. Burt Co., 1928).
Ruth, Babe, and Bob Considine. *The Babe Ruth Story* (New York: E. P. Dutton, 1948).

General Sources

Abrams, M. H., ed. *Literature and Belief* (New York: Columbia University Press, 1965).
Adelman, Melvin. *A Sporting Time: New York City and the Rise of Modern Athletics 1820–1870.* (Urbana: University of Illinois Press, 1986).

Aeschylus. *Agamemnon*. Trans. Herbert Wier Smith, ed. Hugh Lloyd-Jones (Cambridge, Mass., and London: Harvard University Press, 1963).

Allen, Frederick Lewis. *Only Yesterday* (New York: Harper & Brothers, 1931).

Ambrose, Stephen. *Citizen Soldier: The U.S. Army from the Normandy Beaches to the Bulge to the Surrender of Germany June 7, 1944* (New York: Simon & Schuster, 1997).

_____. *D-Day June 6, 1944: The Climatic Battle of World War II* (New York: Simon & Schuster, 1994).

Anti-Saloon League. *Proceedings Fifteenth National Convention of the Anti-Saloon League of America Twenty Year Jubilee Convention* (Westerville, Ohio: n.p., 1913).

Asbury, Herbert. *The Great Illusion: An Informal History of Prohibition* (Garden City, N.Y.: Doubleday, 1950).

Aristophanes. *Four Comedies*, ed. William Arrowsmith (Ann Harbor: University of Michigan Press, 1961, 1994).

Augustine. *The City of God*, 7 vols. (Cambridge, Mass., and London: Harvard University Press, 1966).

Baker, Ray Stannard. *Woodrow Wilson Life and Letters*, 8 vols. (New York: Doubleday-Page, 1927–1939).

Bernstein, Michael. *The Great Depression: Delayed Recovery and Economic Change in America, 1929–1939* (New York: Cambridge University Press, 1987).

Bordin, Ruth. *Women and Temperance: The Quest for Power and Liberty* (Philadelphia: Temple University Press, 1981).

Burns, James McGregory. *Roosevelt: The Lion and the Fox* (New York: Harcourt, Brace, 1956).

_____. *Roosevelt: The Soldier of Freedom* (New York: Harcourt Brace Jovanovich 1970).

Caren, Eric, ed. *Baseball Extra: A Newspaper History of the Glorious Game from its Beginnings to the Present* (Edison, N.J.: Castle Books, 2000).

Carrithers, Gale H., Jr., and James D. Hardy, Jr. *Age of Iron: English Renaissance Topologies of Love and Power* (Baton Rouge: Louisiana State University Press, 1998).

Chandler, Lester. *America's Greatest Depression* (New York: Harper & Row, 1970).

Cherrington, Ernest. *The Evolution of Prohibition in the United States of America* (Westerville, Ohio: American Issue Press, 1920).

Clark, Norman A. *Deliver Us from Evil: An Interpretation of American Prohibition* (New York: W. W. Norton, 1976).

Cook, William A. *Waite Hoyt: A Biography of the Yankees' Schoolboy Wonder* (Jefferson, N.C.: McFarland, 2004).

Cramer, Richard Ben. *Joe DiMaggio: The Hero's Life* (New York: Simon & Schuster, 2000).

Dabney, Virginius. *Dry Messiah: The Life of Bishop Cannon* (New York: A. A. Knopf, 1949).

Daly, Peter. *Literature in the Light of the Emblem: Structural Parallels Between the Emblem and Literature in the Sixteenth and Seventeenth Centuries* (Toronto: University of Toronto Press, 1979).

Dante Alighieri. *Commedia*. Trans. and ed. Mark Musa (New York: Penguin Classics, 1986).

Davis, Kenneth S. *FDR*, 4 vols. (New York: Random House, 1945–1993).

Donne, John. *The Complete English Poems of John Donne*, C.A. Patrides, ed. (London: Dent, 1985).

Downes, Randolph C. *The Rise of Warren Harding: 1865–1920* (Columbus, Ohio: n.p., 1970).

Eliot, T. S. "Little Gidding" *Four Quartets* (London: Faber & Faber, 1943).

Elson, Ruth Miller. *Guardians of Tradition: American Schoolbooks of the Nineteenth Century* (Lincoln: University of Nebraska Press, 1964).

Finan, Christopher H. *Alfred E. Smith: The Happy Warrior* (New York: Hill and Wang, 2002).

Fitzgerald, F. Scott. *The Great Gatsby* (New York: Scribner's, 1925).

Flexner, Eleanor. *Century of Struggle: The Woman's Rights Movement in the United States* (Cambridge, Mass.: Harvard University Press, 1975).

Frazer, Sir James George. *The Golden Bough: A Study in Magic and Religion*, an abridgement of the second and third editions (London: Oxford University Press, 1942, 1976).

Freidel, Frank. *Franklin D. Roosevelt*, 4 vols. (Boston: Little, Brown, 1942–1976).

Galbraith, John Kenneth. *The Great Crash* (Boston: Houghton Mifflin, 1955).

Goodwin, Doris Kearns. *Wait Till Next Year: A Memoir* (New York: Simon & Schuster, 1997).

Gould, Stephen Jay. *Bully for Brontosaurus: Reflections on Natural History* (New York: W. W. Norton, 1991).

_____. *Wonderful Life: The Burgess Shale and the Nature of History* (New York: W. W. Norton, 1989).

Grant, Michael. *Myths of the Greeks and the Romans* (New York: New American Library, 1964).

Hardy, James D., Jr. *The New York Giants Base Ball Club: The Growth of a Team and a Sport, 1870–1900* (Jefferson, N.C.: McFarland, 1996).

Hesiod. *Hesiod Works and Days Theogony*, Stanley Lombardo, trans., and Robert Lamberton, intro. (Indianapolis: Hackett, 1993).

Hexter, J. H. *Doing History* (Bloomington: Indiana University Press, 1971).

Holmes, Oliver Wendell. *The Mind and Faith of Justice Holmes: His Speeches, Essays, Letters, and Judicial Opinions*, Max Lerner, ed. (New York, 1943; repr., New Brunswick, N.J.: Rutgers University Press, 1988).

Homer. *The Iliad*. Trans. Richard Lattimore (Chicago: University of Chicago Press, 1951).

Hopper, DeWolfe, and W. W. Stout. *The Reminiscences of DeWolfe Hopper: Once a Clown Always a Clown* (Garden City, N.Y.: n.p., 1925).

Humphries. Rolfe. *The Summer Landscape* (New York: Scribner's Sons, 1944).

Jonson, Ben. *The Staple of News*, ed. Devra Rowland Kifer (Lincoln: University of Nebraska Press, 1975).

Kennedy, David. *Freedom from Fear: The American People in Depression and War 1929–1945* (New York: Oxford University Press, 19080).

_____. *Over Here: The First World War and American Society* (New York: Oxford University Press, 1980).

Levy, Alan H. *Joe McCarthy: Architect of the Yankee Dynasty* (Jefferson, N.C.: McFarland, 2005).

Liebman, Glen. *Baseball Shorts* (Chicago: Contemporary Books, 1994).

Lindberg, Stanley W. *The Annotated McGuffey: Selections from the McGuffey Eclectic Readers 1836–1920* (New York: Van Nostrand Reinhold, 1976).

Levine, Peter. *A. G. Spalding and the Rise of Baseball: The Promise of American Sport* (New York: Oxford University Press, 1988).

Machiavelli, Niccolò. "Capitolo on Fortune," in Allan Gilbert, ed., *Machiavelli: The Prince and Other Works* (New York: Hendricks House, 1946).

Marzano, Rudy. *The Brooklyn Dodgers in the 1940s: How Robinson, MacPhail, Reiser and Rickey Changed Baseball* (Jefferson, N.C.: McFarland, 2005).

McNeil, William. *Gabby Hartnett: The Life and Times of the Cubs Greatest Catcher* (Jefferson, N.C.: McFarland, 2004).

Mee, Charles L., Jr. *The Ohio Gang: The World of Warren G. Harding* (New York: M. Evans, 1981).

Mencken, H. L. *Prejudices*, 6 vols. (New York: A. A. Knopf, 1919–1927).

Merz, Charles. *The Dry Decade* (New York: Doubleday, 1932)

Milton, John. *Paradise Lost*. Ed. Scott Elledge (New York: W. W. Norton, 1975).

Minnich, Harvey C., ed. *Old Favorites from the McGuffey Readers* (New York and Cincinnati: American Book Company, 1936).

Morford, Mark P. O., and Robert J. Lenardon. *Classical Mythology* (New York: Oxford University Press, 1971).

Mosier, Richard D. *Making the American Mind: Social and Moral Ideas in the McGuffey Readers* (New York: Russell & Russell, 1947).

Murry, Robert K. *The Harding Era: Warren Harding and His Administration*

(Minneapolis: University of Minnesota Press, 1969).

Nahm, Milton C. *Selections from Early Greek Philosophy* (New York: Appleton-Century-Crofts, 1964).

Noggle, Burl. *Into the Twenties: The United States from Armistice to Normalcy* (Urbana: University of Illinois Press, 1974).

Noverr, Douglas, and Lawrence Ziewaiez. *The Games They Played: Sports in American History 1865–1980* (Chicago: Nelson-Hall, 1983).

Ong, Walter. *Orality and Literacy: The Technologizing of the Word* (New York: Methuen, 1982).

Ovid. *Ovid: The Metamorphoses.* Horace Gregory, trans. and ed. (New York: New American Library, 1958).

Perrett, Geoffrey. *America in the Twenties: A History* (New York: Simon & Schuster, 1982).

Reisler, Jim. *Before They Were the Bombers: The New York Yankees' Early Years 1903–1915* (Jefferson, N.C.: McFarland, 2002).

Riess, Steven. *City Games: The Evolution of American Urban Society and the Rise of Sports* (Urbana: University of Illinois Press, 1989).

Riggs v. Palmer et al. 115 NY, 506 (1989).

Ripa, Cesare. *Iconologia,* ed. Stephen Orgel (Ithaca, N.Y.: Cornell University Press, 1976).

Roosevelt, Franklin D. *The Public Papers and Addresses of Franklin D. Roosevelt,* 13 vols. (New York: Random House, 1938–1950).

Rose, H. J. *A Handbook of Greek Mythology,* 6th ed. (London: Routledge, 1958).
_____. *Religion in Greece and Rome* (New York: Harper & Row, 1959).

Rubin, Louis D., Jr. *The Quotable Baseball Fanatic* (New York: Lyons Press, 2000).

Russell, Francis. *The Shadow of Blooming Grove: Warren G. Harding in His Time* (New York: McGraw-Hill, 1968).

Ryan, John K. *The Confessions of Saint Augustine* (Garden City, N.Y.: Doubleday, 1960).

Schortemeier, Frederick E. *Rededicating America: Life and Recent Speeches of Warren G. Harding* (Indianapolis: Bobbs-Merrill, 1920).

Seidel, Michael. *Streak: Joe DiMaggio and the Summer of '41* (New York: McGraw-Hill, 1988).

Seymour, Harold. *Baseball in the Early Years* (New York: Oxford University Press, 1960).

Shakespeare, William. *The Norton Shakespeare,* gen. ed. Stephen Greenblatt (New York: Norton, 1997).

Sinclair, Andrew. *The Available Man: The Life Behind the Masks of Warren Gamaliel Harding* (New York: Macmillan, 1965).

Skipper, John C. *The Cubs Win the Pennant: Charlie Grimm, the Billy Goat Curse and the 1945 World Series Run* (Jefferson, N.C.: McFarland, 2004).

Spalding, Albert G. *America's National Game: Historic Facts Concerning the Beginning, Evolution, Development, and Popularity of Baseball with Personal Reminiscences of its Vicissitudes, its Victories, and its Votaries* (New York: American Sports Publishing, 1911).

Spatz, Lyle. *New York Yankee Openers: An Opening Day History of Baseball's Most Famous Team, 1903–1993* (Jefferson, N.C.: McFarland, 1997).

Stein, Fred, *Mel Ott: The Little Giant of Baseball* (Jefferson, N.C.: McFarland, 1999).

Sullivan, Mark. *Our Times: The United States 1900–1925,* 5 vols. (New York: Scribner's, 1925–1935).

Sutton, Walter. *The Western Book Trade: Cincinnati a Nineteenth-Century Publishing and Book Trade Center* (Columbus: Morgan Library of Ohio Imprints, 1961).

Terkel, Studs. *Hard Times: An Oral History of the Great Depression* (New York: W. W. Norton, 2000).

Thucydides. *The Landmark Thucydides: A Comprehensive Guide to the Peloponnesian War,* Robert B. Strassler, ed., and Victor Davis Hanson, intro. (New York: Free Press, 1996).

Vail, Henry Hobart. *A History of the McGuffey Readers* (Cleveland: Burrows, 1911).

Voigt, David Quentin. *American Baseball: From Gentleman's Sport to the Commissioner System* (Norman: University of Oklahoma Press, 1966).

Walker, Stanley. *City Editor* (New York: Frederick A. Stokes, 1934).

_____. *Mrs. Astor's Horse* (New York: Frederick A. Stokes, 1935).

Westbrook, Deanne. *Ground Rules: Baseball and Myth* (Urbana: University of Illinois Press, 1996).

Westerhoff, John H., III. *McGuffey and His Readers: Piety, Morality, and Education in Nineteenth Century America* (Nashville: Abingdon, 1978).

Index